TALKING TO
CANADIANS

TALKING TO
CANADIANS

a memoir

RICK MERCER

Doubleday Canada

Doubleday Canada and colophon are registered trademarks of Penguin Random House Canada Limited

Library and Archives Canada Cataloguing in Publication

Title: Talking to Canadians : a memoir / Rick Mercer.
Names: Mercer, Rick, 1969- author.
Identifiers: Canadiana (print) 20210244798 | Canadiana (ebook) 20210244801 |
ISBN 9780385696234 (hardcover) | ISBN 9780385696241 (EPUB)
Subjects: LCSH: Mercer, Rick, 1969- | LCSH: Comedians—Canada—Biography. |
LCSH: Television personalities—Canada—Biography. | LCGFT: Autobiographies.
Classification: LCC PN2308.M46 A3 2021 | DDC 792.702/8092—dc23

Every effort has been made to contact copyright holders.
The author and publisher would be glad to amend in future
editions any errors or omissions brought to their attention.

Jacket design: Terri Nimmo
Jacket photograph: Justin Hall
Author photograph: Jon Sturge

Printed in Canada

Published in Canada by Doubleday Canada,
a division of Penguin Random House Canada Limited

www.penguinrandomhouse.ca

10 9 8 7 6 5 4 3 2 1

Penguin
Random House
DOUBLEDAY CANADA

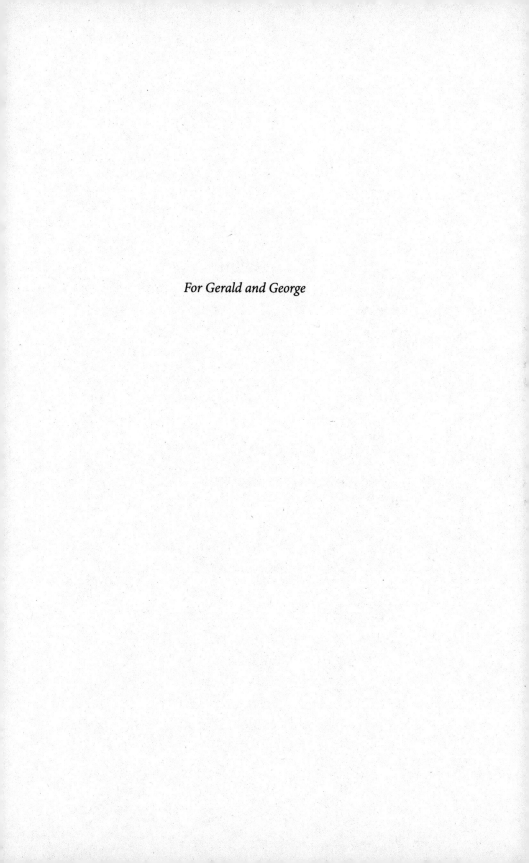

For Gerald and George

Contents

The school of Lois: Prince of Wales Collegiate drama club

Introduction

This is a memoir. Because of that I relied on my own expert testimony.

It is the truth, the whole truth and nothing but the truth. Kind of.

Three people walk into a bar and spend an evening together. Twenty-five years later each of them will have a very different version of what occurred on that night. Or I should say, two of them will. One of them will swear, on their mother, they were not in attendance and in fact out of the country at the time. When faced with photographic evidence to the contrary they will simply say, "Well, that's not how I remember it."

Under the guise of research, while writing this book I called up many old friends and colleagues and questioned them on their version of events, curious to see whether theirs conformed with mine.

For the most part they did, but sometimes they did not. Always the conversation took strange and wonderful turns and we always went down roads entirely irrelevant to anyone but us.

It was grand.

For those calls, those catch-ups, I shall be eternally grateful. If I have any advice, it's pick up the phone and place those calls—you don't need to be writing a book to do so.

Like most Canadians in the entertainment business and all Newfoundlanders in any business, all I ever wanted in life was the opportunity to go to work. And work I did. And I was fortunate to work in
the field of my choosing. I understand this is the equivalent of winning the lotto. That it happened was only possible because I stand on
the shoulders of giants. I speak of the actors and writers and show-
business pioneers in Newfoundland and Canada.

This is my version of events. Some names have been changed, some
locations have been altered, some reputations have been protected.

Regards, and thanks for reading and thanks for watching.

Chapels Cove, Newfoundland
and Labrador, 2021

Prologue

October 1990. Ottawa

The hotel is called the Beacon Arms, but I've only heard it referred to by locals as the Broken Arms. It's the kind of place where you know, instinctively, upon entering your room that you should keep your shoes on. The carpet looks like a crime scene.

For the past three days a small Kentucky Fried Chicken box has been sitting on the floor of the elevator. The cover is off, and inside there is a single chicken breast and a french fry on a plastic fork. Earlier this morning, on my way down for coffee, I noticed the box was still there, but someone had absconded with the chicken.

There is a Yuk Yuk's comedy club in the basement. I wonder which Canadian comedy legend was peckish last night before bed.

I'm up at this hour because my one-man show is about to be reviewed on CBC Radio.

The publicist from the National Arts Centre is up early as well. She wants to pull a quote from the review for ads that are being placed in tomorrow's newspapers. The quote will also be plastered on the show posters that will go up all over downtown Ottawa. They are hoping for something along the lines of "Run, don't walk, to the NAC."

At home in Newfoundland the CBC morning show is going to carry the review as well. Newfoundlanders are always proud of anyone who does well on the mainland, and they love the narrative of a young Newfoundlander having a hit show in, of all places, the National Arts Centre.

The host of the Ottawa morning show teed up the segment with a pretty flattering introduction. "There is a one-man show at the National Arts Centre which is getting a lot of attention in political circles. Why? Well," he continued, "it's a comedy about, of all things, the Meech Lake Accord! Can a constitutional crisis be funny? Well, let's find out. In the studio is theatre critic Brian Gosnell. He is here to review Rick Mercer's *Show Me the Button: I'll Push It—or Charles Lynch Must Die.*"

A very kind set-up. I was feeling pretty good about this. The show the night before had gone really well. Great, in fact. We had a full house, people laughed in the right spots, I didn't rush (which I tend to do). I felt like I killed it. It might have been the best night of my life.

The reviewer began to speak. "Actually, I'm not going to review the production I saw last night at all."

That got my attention. I'm out of bed now, bare feet on the dubious carpet.

"Instead of a review I am going to read an open letter to Mr. Mercer. I hope he is listening."

I was listening.

He cleared his throat for effect. "Dear Mr. Mercer. *Show Me the Button: I'll Push It* is not a play. You are not a playwright. Nor are you an actor. Please leave the theatre. You have nothing to offer."

This was followed by literal radio silence.

It was both the shortest and the worst review in the history of Canadian theatre. How lovely that the folks at home were able to hear it.

Leave the theatre. You have nothing to offer.

I stared at an unsettling stain on the ceiling and thought, "The hell with this. I'm going into television."

Which I did.

Luckily the standards are much lower there, so it worked out well.

1

Middle Cove

Opening night for me was October 17, 1969. I share a birthdate with Broadway legend Angela Lansbury and stuntman Evel Knievel. Show business was in the stars.

I arrived exactly on my mother's due date. Being punctual is something I have continued to be my entire life.

Eventually mother and child travelled twenty-five minutes outside of the city of St. John's to the community of Middle Cove. This is where my father was putting the finishing touches on the house he was building. My father is not a carpenter and would never describe himself as such. He just built our house with his own hands because that's what men of his generation did.

He also dug the hole for the well. Tricky work. They don't call Newfoundland and Labrador "the Rock" for nothing. A few feet below the topsoil you hit the earth's crust. In order to get to the water below, Dad crawled into the shallow hole, packed it with dynamite, crawled back out, hid behind the pickup and lit the fuse.

Having no experience with dynamite, he took the precautionary step of nailing sheets of plywood over the living room windows in case he blew the front of the house off. Inside, behind the plywood, my brother and sister would have been doing whatever it is that four- and six-year-olds do. Family lore has it that I slept peacefully in my mother's arms through multiple explosions while the earth rumbled and rocks rained down on the house.

I've always been a good sleeper. My ability to sleep through anything and everything is legendary. And my knack for sleeping while sitting up has been a huge asset in my career. When you spend twenty-plus years banging around the country in planes, trains and automobiles, it's a lifesaver. Show me a seat in a single-engine Cessna? I'll show you a good spot for a nap. Wake me when the storm is over and we're on the other side of the Rockies. Sleeping sitting up is a skill I honed to perfection during my entire scholastic career.

I have no memory of my father building the house. But growing up I watched him not only head to work for the provincial government every day but also build barns and fences, pour concrete, do electrical and plumbing work and roofing and masonry. I watched him replace a motor in a car in the driveway. I watched him bake literally tens of thousands of loaves of bread. Currently in his eighties he's building the boat he's been threatening to build his entire life. The boat, nearly finished, is in the shed he built for the purpose. Next to the shed is his garden of potatoes, tomatoes, carrots and lettuces.

I can do exactly none of the things my father can do. My occupation is that of pretending and talking. Also typing. I have the hands of an Egyptian princess.

During the pandemic, when everyone was locked away in their homes, it became very evident to me just how useless I was. My lack of true skills was alarming. I called my father and said, "My water boiler broke and repair people are not allowed to come inside the house." He said, "Do you have any tools?" I thought about it and replied, "Yes, I have a corkscrew and some glow sticks left over from Pride."

In a crisis or a pandemic nobody ever shouts, "Is there somebody pithy in the house?"

Fraser Ellis, the father of my great school friend Don Ellis, once said to me, "I remember when you and Donald were teenagers, comedy skits and punk bands is all you cared about. I used to watch the two of you walk up the driveway and I would think to myself, what in the name of all that is holy will become of those two?"

And then this compliment years later: "For a man with no discernible skills, you've done well for yourself."

It's true. And nobody is more surprised than me.

I was not what you would call a gifted child. It would have been a stretch to call me an average child. On paper I was, if anything, well below average. Not that long ago my mother surprised me with a memory box of report cards. She had, it seems, lovingly saved almost all of them. She passed them over with a great measure of pride. Why? I have no idea.

These were not yearly progress reports, they were a cry for help. Not so much from me as from the teachers.

Going by the teachers' comments alone I am sure I would, by today's standards, qualify for every juvenile psychiatric condition going. I appeared to be the poster child for hyperactive attention deficit disorder. Year after year through elementary school the same phrases popped up: "undisciplined," "underachieving" and "distracting." Through junior high the word "disappointment" appeared a fair bit.

Reading the report cards, I felt terrible, for my teachers and for my mother. She said parent-teacher meetings were the worst. In grade six a teacher, allegedly joking, suggested that unless something "changed at home" I would eventually be tried as an adult. Classic blame the parents or, let's face it, the mother.

My mother said, "From grade one on they were always wanting to diagnose you with something. I wouldn't let them. One of them wanted me to put you on downers because you talked too much. It's a good thing you were well liked," she added, "otherwise you would have ended up in special ed."

On paper, certainly, that's where I belonged. My academic results were abysmal. How, I wondered, could one child get 50 percent in so many subjects?

"I think they call that 'pushing you ahead,'" Mom said. "You just didn't seem interested in anything at school and you can't force a child to be interested in something."

In hindsight I don't think I was suited for childhood; if childhood was a movie, I was miscast. I was a happy enough kid. Carefree, even. I don't ever remember being sad or anxious, but I do remember being astounded at how the other kids took such joy in "stuff."

I liked "stuff" but within limits. Sure, I liked playing with Hot Wheels cars, but they certainly weren't the be-all and end-all of the world. Yes, I was happy enough to get down in the dirt and push a Dinky Toy around while making the vroom-vroom sound, but I wasn't going to do it for hours on end.

And I concede now, as I did then, that dinosaurs are impressive. But not impressive enough to spend all of primary school memorizing a doctorate's worth of statistics about seven hundred species of prehistoric animals. There was a period when it seemed like the entire school was infected with a virus that led to obsessive talk about dinosaurs. Every bus ride would be punctuated with over-the-top debates about the *Velociraptor* versus the *Triceratops*, or stuttering blustery braggarts announcing to the world, "The *Tyrannosaurus rex* is *not* the largest dinosaur. There was one bigger, it was the *Argentinosaurus*, it was bigger than six elephants! Its poo was the size of a grown man!"

All I could think was, "What is the point of this? They're all dead, right?"

In primary school my very best, very daring friend was Timmy Green. He was a bit of an outlier because his obsession was not dinosaurs but trains. I liked trains too and was more than happy to play with his train set in the privacy of his basement. But I wasn't so in love with trains that I would wear a conductor outfit to school. Timmy did this on numerous occasions and it would always end in tears. The non-train-obsessed kids would mock his outfit but he didn't care. He may have cried on the way home, but the next morning he would get back on the bus, conductor's hat on head, overalls akimbo. I admired his commitment and his courage but couldn't relate.

And I never got the appeal of "running around." My father was always saying, "Go outdoors and run around." My reaction was always the same. "What an absurd thing to say. How is running around even a thing?"

Sports I could take or leave. I liked to play pickup hockey on the pond but I wasn't going to sit around with the others and talk for hours about which team we would rather play on, the Habs or the Leafs. Yes, Tyler Roach, aged eleven, he who cannot walk up a flight of stairs without falling over and banging his head, you will certainly be a first-round draft pick. Being drafted will be huge inspiration to all the other kids out there with chronic asthma and lousy eyesight.

If I excelled at anything in childhood, it would have to be at what parenting experts now call "free" or "undirected" play. The theory being that a child can't thrive properly if every moment of their day is scheduled with music lessons, volleyball camp and advanced Mandarin. The key to a well-developed, confident child is undirected play and self-directed learning.

Well, one thing my friends and I had loads of in Middle Cove was undirected play, or should I say misdirected play. It was an education, all right. We learned how to light fires, build forts and to hide towels by the pond so nobody knew we were swimming unsupervised. We learned how to play games that involved throwing pocketknives at each other's feet. We learned which barns and garages were left open. We learned how to steal crabapples from trees and carrots from gardens. We learned where Gina's brother kept his copies of *Playboy*. We learned that at a certain point in a male adolescent's life there is nothing quite as exhilarating as the sound of broken glass. We learned how to build poorly constructed go-karts and race them with abandon down Kelly's Hill. We threw rocks on the beach and explored the river. We rode bicycles everywhere and for the first fifteen years of my life I never once clapped eyes on a bike lock or a helmet. Children and dogs roamed wild and in packs.

I'd rather not dwell too much on this part of my childhood because it's too painful. Not for me but for those not lucky enough to be raised where I was, how I was and by whom I was. It was glorious.

How glorious? We had both a pony and a goat: Thunder and Lightning.

In Newfoundland at the time there was a system of denominational education. This meant if you were Catholic—and the vast majority of families in Middle Cove were—you went to a local school called St. Francis of Assisi, named after a monk who was known to wander around in the woods talking to animals.

If you were Protestant, you were bused into the city of St. John's to attend Macdonald Drive Elementary, named after Canada's first prime minister. He too was known to have conversations with animals, once dictating an entire speech to a raccoon he drunkenly mistook for his principal secretary.

The Mercer children were the exception to the rule. Despite being Catholic we went to the Protestant school. Which was essentially unheard of.

My parents had a mixed marriage, or what would be described as a mixed marriage in those days. Mom was Catholic and Dad Protestant. In order to be married in the one true church my father agreed that any children would be brought up Catholic.

And we were, kind of. We were all baptized, and we attended Catholic church on some Sundays, but when it came to school, we were sent down a different path on a different yellow bus.

My father couldn't care less where we went to school but my mother cared. I remember asking her why we didn't go to Catholic school. Her answer: "Because I went to one."

In general, it didn't cause much consternation, but the subject did come up on occasion. I went to play at my friend Danny's house one Saturday and was surprised to see him scrubbed up and dressed in his Sunday best. Turns out it was Danny's first day of altar boy training. For some reason the idea appealed to me. The robes, the ringing of the bells, the wine, it all seemed very glamorous. Danny's mother could tell I was intrigued. Certainly more intrigued than Danny, who looked like he was about to walk the plank. She told me to ride home, put on a pair of good pants, wash my face and come right back. Danny and I would be altar boys together.

I rode home, ran in the house screaming about pants and telling Mom the good news. I was going to be an altar boy.

"Indeed you're not," she said. "That is not happening."

Maybe it was the tone of her voice, but I knew I had touched a third rail. Also, the idea had become less appealing now that it involved pants. On the way out the door I heard her tell my father exactly why she had said no. So back I went to Danny's, where I found his mother waiting by the car.

She asked me why I wasn't dressed.

"I'm not allowed to be an altar boy," I reported. "Mom doesn't want me around the priests."

She went into full vapours. Her left hand reached out to the car mirror for balance. She wobbled. I took my exit.

As I was pedalling away, I yelled over my shoulder, "See you after altar boy class, Danny!"

"Daniel is busy!" his mother yelled back, still gripping the car's mirror. "For the rest of the day."

And he *was* busy. That day and the next, and then for a few weekends after that. It was quite a while before we were allowed to play with each other again.

The price you pay for taking the Protestant bus.

For obvious reasons, I'm glad my mother made that call. It's not surprising that she did. Pat Mercer is the strongest, most independent woman I know. She never suffered fools gladly.

I recall as a boy being dragged by my mother to the Bank of Montreal on Water Street in downtown St. John's. Mom had an appointment. Could anything be more boring than having to accompany a parent to the bank? We sat in a waiting area longer than anticipated and I could see she was not impressed. Eventually we were called to an office, where my mother presented some papers to the man and was preparing to sign. My mother, who worked full time as a nurse, was partially financing the purchase of a new car. When she passed over the papers, the man said something to the effect that everything was in order, the loan would be no problem, but, he said, reaching for his phone, "I'm just going to give your husband a call and see if he's okay with you getting a new car."

Well, things were no longer boring. I had never seen a person with such little regard for their own life than this man in front of me. A suicide bomber would have a better chance of emerging unscathed from a mission than some guy in a bad suit telling my mother she needed her husband's permission to do something.

"This poor dumb creature," I thought. "He has no idea what he has done."

Long story short, after the guy had been given what can only be called a brutal re-education in gender equality, we ended up marching across the street to the Bank of Nova Scotia. In her wake Mom left a man forever changed. A man who would think long and hard before ever again suggesting a woman get her husband's permission to buy a car.

The school I attended was the most modern in the province. It opened in 1971, so it was essentially brand new when I showed up for kindergarten in 1974. It still had that new-carpet chemical smell. It was modern in both its design and its cutting-edge approach to education. Macdonald Drive Elementary was to be the template for how schools were designed and run in the future. We were guinea pigs.

For starters there were no grades. Grades were a thing of the past. Grades did something to one's confidence, so instead we had "pods." Do you see the difference? "I am *not* in grade four. I am in *pod* four!"

But by far the biggest innovation at Macdonald Drive was the lack of walls. Each pod consisted of one hundred children. The pod system recognized that if you have one hundred children to educate, dividing them into three or four smaller groups in separate classrooms with privacy and walls was cruel and unusual. Far better to put all one hundred children in one giant classroom with three teachers. Free-range children.

The entire thing was conceived by an educational consultant who had clearly never met a child and currently resides in a hospital for the criminally insane.

By the time I hit grade one—sorry, pod one—battle-weary teachers had already started to erect small barricades and faux walls in direct contravention of the no-walls philosophy. These attempts were mostly for naught. The din was constant and punctuated by random screams from elsewhere in the pod. It was like being in an abattoir. You might be in math class with thirty kids and over to your right another thirty kids could be having a singalong, while to your left, kids were watching a slide show. There was no pattern in the chaos.

I was neither popular nor unpopular in school. I was middle of the pack. Like at most schools, the very top of the food chain was reserved exclusively for those who excelled at athletics.

I've never known what it feels like to throw the ball the farthest or run the fastest. But mercifully I was never dead last. And while I could hold my own in a game of soccer in the school gym, I never joined the real pickup games during recess. I would have liked to join in the skipping games, but my sense of self-preservation stopped me.

To ensure that only athletic children achieved true popularity, the government of Pierre Trudeau strong-armed the provinces and introduced a series of standardized physical education tests that were mandatory for children. I speak of the Canada Fitness Award Program. Testing took place over two weeks near the beginning of every school year. The results, carefully documented and posted in the school for all to see, were either a confirmation of your excellence and popularity or the gateway to a year filled with post-traumatic stress.

Any child could walk up to that big poster and learn exactly how many push-ups Ricky Mercer could do in one minute versus how many Wayne Thorne could do. You might look at little Keith Whalen and think, "He's probably good at sports," but then on checking the results discover he was actually as weak as a kitten. There were tests for speed sit-ups, the standing long jump, the shuttle run, the fifty-yard sprint, the three-hundred-yard dash and the endurance run, which if memory serves was 126 kilometres.

The endurance run meant an entire gym class would be spent doing laps around the soccer field. Naturally, some kids could do this in their sleep, while others struggled mightily but managed to make it in an acceptable time. Together these two groups would sit at the finish line and heckle the real stragglers who panted and limped across the finish line like they were the miraculous survivors of a death march.

Nothing, however, separated the men from the boys, the lives worth living from those better off gone, like the flexed arm hang.

The flexed arm hang is a military testing exercise originally developed by the US Marines. The difference being that adults volunteer to join the marines. Children in the Canadian school system are conscripted. Marines pride themselves on tearing down and destroying the individual and building them back up as soldiers. Elementary schools aren't really supposed to be up to that.

On flexed arm hang day everyone in gym class would sit around on the floor as the gym teacher called each student up one by one for this ultimate upper body strength exercise. The teacher, stopwatch in hand, would time how long a child could hang vertically with their chin above a bar protruding from the wall. The results would be announced in a loud voice by the teacher before noting the child's triumph or shame in his or her permanent record.

A bad result in any of the other events could be explained with a variety of plausible excuses. "I didn't do well in the shuttle run because I stood on a nail last Wednesday." "I didn't do well in the speed push-ups because I hurt my back in a karate tournament."

But the flexed arm hang was about one thing only—upper body strength. There were no excuses. You were strong or you were weak. I won't sugar-coat it: yes, as an adult my arms and pectoral muscles became toned from vigorous typing, but as a child I was weak.

One harrowing flexed arm hang competition is seared in my memory. Our regular gym teacher, a lovely woman who excelled at the genteel blood sport of field hockey, was away. No doubt off breaking down gender barriers in the multitude of sports she excelled at. Her substitute supply teacher for a period of a few weeks was a giant bull of a man who we secretly called Swamp Thing. A name inspired by his eerie likeness to the DC Comics character. He was all muscle from the waist up, relished mocking the weak and infirm and had a fitness and diet regime that was rumoured to involve a daily omelet made from the eggs of song birds.

On this particular day, Swamp Thing spent an inordinate length of time explaining just how important the flexed arm hang was. To succeed at it was to succeed at life. To fail? Well you know the rest. To illustrate just how easy the exercise was, Swampy called up a "random" child volunteer. No surprise the random child just happened to be a genetically superior whippet-like being who weighed less than a bike tire. In my grade this would be Jamie Holden. He with the long hair, the best sneakers, and the coolest orange-and-black Adidas track suit anyone had ever seen. He who routinely had his picture in the actual newspaper for excelling at both athletics and Lego.

There was a stool that kids could stand on to get in position, but Jamie didn't need that. One nod from Swamp Thing and up he jumped, grabbed the bar and pulled himself up, his chin perfectly placed, his eyes laser-focused on the bar in front of him. Swamp praised his excellent form and predicted a future that would include great wealth and beautiful ladies. All the while, Jamie hung in place, not wavering, not breaking a sweat or making a sound. He appeared as if he was not only born there but lived there as well. He didn't so much as twitch, though after a few minutes he did remove one hand and nonchalantly run it through his hair.

Eventually, when it became obvious that Jamie could hang there all day, Swamp blew his whistle, indicating it was time for Jamie to jump down, having broken a provincial record.

If your secret shame was that you thought a pencil case was heavy, this was the stuff of nightmares. I knew damn well that when my turn came I would be lucky to last five to eight seconds in that position.

That, however, was a walk in the park compared with how the overweight kids fared. The heavy kids could simply not last a second. One by one they were called up to take their position on the stool. They stood there with their chin in place, their chubby little arms in the flex position, holding the bar for dear life. The kids watching were rolling around on the floor in hysterics. Swamp shouted them down to make them quiet. And when silence was achieved he counted down from three, winked at the class and then kicked the chair out from under the portly pupil.

And despite the determined look on the child's face, and his very best effort, his arms would fail him, and he would plummet downward as fast as a condemned man falls through a trap door on the gallows.

Except the child would not enjoy the sweet release of darkness. Instead, he would end up on his back, helpless as a flipped-over turtle. The laughter of twenty-nine children ringing in his ears. All thanks to Prime Minister Pierre Trudeau—sadist. Gym class meets *Lord of the Flies*.

Over two weeks the scores would be tallied and then at a school assembly each child would be presented with a medal and a patch depending on their level of fitness. The very best received the Award of Excellence. Only a handful of boys and girls would reach this level of social glorification.

Then the gold medals would be passed out, each child whooping and hollering and punching the sky with their fists. They would look at their cloth badge with great satisfaction, knowing their mother would soon sew it onto their jean jacket so they could proudly wear it every day for the remainder of the year.

The silver medallists, by far the biggest group of all, would celebrate as well.

Then the bronze medallists would be called, most of them not happy with their result, some too dim to know that they had come in last.

But of course they hadn't really come in "last." There was yet another category. A category for those of us who didn't own the podium but did manage to trip over it and get a nosebleed.

Those of us who were too weak, too heavy or too uncoordinated to warrant a bronze received a little plastic pin with the letter *P* on it. P for participant.

Cue the public shaming.

2

The Hippies in the Van

At Macdonald Drive Elementary each pod had distinct areas for the three classes plus one staff room. Even the staff rooms were open concept. The teachers would enter and exit through a large open archway.

By the time grade three rolled around, eight-year-old me was spending a lot of time on the floor outside of that archway. That is where you were sentenced to sit if you were deemed a distraction in class. It was believed that making kids do time by the staff room during recess or lunch was a great deterrent.

Personally, missing recess suited me fine. I think many people have glorious sepia-toned memories of time spent on the school playground. The sun is shining, the grass is green, the air is filled with squeals of laughter. If you went to Macdonald Drive Elementary and you think that way, you're experiencing false memory syndrome.

The truth is, at my school once you crossed the threshold and hit the playground you were far more likely to encounter gale-force winds and some form of sideways precipitation. The air was filled not with squeals of laughter so much as the sounds of children being pushed into puddles. That and the constant staccato of metal chains rattling on the flagpole in hurricane winds. Throw in a dented apple and a box of raisins and that's recess. Fill your boots.

Punishing kids by taking away playground access makes a lot of sense. Everyone agrees that kids need exercise. It helps them focus in class, keeps them healthy and hopefully leads to a lifetime habit of regular daily activity. To take a child who is acting out in class and punish them by taking away their chance to go outside and blow off steam is pretty clever. As a bonus it might lull the child into pursuing a sedentary lifestyle. A lifestyle that will lead them down the road to obesity, high blood pressure and early-onset diabetes. But hey, if you can't do the time, don't do the crime. This is the price you pay for making Timmy Green laugh by gluing your own hand to your forehead during art class.

I liked spending time on the floor outside the staff room because I learned that if you were very quiet and very still, the teachers inside would forget you were there and start talking with impunity. Sometimes they would swear. Hearing adults swear was always a forbidden thrill. Sometimes they would talk about other teachers. And always they would talk about the kids. I found this exhilarating. It was impossible for me to shut up and pay attention in a normal class, but when given the opportunity to overhear a grade four teacher refer to a specific child as a spoiled little shit, I had the discipline of a Tibetan monk.

Eavesdropping on teachers also allowed me to pick up information that might prove useful. In much the same way a prisoner who works in the warden's office might find out about an impending lockdown, students on the shaming floor might learn in advance of an impending field trip to the local brewery. Information is power. True then. True now.

So you can imagine how excited I was when halfway through a lunch-hour punishment stint I distinctly heard one teacher confirm to another that there were to be no classes that afternoon. No classes! A mind-boggling development. And I was the only one who knew. This must have been how Churchill felt when he found out before anyone else that Germany was preparing to surrender.

I couldn't wait until after lunch and the other kids came in from the playground red-cheeked and winded. I would casually say, "Did you do your homework? I didn't. I've got a feeling there will be no school this afternoon anyway." I was so confident in my information that if anyone questioned this I might even say: "Bet you a dollar?"

What I didn't know was why there would be no school. All I knew was that all three classes in the pod were to be brought together on the floor in the library and we would, in the words of Mr. Brace, be subjected "to those hippies in a van."

It sounded ominous.

Unexpected disruptions in the school day were not without precedent. Just a few months previously, all classes after lunch one day were cancelled without warning. We were all lined up in the gym and told that we were to stay away from one another at a distance of two feet—early shades of what we now know as physical distancing. Two long lines slowly snaked into both the girls' and boys' change rooms. Inside, strangers in face masks stood over us as they combed through our hair in search of lice. Once you were inspected you were given a blue card or a red card. The blues went back to class and the reds were sent out to sit on the floor of the gym.

I remember a lot of consternation on the part of the lady who was picking through my hair. I don't blame her. In those days I refused to cut my hair at all. It never grew long; it just grew high and wide. From behind I looked like Diana Ross. Field mice could have been living in there for all I knew.

Once inspected I was issued a red card and sent back to the gym. It became pretty evident that the red-carders were actually in quarantine. There were about fifty of us sitting at centre court furiously scratching our scalps. A few kids were sniffling back tears. I assume out of embarrassment or maybe horror.

Eventually the principal came and spoke to us from about thirty feet away. In a calm, reassuring voice, she told us that tiny wingless creatures had burrowed into our scalps and were drinking our blood. But other than that, everything was fine. Also our parents had been called. At this news Bianca Hickey burst out crying and ran towards the principal, arms spread wide, looking for a hug and reassurance. The principal screamed and recoiled in terror as if she was being attacked by something rabid. She sought safety behind the gym teacher and hissed at Bianca to get back "with the rest of them," dry-heaving for good measure.

"Your parents have been given instructions on how to bathe you in chemicals. In the meantime you will stay in the gym until end of school, no more classes."

Most of us greeted this news with cheers and high-fives. Bianca continued to sob, head in hands, her long, curly blond hair hiding her face. The next day with her smart new bob she was practically unrecognizable.

After lunch many people were suitably impressed that I had divined we were getting the afternoon off. "What's happening?" they said, as we were marched to the library. "Hippies in a van is my guess," I said. "What's that mean?" they asked.

"If you don't know what that means," I said, "I can't help you."

In the library the tables and chairs were all pulled back and we were told to sit on the floor in front of what looked like a curtain made from hundreds of different pieces of fabric. It looked exactly like one of my grandmother's quilts.

From behind the curtain came a man we hadn't seen before. He told us his name was Uncle Val. And he told us he was there to tell us an incredible story of a boy named Jack and an adventure like none other.

I now know that Uncle Val is the creation of Canadian comedy legend Andy Jones. He of CODCO. A true comedic genius. But right there, in that moment, he was 100 percent Uncle Val.

He had me at hello.

The company of actors was a local theatre company called Sheila's Brush. Their passion for collecting, preserving and performing traditional stories from Newfoundland and Labrador is legend. The Jack Tales are performed to this day because of their work. Andy would go on to write a series of award-winning children's books about Jack and his adventures.

On this day, as the story unfolded, one after another of the characters mentioned emerged from behind the colourful curtain. Some of them danced a jig, one did a handstand, one shook his fist and bared his teeth. In due time we met our hero Jack, his greedy mother, a brave princess, a benevolent king, a band of pirates, an insane horse and one hell of a devious cat.

I was hypnotized. This was better than anything I had ever seen. I couldn't believe these actors could make a story like this come to life. It was also the funniest thing I had ever seen. And the scariest thing too. Uncle Val made us fall over laughing and then jump out of our skin with fright. And who were these actors? If this was what it meant to be a hippie in a van, sign me up. The hell with being a firefighter, a nurse, a doctor or an astronaut, I wanted to live in a van with a bunch of people with long hair and travel around the Avalon Peninsula.

I thought my head would explode and my heart would burst. I didn't know what it was I was experiencing but I knew I wanted more. Is this how Timmy felt about trains? That explained a lot. Transfixed, I heard myself whisper, "That should be me up there."

And no sooner had I uttered that famous show-business incantation than Uncle Val asked, "Are there any pirate children in the crowd?" He then implored the wildly clapping horse to find him some child pirates! All around me kids were raising their hands. The horse was coming into the audience. This was really happening. Kids were scooting closer to the stage on their bottoms, eager to be chosen.

I saw the horse's mouth open and grab Laura Doobie by the arm. He pulled her up on the stage and deposited her behind the curtain. And then he was back. The horse was coming my way. He was looking for another pirate. I could see the actor inside the giant head looking directly at me. Or was he looking at the little girl next to me who was also waving her hands? Everything seemed to move in slow motion as the horse's jaws opened and came even closer.

I am not proud of this, but at that precise moment, I body checked Adelle Parsons sideways and threw myself with all my might into the horse's mouth. Nothing was going to stop me.

And suddenly I *was* up there.

The horse "dragged" me to the stage. I struggled mightily because, as eager as I was, I knew instinctively that was what the part called for.

And then I was behind the curtain. One of the actors grabbed me and wrapped me in a large shirt with Velcro in the place of buttons. Velcro! Who'd thought of such a thing! She tied a bandana on my head and put a patch over one eye. I was being transformed. All around me the actors were furiously changing from one character to another. The man who only moments ago was the king was now wearing a red dress, a blond wig and a crown. From the other side of the curtain I could hear Uncle Val shouting, the accordion playing and the audience screaming. I wanted to know what was happening, but I was even more intrigued by the action around me. Backstage! To this day there is no more exciting place in the world.

Moments later I made my amateur theatrical debut in the role of pirate child number two. I was told to follow the adult pirate and do exactly as he did. And did I ever. When he danced, I danced. When he shouted, I yelled. And when called upon to do so, I quivered in fear like there was no tomorrow. The audience ate it up. It was the greatest three minutes of my life.

"This," I thought, "I could do forever."

That Christmas, still buzzing from my experience with the hippies in a van, I auditioned for and landed the part of the Roly Poly Teddy Bear in the school concert. A pivotal role, my job was to walk out and flop on the floor while a choir of children sang a song about toys. I spent days practising the move. And come showtime, my bear did not so much flop on the floor as perform a long-drawn-out death scene in the best theatrical tradition. I was flopping around on the floor long after the choir's song had ended. I was a total ham. You could smell the pineapples and cloves for miles.

3

Just Kids

For the longest time at home there were three of us, me being the youngest. My brother Gilbert was five years older than me, my sister Susan three years older than him. This was the set-up until, when I was nine, my younger sister arrived out of the blue. She weighed eighty-three pounds, six ounces and was seven years old. She was no accident. She was very much planned.

The gestation period is a bit hazy. One day my mother was telling me that she had met a little girl, younger than me, who didn't have a family. My mother asked if it would be all right if this little girl came to visit for a few hours on the weekend. I would not, she assured me, have to play with her or entertain her. It was suggested that I could introduce her to the dog.

I didn't know much but I did know I had no interest in playing with a seven-year-old girl. That said, I wasn't dead inside. I couldn't begrudge a kid without a family a few hours with our dog. I agreed to the visit.

Tonia showed up that Saturday and revealed herself to be a very talkative, very excitable redhead who had a habit of spelling random words. "Last summer I was on a T-R-A-I-N! Have you ever been on a train, R-I-C-K-Y?" To give her credit, for a little kid she was under a lot of pressure. She must have felt that this was some sort of audition.

Tonia was soon spending every Saturday at our house. It became part of our routine. Eventually it was suggested that she could spend Saturdays and Sundays. I agreed that it made sense. The weekends soon became full time and Tonia became my foster sister. It seemed like the most natural progression in the world. Soon she had her own friends on the street. We adopted her sometime after that, and she chose to change her last name to ours.

The dining room was turned into a bedroom and from then on, all meals, including on Sundays, were eaten at the kitchen table. How six people fit in that room for meals astounds me to this day. The room hasn't gotten smaller but today there is barely room in there for Mom and Dad and two cups of tea. Biscuits have to sit on a tray in the hallway.

I think my parents were mostly concerned with how Tonia's joining the family would affect me. I was the baby, and suddenly that position changed. I was the one closest in age to Tonia, so we would be going to the same school. When Tonia showed up, my sister Susan was busy applying for her first year at Memorial University and actively planning an escape to the mainland to finish her degree. My brother was in high school and was hiding in his room and listening to Clash records.

Tonia was a welcome addition to the family. And nobody was less surprised than me. In fact, from the first time my mother mentioned that she'd met a little girl without a family, I assumed she would end up joining ours. My parents are like that.

And Tonia clearly took to the dog I'd introduced her to on day one. Of course, he's now long gone, but there's not a dog on this earth that she won't rescue. As I write this she is probably figuring out how to airlift strays from the Dominican Republic.

Susan paid me the ultimate compliment by allowing me to hang around with her and her friends. Astounding when you think about it. Unlike many of my friends' teenage sisters, Susan was always super nice to her little brother. Later she would become my biggest fan, attending any show she could over and again. Also, when she got her first real job, she would slip me money on occasion. She always had a great maturity and independent streak that probably came from the fact that from the age of seven she had to dutifully inject herself with insulin two or three times a day.

Because of her I was "raised as a diabetic." No desserts in our fridge and no processed food either. I can remember yelling, "I've been to other houses, you know. Cottage cheese is not a treat!"

My sister would go on to be a social worker and spend the early part of her career working with chronically psychiatrically ill street people in the nation's capital.

Early in my TV days, we both approached the Air Canada desk in St. John's airport. I was flying to Halifax, where we were shooting *This Hour Has 22 Minutes*, and Susan was on a flight to Ottawa, where she was working. The young man behind the counter saw me and said, "Oh my gosh, I love your show, let's take a look at your ticket and see if we can find you a seat in business class." A few flicks on his keyboard and he passed me a new and improved ticket. I thanked him profusely and then leaned in and said conspiratorially, "This is my sister. She's flying out today as well, on another flight. Do you think you could find her a seat in the front of the plane?"

He turned to my sister and said, "Do you work in TV too?"

She said, "No, I work with the homeless."

"That's too bad," he said sympathetically as he passed over her economy ticket. But then he glanced at me, then back at her, and said, "Oh what the hell," took back her ticket and magically gave her an upgrade.

The point being, she's a better person than me and has always worked to help the underdog. Meanwhile I get the better seats.

Out of all the siblings, my brother had the best deal. Mostly because he had me as a younger brother. That's not a comment on my personality so much as a comment on how handy a little brother can be. For example, when he was ten and I was five I would, without hesitation, do whatever he told me to do. If he said, "Go get a butter knife and put it in the electrical socket," I would have started running to the kitchen drawer in a heartbeat. If he started counting, I'd have gone twice as fast.

Now to be clear, he never did instruct me to put a knife in a socket, as that would have been far too dangerous. Either that or the thought never occurred to him.

When he built a ramp out on the road with plywood and cinder blocks, I in my capacity as little brother proved indispensable. The whole thing was inspired by stuntman Evel Knievel, whose most recent TV broadcast showed him crash his motorcycle after attempting to jump over a swimming pool filled with sharks. He cleared the pool but went off the landing ramp and hit a cameraman. We heard that he poked the cameraman's eye out with his handlebar. Somehow the eye ended up in the tank and now the sharks had a taste for human flesh. Most experts now agree that the fundamental mistake Evel made while attempting to execute his stunt was being snapped on whiskey and pills.

Gilbert didn't have a pool of sharks to jump but he did have me. It was my job to lie on the ground, giving him something to clear. Jump after successful jump I would be repositioned farther into danger. Seeing my little body lying on the pavement on the wrong side of a ramp was all the inspiration he needed to pedal harder and soar farther.

After a few successful jumps it did dawn on me that if Evel Knievel had come up short, he would have been devoured by fish on live TV. Had Gilbert came up short, he would be fine—he might take a spill off his bike, but I would have a broken femur or perhaps lose the use of a hand. When I floated this notion, my older, wiser brother responded by quoting one of the famous stuntman's great catchphrases about his own self: "When he's not in action, he's in traction." Fair enough, I thought and lay down on the pavement again.

We never did find out which part of me would have cushioned Gilbert's bike had the stunt failed. A man in a pickup truck saw me on the ground and pulled over. He got out and started screaming that I was going to be killed. As he approached, we did what we always did. We ran. We watched from a distance as he picked up the plywood and cinder blocks, threw them in the back of his truck and drove away.

Gilbert wasn't the only one to benefit from the relationship. There were advantages to having an older brother. Kids don't mess with you on the bus if you have an older brother. That's just a fact of life. Also, on the home front, because of the age difference and the substantial difference in our maturity levels, anything we did wrong was, statistically, his fault. He was older and thus theoretically more sensible.

History has proved this was not entirely true. Certainly it wasn't when, at the ages of seven and eleven and a half, we headed out alone into the woods with an axe and a saw and the goal of finding the perfect Christmas tree. Two children armed with medieval cutting tools. What could go wrong?

In our house, the tradition was for the tree to go up the day before Christmas Eve. This infuriated us because many people on the street would have trees up a full week before Christmas. Now of course people put them up way earlier than that. I have neighbours in Toronto who have their Christmas tree up and decorated on November 12 and they are Jewish.

So it must have been just before the holiday when our nagging got us the go-ahead from Dad to go find the perfect tree. And this year we were being trusted to do it entirely on our own. This is typical of my father. And while I know now he would have been happy with whatever tangly mess we brought back, we took the challenge very seriously. So, axe in Gilbert's hand, saw in mine, we set out for all the spots we imagined we might find a magnificent fir.

We were young, but we knew the rules. Trees could only be taken from Crown land and not near any road. Also, you should look for younger trees that are in clumps of other younger trees. That way, when you take one, you're essentially making room for the other young trees to grow. You are not, under any circumstances, to cut down a larger mature tree and just take the top off. It's wasteful, environmentally unfriendly and just plain wrong. We knew this because

Dad had said it many times when, every year at Christmas, we would come across a large felled tree with no top.

Of course, unsupervised, it was the very first thing we did.

We started out with the best of intentions. We were on Pine River Lane, a dirt road about a kilometre from the house that cut through multiple meadows. We were looking at the small firs that ringed the fields, but none of them looked quite good enough. Eventually we started looking at the tops of the larger, more mature trees; we could see why some jerks would go that route. The tops were perfect. We sized up a monster with an attractive tip, agreed to "never tell," and started cutting.

It took us forever. The trunk was huge, and taking turns was suddenly the worst kind of manual labour. We didn't have a bucksaw, just a regular wood saw—a saw suitable for cutting down the young trees we were supposed to be hunting. The thick branches of the mighty fir prohibited us from using the axe. We tried to cut the lower limbs off to make room so we could swing at the trunk, but that was also exhausting. Halfway through the trunk we gave up. We half killed a tree for nothing. Is it any wonder they say the brains of little boys take forever to form?

In the face of our defeat we ran.

It was getting dark as we headed up Middle Cove Road. Miserable. Two saps covered in same. It was Gilbert who stopped. Grabbed my arm and said, "I see it!"

"You see what?" I said.

"Right there, look. It's perfect."

And he was right. It was a young tree, six or seven feet tall, standing alone. It was the classic Christmas tree. In all my years I had never seen such a perfect one.

Perfect except for one small problem. The tree was pretty close to the road. Also, it was behind a fence, and so the tree was in someone's yard. And not just any someone. It was in Timmy Green's yard. My best friend. The Greens had one of the largest pieces of land in Middle Cove. A house and barn and two large meadows. This tree was in front of that barn. Certainly not Crown land.

The Greens' yard was always immaculately mowed. Their grounds were heavily landscaped, with many different types of flowering bushes and trees. They took this stuff seriously. They were both professionals, university professor types, in fact. I suspected that they lacked a sense of humour. That said, no sense of humour would allow them to see the lighter side of what Gilbert was about to suggest.

"It's not even really in their yard," he said. "It's more by the barn. I bet they wouldn't even notice."

They probably wouldn't, I agreed.

Their "not noticing" was magical thinking at its best. This was not even a tree that was growing wild on their property. This tree had come from a nursery. This was a tree they had planted, in a lawn that they mowed regularly. When spring came there would be a ring of daffodils at its base.

"It's really young. The trunk is small. We can have it out of there in minutes."

I had to admit it was a pretty good-looking tree. The chances of our finding another one like it were slim to none.

"You stand guard," Gilbert said.

And with that we were over the fence and on our bellies crawling towards the target.

I lay in the snow and put their house under surveillance. I was to whistle or cough if I saw anyone coming. The lights were on, but nobody came out to investigate the sounds of a saw and a panting boy.

Within a few minutes it fell.

"Grab the end," Gilbert said, and we heaved it over the fence. Now we were on the road. We looked back where the tree once stood. It was *glaring* in its absence. How we thought for a second that it wouldn't be missed was truly absurd. It was like a car thief thinking that a homeowner wouldn't notice the missing Subaru because there was also a Range Rover in the driveway.

This was new territory for us. We had committed a true act of vandalism. We were vandals and juvenile delinquents.

Suddenly Gilbert's eyes widened like saucers. "Our footprints!" he said. Sure enough, all around the base of the naked stump were footprints. Boys' footprints. We might as well have left a signed note.

Together we climbed over the fence again. All criminals return to the scene of the crime but usually they wait for a week to ten days. We were back within minutes. Together in the fading light we got down on all fours and wiped away our footprints with an intensity bordering on manic. Eventually the tracks were covered.

Back out on the road it was an adventure to get home. We had probably half of a kilometre of ground to cover, and every time a car approached we would throw ourselves into the ditch with an increasingly dramatic flair, like soldiers diving into the trenches to avoid a hand grenade.

On the walk we covered a wide range of topics. Everything from "Whose idea was this anyway?" to "Do you think we will go to jail?" to "Will the Greens be mad?" and of course "the Santa factor."

Oddly the one option we didn't consider was just dumping the tree and running. Possession is nine-tenths of the law, but we didn't know that. We were too naive to realize the smart move was to ditch the evidence, throw the gun in the creek and bolt, or in this case, the tree in the ditch and skedaddle.

Our arrival in our yard was greeted as a triumph. The entire family agreed that we had found the perfect tree. So perfect, in fact, that Mom and Dad agreed to put it up and decorate it that very night, a full two days early.

When we were asked "Where did you find it?" we answered simultaneously and with great confidence. "Pine Line," said Gilbert; "By the pond," I blurted.

You'd think on the walk home we would have bothered to get our stories straight.

In any event, when the tree was lit and decorated, Mom declared, as she did every year, that this was the best tree yet. For the first time she was not lying.

Over the next few days, we began to relax. Nobody came around and asked questions. No SWAT team surrounded the house. We started to get comfortable with the idea that we had pulled off the perfect crime. We still avoided walking past the Greens' house in case someone was watching over the stump. I avoided calling Timmy to go sliding because the hill was on the Greens' property. All of the children in the neighbourhood were free to toboggan on their hill. In hindsight that was awful nice of his parents. Sometimes Mrs. Green would make hot chocolate for everyone. I tried not to think about that. Also you could always count on Mr. Green to pull over and give you a ride if he saw you walking up the street. The guilt was killing me.

The plan was to avoid the Greens altogether until perhaps the new year. So it came as a complete shock when Gilbert and I marched into the house after dinner on Christmas Eve and found John and Jane Green in our living room with our parents, drinking tea.

It's a wonder I didn't projectile-vomit right there on the spot.

I had known the Greens my entire life, but never to my knowledge had Timmy's parents been in our living room before. The thought that they would ever be in our house had never even occurred to me. And yet here they were, on the couch, next to the perfect Christmas tree.

"Look who popped by," said Dad.

"Hello," I said, although no real sound came out.

And then the most astounding thing happened. Mrs. Green turned back to my parents and continued with the conversation they'd clearly been having before we came in.

It was small talk.

Gilbert and I sank to the floor looking at each other with bewilderment while the adults continued to have a pleasant conversation about nothing in particular.

Twenty minutes later my heart rate was approaching normal when Mr. Green, on standing and getting ready to leave, suddenly turned the conversation to theft. "Have you ever had anyone cut any trees off your land, Ken?" he asked. "Someone took a tree by our barn this week, practically in broad daylight."

My mother and father reacted to this news the way someone would react if they found out an axe murderer had moved in next door.

"In your *garden*?" Mom said, aghast. "Can you believe it."

"Brazen," Dad said.

"Who in God's name would do that?" Mom asked.

I thought I was going to die. "They have to know," I thought. This was an elaborate torture. The tree was literally under their noses. The entire house reeked of fir and guilt. Of course they knew it was us.

It dawned on me that I had never ever been in this much trouble before. I was about to speak when my eyes caught those of my brother. As he reached up to scratch his neck he ever so subtly made the universal symbol for "do not say a word," his index finger crossing his windpipe like a knife.

And suddenly the Greens were reaching for their coats.

"Well, that was nice. Thanks for the tea," said one of them.

"Come again," said Dad. "Don't be strangers."

"Merry Christmas," said the Greens directly to my brother and me. And as if they meant it, "Hope Santa finds you."

"You too," I croaked. Was my voice choosing now to change?

"Lovely tree," said Mr. Green.

"Isn't it," said his wife.

And then they were gone. And Mom and Dad were taking the empty cups to the kitchen.

I was hyperventilating on the floor but Gilbert threw himself on the sofa with total confidence. Cool. Collected.

"Told ya," he said. "They didn't suspect a thing."

To this day I have no idea whether they knew it was us who cut down the bloody thing. If they did, why did they remain silent? Maybe they thought it better to just let the guilt punish us. Or maybe because of their decency they never considered in a million years that the tree from their land was the one standing in our house with an angel on top.

I do know that many times over the years I've considered confessing to them. They still live down the street in the same house.

In our defence all I can say is that in all honesty we never took a tree on anyone else's property ever again. My parents were legitimately horrified when the truth came out in our house many decades later. They were shocked to learn they had raised history's greatest monsters and didn't know it. And they couldn't believe we had both sat there in the room with the Greens while the tree was discussed and we didn't crack.

"Terrible," Mom said. "Although it *was* a nice tree."

If you are reading this, John and Jane, my abject apologies. I'll drop off a sapling in the spring.

4

The Idiot Box

As a child my relationship with television was limited. So many people who work in television report that while growing up TV was their dear friend. For some, directors especially, it was their only friend.

For me TV wasn't a dear friend or a trusted companion. It was more like a distant uncle who would show up on occasion. The kind of uncle you weren't supposed to spend much time with unsupervised.

We were not what you would describe as a TV family.

I had friends whose families had colour sets that were never turned off. I had friends with TVs that were so large they sat in mahogany cabinets that took up half the living room. Some friends were allowed to eat in front of theirs on tables designed just for that purpose. I had never met one, but I had heard rumours that some kids had TVs in their bedrooms. The rumours were consistent, so I assumed they were true, like the one about the dog in Torbay that had kittens.

Television and my parents didn't get along.

My parents were of the opinion that TV was only a negative influence, one that needed to be managed and doled out in very small portions. It was tightly rationed, like nylons and chocolate in the war.

For years there was no television set in the house at all. This was not because they hadn't been invented. Philo Farnsworth did that in 1927. By the time I was born, TV sets were ubiquitous—it was rare that a middle-class home in North America would be without one. In most homes the TV was the centre of attention. My parents eschewed that notion.

Ken and Pat Mercer, after starting a family, decided that they would not buy a television for the house until they could afford to purchase a piano first. Who thinks like that?

For the most part I believe that my parents are two of the finest people on earth. Wonderful human beings who raised their kids with unconditional love and support. But where they came up with their ridiculous views about television, I have no idea. Had there been a Kids Help Phone line back in those days I would have reported them.

Their desire to own a piano had nothing to do with status. My parents had no interest in status symbols of any kind. Cars were always second-hand, a goat mowed the lawn, and when the greatest status symbol of them all came to Middle Cove—the paved driveway—ours remained crushed stone.

That was what separated the haves from the have-nots in Middle Cove: asphalt and a colour TV. We had neither.

My parents chose a piano over a TV because as far as they were concerned, time spent watching TV was time wasted. It was brain cells disintegrating. They envisioned a family where the children read books, played music and frolicked in the fresh air.

Who did they think we were? The von Trapps?

It was my older brother and sister who went the longest time without TV. The piano was purchased just when I was at the age where it was dawning on me that there was a gaping hole in our life. My aunt had a magic box that played cartoons. Where was ours? When it was explained that we couldn't have a television because we were saving for a piano, I felt like I was being raised in an insane asylum.

And when the piano arrived? I had no interest. If anything, I had a resentment towards the instrument. Susan took lessons and liked them. My brother is musically gifted, and he began playing by ear.

Tonia took to the thing the day she arrived and today plays beautifully. Me? Out of spite I learned exactly two, irritating songs. These were the A&W Root Bear song and a classic Gilbert Mercer composition with the lyrics:

I think, I think I smell a stink.
I think, I think I do.
I think, I think I smell a stink.
It's coming out of you.

It just has the one chorus but it's the kind of song that is designed to be sung and played with great gusto over and over again—it can be repeated for as long as it takes the average seven-year-old to cease finding the lyrics funny. Which meant I played that song as often as Glenn Gould played the *Goldberg Variations*. My goal was to play it just enough to make my parents regret the purchase and trade it in for a floor-model Magnavox.

No such luck.

Eventually a friend of my father's came to our rescue. Danny Shea owned a TV repair shop and with the advent of colour television, black-and-white units quickly became obsolete and worthless. He took pity on us and gifted us a black-and-white portable orphan in need of a good home.

Some family's trash was my family's treasure.

The portable came with strict rules imposed upon us by our parents. We couldn't watch it too much, as it rots the mind, and we couldn't sit too close to it, because that would make us go blind. (Why is it that every worthwhile pastime in a young man's life leads to the loss of sight?) TV was not something that could be watched every night or every day after school. One or two shows a week was all that was allowed. And there had to be consensus among the kids.

Mom and Dad pushed us towards wholesome and family-oriented shows such as *The Waltons* and *Little House on the Prairie*. Personally, I could never get past the thing on John-Boy's face, and Laura Ingalls left me cold.

My parents were particularly strict about anything violent. After just one episode my parents were convinced that *The Incredible Hulk* was the cause of my recent bad dreams. Despite my protestations, the Hulk was banned.

I did have some odd dreams about the Hulk, but they could hardly be described as nightmares. Confusing yes, nightmarish no.

But were my parents right? Could TV be a bad influence on a child? Well, to this day I have a penchant for non-verbal olive-skinned thugs with anger issues. For this I blame CBS.

But eventually the Hulk, Magnum and Bo and Luke Duke ceased to be relevant. Because when I was ten years old the most extraordinary thing happened.

The Wonderful Grand Band appeared on television for the first time. And nothing was the same again. Never again would the kids argue over what to watch. Suddenly there was actual consensus. Not just in our family but in the entire province.

The Wonderful Grand Band was a CBC Newfoundland and Labrador production. And as everyone other than the CBC board of directors knows, the network's mandate is to reflect Canadian culture back to Canada. For most of its life the CBC interpreted this mandate to mean that they needed to produce not only Canadian content for a national audience but also local content for a regional audience. To that end there were regional production centres all across Canada.

Newfoundland and Labrador was a region unto itself, and for decades CBC TV produced non-stop original programming. It being Newfoundland, music and variety was a mainstay. Local programming was always successful, but in 1980, with the premiere of *The Wonderful Grand Band*, it was taken to a whole new level.

It was a show that featured and was about the eponymous Wonderful Grand Band. They were a supergroup of Newfoundland musicians. Ron Hynes, to this day our greatest songwriter, was the lead singer. The band could play anything. They would cover hit songs of the day, perform original compositions and play traditional Newfoundland music with a modern rock and roll twist. They were the original Great Big Sea.

But what really set the show apart were the comedians. Tommy Sexton and Greg Malone, two members of the CODCO comedy troupe, were as essential as any member of the band. They each played multiple characters every week. An entire fictional world surrounded the band, and it had been created entirely by Tommy and Greg.

They were gender-bending before the term was coined. Together or alone, they played the band's managers, groupies, mothers and fathers, grandmothers and grandfathers. They impersonated famous Newfoundlanders and Ronald Reagan. And much to the chagrin of the church they played a non-stop cavalcade of nuns, priests and Christian Brothers. The show was outrageous and funny as hell.

And it oozed Newfoundland culture. The music was ours and the voices and references were ours. It parodied and satirized everything that was wonderful about and everything that was wrong with Newfoundland and Labrador.

From the moment it aired it was the most popular show on the schedule. Suddenly the biggest TV stars in the world were not those of *Dallas* or *Falcon Crest*. They were not living in Los Angeles or New York. The biggest stars were living down the street.

I can remember being in the Avalon Mall as a kid when a rumour started to spread that Tommy and Greg were in the building. Suddenly an avalanche of kids were running through the mall screaming their names. Some kid yelled "They went that way!" and pointed to Zellers. Hundreds of youngsters trampled through the ladies' department looking for their comedy heroes. It was like *A Hard Day's Night*, but with baymen, not Beatles.

The musicians in the band were also huge stars. Alan Doyle, lead singer of Great Big Sea, is exactly of my vintage, and he too says his life changed when *Grand Band* came on. When asked in an interview to describe how popular the band was, he said, "Elvis never played in Newfoundland, but if he did, he would have opened for the Wonderful Grand Band."

The show was appointment viewing for everyone in the province, whether you were eight or eighty. Each episode would get 220,000 viewers in a province of 330,000 people. Per capita it was the most successful regional TV project in the history of CBC.

People loved it, but I adored it. To me it was the most brilliant, funniest thing in the world. My first fan letter was to the Grand Band, telling them how much I liked the show and outlining a few ideas I had to maybe improve it.

Tommy and Greg became my idols. I wanted to do exactly what they were doing.

One day my father referred to the TV as "the idiot box."

I said, "Yeah, well when I grow up, I want to be an idiot."

Which is exactly what I did.

5

Class Act

For high school, grades ten through twelve, I attended Prince of Wales Collegiate. PWC was considered one of the more prestigious schools in the city. Its catchment consisted of the wealthier St. John's neighbourhoods, and it was situated next door to the university. This was where the St. John's professional class originated. In those days PWC was known for producing our province's doctors and engineers, our teachers and bureaucrats and eventually its clowns.

For the first time we had some latitude in what classes we studied. In my first year I could choose two electives. I chose Creative Writing and World Affairs. I loved both. PWC did offer a theatre class, but I did not take the plunge. I had heard that it was, for the most part, filled with older students, those in grades eleven and twelve. Why that was a factor in the decision I have no idea. Curious is the mind of a kid in grade ten. *Curious* being the operative word. Because I was certainly that—about a lot of things.

At my school there was no such thing as a gay-straight alliance, but there was the drama club. Which was basically the same thing. Or at least that was my suspicion. I couldn't wait to sign up.

Unfortunately, I wasn't the only one with suspicions.

In the early days of grade ten, it was announced over the PA system that the drama club would be having their first meeting of the year in the library. This announcement was met with a chorus of catcalls and a handful of students began waving limp wrists in the air. Their leader, in a Daniel Hechter polo shirt and with a forehead like a ski hill, said, "Attention, all fags, flakes and weirdos—the drama club has started." This got big laughs and no reprimand. His buddies high-fived him as if congratulating him on a job well done. And in hind-sight maybe they were. It was a complete sentence, which, I would come to learn, was never an easy task for him.

But for me the catcalls and the high-fives suddenly made it impossible to breathe. It was one of those horrible teenage moments where you are convinced that everyone is about to find out what club you belong in.

I immediately concluded that signing up for the drama club was not going to happen. It was clearly the equivalent of social suicide. The idea that these guys would somehow see me heading into the meeting was inconceivable. Of course, in order for any of them do that, they would have had to have found the library first. That was unlikely.

I'm embarrassed to say that at that point in my life, in grade ten, I was not brave enough to ignore the mob and seek out the "fags, flakes and weirdos" who, secretly, intrigued me no end. "Head down" was my mantra, and it's my guess it was the mantra of the majority of kids who were figuring out how to function in the new hellscape that was high school.

I did stick my head up long enough to run for student council. It wasn't the idea of student government that appealed to me so much as the process. Each candidate was expected to take part in something called a "speak out" contest. We were each to give a three-minute speech on an issue dear to our heart. So, while I didn't put up posters or campaign in any way, I did give a speech.

All of the candidates took the "speak out" seriously and prepared dire speeches on subjects of the utmost importance—the cultural imperative of the seal hunt, why we should say no to drugs and of course multiple talks on our impending death from the hole in the ozone layer.

The entire school population gathered in the gymnasium for the occasion. They sat in silence, watching and listening with the enthusiasm of Chinese dissidents in a re-education camp.

It didn't occur to me to take the exercise seriously. I viewed it as an opportunity to do three minutes of stand-up. So that's what I did. I would like to say I wrote my speech entirely on my own, but the truth is, it was very much an homage to, and may have even been gently plagiarized from, the great American humorist Dave Barry.

At least I think it was him. My father's sister, my aunt Eva, lived in Virginia. She was one of many Newfoundland women who married American servicemen stationed in Newfoundland during and after the war. She regularly sent letters and care packages to us and included in them clippings from a humour columnist who I now think was Barry. I loved them.

One of the columns I remembered from childhood was filled with puns based entirely on the names of fruits and vegetables. I resurrected that idea for my "speak out," and it worked like a charm. I don't know if it was the content or the delivery or the fact that I was providing a break from dire predictions of our future, but it worked. I got big laughs with bad puns. The laughs translated into electoral victory.

At the end of the year when the yearbook came out, I received my first and, to date, my finest review. "Who can forget Rick Mercer who had the audience 'eating' out of his hand."

Thank you, Dave Barry.

It was for the most part an uneventful school year. My duties at student council were not overwhelming. Like so many of today's cabinet ministers, once elected I lost interest in governing. The campaign was fun, but work was not for me. Any time there was a call for volunteers at council I would mumble something about not being able to because "I had to catch a bus." A tactic I plan on revisiting if I ever take leave of my senses and decide to run for Parliament.

By high school standards, grade ten was a success. A success in that I didn't get punched in the head, didn't get bullied and managed to avoid any run-ins with the school's administration. That is, until the final week of school.

Just as we were wrapping up the year, it was announced that a meeting would be held to determine the executive of next year's school newspaper. The idea was that the newspaper staff would have to be in place in order to produce the first edition at the very beginning of the school year. Admission to this meeting was open to anyone who was currently a member of the newspaper staff or anyone who would like to take part the next year.

I had been toying with the notion of maybe trying to write for the school newspaper in grade eleven, but suddenly the idea of running a newspaper seemed more appealing.

Together with Timmy Green and my very creative friend Terry Burt we rounded up twenty warm bodies and headed to the meeting. When the teacher advising the paper asked who would like to run for editor, my hand shot up. As did the hand of the current editor.

The teacher looked at me like I had soiled myself on a public bus. He suggested the editor should be someone with some experience working at the paper. I asked if that was a rule and was informed, reluctantly, that it was not. I didn't see any issue at all with my not having experience. It was a newspaper. How hard could it be? Also, I was in grade ten. I didn't have any experience at anything.

Our motley crew outnumbered the establishment. Within minutes I was elected editor, and I appointed Terry and Tim co-editors. Just like that, with just a few sleazy manoeuvres and no investment on our part, we had ourselves a newspaper. We were like a trio of Conrad Blacks. (Sadly, there was no pension plan to plunder.) This was a prestigious vessel whose masthead proudly noted that it was founded in 1921. A historic organ was ours to do with what we pleased. I immediately began formulating our first self-aggrandizing editorial.

It was a short-lived triumph. The next day Terry, Timmy and I were called into the principal's office. Mr. Clyde Flight started by asking us straight up if we had stacked the meeting.

I was so relieved to get a question I knew the answer to. I assured him we had. Of course we had! I didn't know much, but I did know that was the entire point of meetings where people got elected. My godfather had run for the Liberals and the Tories provincially and I had attended, with my father, meetings that were clearly stacked by all the candidates. This is how things get done in a democracy. This is how religious ding-dongs get elected to school boards all across Canada. They stack the meetings. This, I argued, was a fundamental cornerstone of our democracy.

Mr. Flight didn't care. As far as he was concerned, we had stolen the paper from students who had worked hard on every issue for the past year, week in and week out. (Clearly, he had never read the thing. There was no evidence anyone had ever worked hard on it.) He unilaterally declared we were no longer editors or involved with the paper in any way. Before we could put pen to paper, we were out. There was no respect for the democratic process in that office; we might as well have been in Beijing.

Before we left the office, he pulled me aside and told me just how disappointed he was in me. He said that after my student council speech at the beginning of the year he'd had high hopes, but no more. Not only because of this newspaper business but because of my final marks. He said I was dangerously behind.

I chose to think he had confused me with someone else.

Two or three days later, report cards were issued and turns out he did indeed have inside information. I had scraped by, barely. I did well in the electives, but past that it was a cavalcade of 53s and 54s. It was becoming abundantly clear that my future would not include an internship at NASA.

The only upside was that in scraping by, there was no talk of the dreaded "summer school." And so the summer was spent in Terry Burt's bedroom listening to punk rock. Our shared like of this music was the original basis for our friendship. Terry was a devotee of the Dead Kennedys and Billy Idol. I was obsessed with the Ramones. This clearly made us outliers. In July and August of 1986, the number one song in the country was "That's What Friends Are For" by

Dionne Warwick followed closely by "The Lady in Red" by Chris de Burgh. The kind of songs that when they come on the car radio you end up getting a ticket for driving too slow.

It was our love of punk rock that brought us downtown during the second week in August for something called the Peace-A-Chord. Billed as a day of music, poetry and peace, it also promised a healthy dose of activism, anarchy and a total disregard for societal norms. In beautiful Bannerman Park, our minds were blown.

The concert was huge. The physical set-up had a completely professional look: an outdoor stage with a sound system that would not have been out of place at the myriad of folk festivals that occurred every summer. The difference being that instead of traditional musicians performing Irish Newfoundland tunes on fiddles and accordions there were hardcore punk bands playing very loudly and very poorly in front of a very excited mosh pit. Some of the bands seemed to be appearing onstage for the first time. Others were slightly seasoned.

They weren't household names, but they were greeted like rock stars one and all. Put your hands together for Tough Justice, Schizoid, Dog Meat BBQ, Potato Bug and Twat! There were also some new wave bands and some solo acts. It was varied but it was all alternative. Nothing approached the mainstream. Nobody attempted a Phil Collins cover.

In between each band a poet would take the stage, followed by activists who talked about everything from apartheid in South Africa to Indigenous rights in Labrador. Crazy notions like a city-run recycling program were floated from the stage. One lunatic was an advocate for bike lanes!

Eventually the organizers of the festival came to the stage. They were a revelation. The entire thing had been put together by four or five women. There was not a guy on the stage. And these were young women, our age it seemed, definitely high school students. They were confident in their delivery. They were the founders of Ploughshares Youth, a peace organization that appeared to have a strict dress code of only black. They told us that with our help they were going to get Nelson Mandela out of prison. Again we cheered. I was in. I made sure to make my way to their table and I signed up to join the organization. Joining—a first.

Before we left the park, we picked up a fanzine called *Wabana Riot*. Fanzines were punk rock publications, usually just photocopied pages stapled together—a low-tech celebration of a subculture. They would carry record reviews, concert reviews, interviews with bands and a celebration of all things skateboarding. Terry had quite a few fanzines, but they were all ordered from California or New York. We had never seen a local fanzine and it was brilliant. It was as saucy and funny as any of the ones from the States but loaded with Newfoundland references. (Wabana is the capital of Bell Island, which is just a stone's throw and a ferry ride from downtown St. John's.) It also contained information on the various bands that played the festival and information on where to order their cassettes.

I loved *Wabana Riot*. So did Terry. So did Timmy. We ranted that if we had been allowed to run the school newspaper like we'd planned, we could have made it look and feel like a fanzine. From there it was a small logical leap to deciding to create our own underground school newspaper to compete with the one we had been so unceremoniously fired from.

Immediately we set up camp in the office of Structural Consultants, the small engineering firm owned and operated by Terry's parents. We commandeered the photocopier, the electric typewriter and the supplies closet and began to write and copy and create. It was a great bit of fun. We could do, and did, whatever we wanted. I certainly worked harder on that paper than any assignment I had ever had in school. Days went by. We slept on the office floor.

We called the paper *The Competition*—you would swear we were Ayn Rand devotees. The masthead was created using cut-out letters from newspapers and magazines, the typeface popularized by kidnappers, blackmailers and the Sex Pistols. It was twenty-plus pages photocopied on each side filled with collages and cartoons and columns on a whole variety of subjects. We had columns on sports, we had music reviews, we had a piece alerting students to the dangers of an impending nuclear war. We predicted with some certainty that such a war would end badly.

The paper's editorial addressed a looming labour disruption at school. Teachers were preparing a work-to-rule prior to a strike vote—we came out firmly in favour of the teachers and against management. That was our official position. Privately we hoped that a long, protracted strike would take place.

We had—and this was my favourite—a substantial spread on the adventures of Robinson Condom, written by me and based on pamphlets from Planned Parenthood. Robinson Condom was illustrated by Terry. (Today his days of creating rubber-clad cartoon penises with eyes and a nose are behind him. He is a commercial airline pilot and a visual artist who specializes in realistic paintings of aircraft.) It's hard to believe but when we were in high school, despite the AIDS crisis and a teenage pregnancy epidemic, there wasn't a stick of information on safe sex or birth control. The idea of making contraception readily available to students had not even been suggested yet. It was pre-internet, and for many students the ins and outs of condom use were a complete mystery. Or the ins and outs of anything, for that matter.

The paper cost fifty cents an issue and we sold out on the first day of school. Each of us manned a different entrance and they flew out of our arms before the morning bell rang. They sold out so fast, in fact, that we had to spend hours that night producing another run.

Coming down from the high of creating the paper and then selling out so quickly meant that preparing the second run was far more tedious than the first. Photocopying both sides, collating them and then stapling them into a magazine was labour-intensive. The copier was constantly clogging. As fast as the attraction of being a newspaper magnate appeared, it began to pale.

My takeaway was, let's do something else. The novelty had worn off. Everyone agreed.

We all had other irons in the fire. Timmy was trying out for the senior basketball team; Terry was training to join the Ironman club.

And me? I was starting to hang with the Ploughshares Youth down-town; we had a jailed dissident in South Africa to free. Also, the impressive young women of Ploughshares Youth had given me the courage to embrace societal ridicule and join the circus. I was headed to the drama club.

And so the next day we sold the remaining papers, split the money and retired from the media business. We had proved our point; we had produced a way better paper than the one that the school pro-duced, and we had made a few bucks while we were at it. A fun and harmless way to start the school year. Or so we thought.

Just a few weeks later we were called to the principal's office. There we found a flustered Mr. Flight, in his hand a copy of our paper. He had found it, of all places, on the coffee table in the staff room.

"Did you think," he said, "you could bring this crap into my school for five minutes and I would not know about it?"

Sometimes when faced with a rhetorical question it's best to keep your mouth shut. This was a lesson none of us had yet learned.

Terry said, "Sure, we did that weeks ago."

I said, "We sold out so fast we had to do a second run."

Timmy added, "A lot of teachers bought a copy."

He went full Marty Feldman on us. His eyes bulged out of his head. He looked down and read the name off the masthead out loud. "*The Competition?*" he said. And then he began to read out loud our mission statement on the front page. Some pretentious promise to be both better and bolder than any newspaper that had come before. I could tell from his delivery that this was his first time reading it. I had a terrible sinking feeling that he had no idea what was inside.

I was right. As he turned each page, he discovered in real time yet another item to send him further into a rage spiral. It was all there. Foul language, a flippant disregard for the school, the edito-rial about the teachers working to rule (it never dawned on me that the poor man was under a terrible amount of stress due to the impending strike).

When he reached the Robinson Condom feature, with its illustra-tions of condoms and penises, he finally stopped reading highlights out loud. I guess he couldn't bring himself to say "The sperm then enters and remains in the reservoir tip" in front of students.

When he got to the end, I realized we were in very serious trouble. On the last page we had a photocopy of a page torn out of the St. John's phone book. We had a note about the importance of transparency concerning school policy and suggested that if students had a question or comment on such they should go to the top. And next to it, circled in the phone book, was the name, address and phone number of one Clyde Flight.

"*What the hell?*" he said. "*My phone number?!*"

He was (and rightly so) apoplectic. Seriously, what was wrong with us?

"My phone number? You put my $%@&#*! phone number in your paper? You think I want my phone ringing at all hours of the night? *I have small children!*"

Timmy said, "I don't think the phone will wake them up, sir."

To which Terry added, "You can turn down the ringer at night. Father does that."

"Out!" he yelled. "Out!"

I began to plead my case. "Mr. Flight, the thing is, it's a joke, everyone knows it's a joke, and you *are* listed in the phone book—"

"*Out!*" he said, pointing to the door. I don't know if I'd ever seen a man so angry. "I will be informing your parents tomorrow of your suspension" were the last words we heard.

An auspicious beginning to grade eleven.

It was a sleepless night. Or it would have been if I were normal. As earlier reported, I tend to sleep through anything.

The next day we were summoned to the office for what we assumed would be our marching orders. They never came. It seems that overnight the governor called and delayed our execution. There would be no disciplinary action. The only caveat was that we could no longer sell our paper on school grounds. That and we were supposed to use our brains next time.

Bullet dodged.

Years later it was suggested to me that some teachers had argued at the board level for clemency on our behalf. Yes, we showed terrible judgment in publishing the phone number, but a substantial amount of time had passed and no crank phone calls had occurred. Also, suspending students for creating a newspaper could be perceived as an infringement on our freedom of speech. And the kicker—if we were suspended, the union would suggest that it had more to do with our editorial supporting the teachers in its current dispute with the board than anything else. And that might be newsworthy.

We were saved by the union. Solidarity forever.

Whether that is true I have no idea. Not long ago I brought up the incident on a call with my old principal. We talked for a long time about what we had been up to in the last thirty-plus years. One of his children grew up to be a renowned opera singer, and he was very proud to talk about that. I took the opportunity to apologize for the phone number business, and he claimed to have no memory of it whatsoever. "Can't remember anyone creating their own newspaper," he said, "let alone putting my number in it," and then he changed the subject.

It's quite possible he simply forgot the entire thing, or maybe his anger at the time was feigned for effect. Either way, I was glad I took the opportunity to say sorry.

And how did I get him on the phone? Turns out he's still in the book.

6

A Tribe Is Found

In the early days of grade eleven I attended my first meeting of the drama club. It was quickly evident that I was in the right place but at the wrong time.

It was the right place because the teacher who ran the drama program and the club was the most fascinating person I had ever met. "Call me Lois," she said at the beginning of the first meeting. Teachers were never to be referred to by their first names. I had never even seen that happen in movies.

Immediately I was entirely taken with her. Lois Brown remains to this day one of the most wonderful and eccentric women I know. She is a brilliant performance artist, choreographer, poet and writer. She has made films and multimedia installations. She has done yeoman's work as an arts administrator. She is a great theatre director, and she has mentored many generations of actors and writers. She is a true artist. And as luck would have it, my years in high school coincided exactly with her brief flirtation with having a real job.

I didn't know anyone in the club. The others were mostly older students who had been members the year before. They were a clique.

The drama club was going to do two shows that year, the first one a classic *commedia dell'arte* called *The Servant of Two Masters*. I say "classic" *commedia dell'arte* but at that point I was as familiar with the art form as I was with the plans for the International Space Station.

When Lois explained that *commedia* was a form of physical comedy popularized in Italy in the sixteenth and seventeenth centuries, I had a sneaking suspicion this was not the place for me. When I looked through the script and saw that it was filled with characters named Pantalone and Truffaldino, my suspicions were confirmed.

When a young actor in parachute pants leapt to his feet and started to read Pantalone's lines in what I can only describe as a faux Looney Tunes-inspired Italian accent, I decided this would be the last drama club meeting I would be attending. When Lois asked who would like to prepare an audition for the play, my hand did not go up. This just didn't feel right.

But the more she talked about the play and the process, the more intrigued I became, not with the production but with Lois herself. By the end of the meeting, I had signed up to work backstage. The fags, the freaks and the weirdos might get me yet.

The task I signed up for was stage manager. I did this without any knowledge of what a stage manager actually does. The key word that appealed to me was *manager*. I have always seen myself as management material, not because of an affinity for management but due to an aversion to heavy lifting. The only job on a construction site I want involves a white hard hat.

Turns out stage managing is actually a hard job. Even at the amateur high school level, it's very detail oriented and involves a lot of note taking. If either was my strong suit I would have brought a pencil to school on occasion.

Unfortunately, my suspicions about *commedia dell'arte* proved to be bang on. I detested the play. Everything about it really, but mostly its lack of humour. Full disclosure: I have since seen a few productions of *The Servant of Two Masters* that have changed my mind entirely about the play and the genre, but at that time it was set in stone.

I stuck with it until the bitter end. On closing night of a triumphant two-show run in the library, I told Lois I was out of the drama club.

There was a long silence. Lois seemed to collect her thoughts and then she told me that leaving was a terrible mistake. She said that this was a decision I might regret for the rest of my life. Even by Lois's standards this was particularly dramatic. Getting drunk and diving headfirst into a pond without looking for rocks is the type of thing you regret for the rest of your life. Dropping an extracurricular activity? Not so much.

Also, given the choice, I'd rather opt for a catastrophic head injury than watch another *commedia dell'arte* butchered by teenagers. I stuck to my guns and told her I had no interest in continuing as the stage manager.

"Oh god no, you can't be the stage manager," she said. "You're terrible at it. The only reason I didn't fire you is because I like listening to you talk while I'm directing."

It was true that I sat next to her during rehearsals. That's what stage managers do. But apparently they are supposed to pay attention to the show and not talk to the director non-stop about everything other than what was happening in front of them.

She told me I should forget about being a stage manager but remain in the club because the next production was an important one. It would be entered into a provincial drama festival of one-act plays.

"What's the show?" I asked, mostly to be polite. I had never read a one-act play.

"I don't know," she said. "You haven't written it yet."

If there are moments in a person's life when everything changes and from that point on nothing will be the same again, this was it for me. Nothing since has come close.

"I don't know anything about writing plays," I said.

"Perfect," said Lois. "Neither do I. And you won't be writing it on your own," she said. "Everyone's writing it. It's a collective."

"Who's everyone?" I asked. Not knowing what a collective was.

"I haven't decided yet," she said. "Interesting people."

Turns out a collective is just that. A group of people come together and create a show, a play or a musical. It's art by jury. Now the idea horrifies me; back then it sounded intriguing.

I didn't want to be in the play, but the idea of writing one was suddenly very exciting.

Within the week I was sitting in the library with a group of people Lois had deemed "interesting." Many of them I was already friendly with, most of them are friends to this day, and two of them would become my future comedy partners—Ashley Billard and Andrew Younghusband.

Ashley was already a great friend. He came from downtown St. John's and for some reason ended up at our school, which was decidedly not downtown. On his first day of grade ten, he went to the principal's office and demanded he be transferred to the school he was supposed to attend. He had friends there, his cousin was there, his brother had gone there. He didn't fit in this school and wanted out.

Unbeknownst to Ashley, his ending up in our school was not an administrative error. There were greater powers at play. The administration had put him in our school precisely to keep him away from the people he wanted so badly to be with. He was, to put it politely, a young person who was "at risk." Someone somewhere figured his only chance at salvation was to be as far away from those kids as possible. So he was sent uptown to the fancier and more genteel PWC.

When the principal told him in no uncertain terms that he was stuck at Prince of Wales, Ashley left the office and went to the smoking area. He was right about one thing: he didn't fit in. At least not on the surface. He was probably a hundred pounds and freakishly skinny with a huge head of hair. He wore tapered jeans and giant black leather biker boots. Among the well-scrubbed preppy kids of our school, he was the only one who had circles under his eyes and looked like he hadn't slept in weeks.

The first two people he saw in the smoking area were me and Don Ellis. Or rather he saw our T-shirts. I was sporting the Ramones and

Don was wearing the Clash. He walked up to us and said, "So, look-ing at the shirts, I guess you're the ones I'm supposed to hang out with." We agreed it looked that way. Later that day one of the school jocks said to me, "I saw you talking to that Ashley guy. Stay away from him. He carries a knife. He'll cut you."

Ashley's reputation as a killer preceded him. Although it was somewhat sullied months later when he accepted Lois's invitation to join the theatre collective.

Andrew Younghusband already had a reputation in the school as a very funny guy. Like me, he would enter public-speaking contests. He had also run for student council that year and gave the best speech. I had given up on student council in my second year, so I never got to know him that well. It never crossed my mind that we might be friends because he wore an Iron Maiden T-shirt and played competitive tennis. He might as well have been an alien.

He came locked and loaded for the collective. He could do killer accents and could juggle. Quickly the Iron Maiden factor was over-looked, and we bonded over our love for *The Wonderful Grand Band*.

All in all, there were about ten of us in the room. Some would come and some would go. None of us had a clue what we were doing and most had never been onstage before.

Lois seemed mostly interested in our writing exercises. I often decried them as flaky, but I secretly loved them. We would practice free-association writing. This is where you put pen to paper and you do not stop writing, no matter what, for fifteen minutes. Whatever comes into your head you put down on paper. The results would be read to the group. The inner monologues of a gang of fifteen- and sixteen-year-olds, our deepest fears and strongest desires, laid bare. In this group there was enough angst for two high schools.

I wasn't revealing too many secrets, but I was getting laughs, and it was exhilarating. I started to think, "If this ends up in the show, I don't want someone else to say it. *I* want to say it."

Over the next weeks we did theatre exercises and improvs. During these exercises I was the one who was writing things down. Suddenly

I was a voracious note taker. Improv wasn't my forte—I preferred to work on written bits and hash those out. But Ashley and Andrew were brilliant at improv together. They were like a seasoned comedy duo. Andrew had complete characters and to me he was like a TV star. He was a student of comedy. He wouldn't just say "Did you see *The Cosby Show* last night?" He would analyze it, break it down, determining *why* it was funny. It is of no surprise to anyone who knew Andrew in those days that show business would literally take him around the world, as host of the TV show *The Tall Ship Chronicles*. He would go on to host and produce some of Canada's most successful reality shows, including *Canada's Worst Driver*.

I was constantly thinking about how we could take all of these different characters and scenarios and put them together in one cohesive package. It was like a giant puzzle. A puzzle I was obsessed with. This was the most fun I'd had in a long time. This was something I didn't want to end.

Eventually we ended up with a play called *The Twenty Minute Psychiatric Workout*. A very simple, straightforward little production with an entirely believable plot. It was set in a fictional television studio in St. John's that was home to a hit call-in show hosted by a pair of quack TV psychiatrists. Donna Pinhorn played Dr. Feelgood and I was Dr. Feltgood. We would take calls from viewers (claiming to be students from other schools) that were ridiculous and embarrassing, often of a sexual nature. We took a call from the premier of the province confessing his idiocy. One caller sounded suspiciously like our school principal. It was tightly scripted, rapid-fire and actually funny.

I seem to remember a subplot about international terrorists secretly convening in St. John's and a suitcase that may or may not have included a nuclear device. But the kicker, the thing that took us over the top, was WAFUT. Our show had a band!

Some of the scenes in the show took place in a bar. Wouldn't it be cool, we said, if the bar had a band? It was Ashley who suggested we ask WAFUT. This was a game-changing idea.

WAFUT—short for What a Fucking Ugly Truck—was a four-piece punk band and a bit of a sensation in St. John's at the time. Two of the members—Don Ellis and Ken Tizzard—went to our school. I was great friends with both of them. WAFUT, along with a few other bands, would occasionally rent a hall at an old age home or a community centre and put on a show. Kids would show up and slam-dance until they were barred from said hall for the rest of their lives. The band was running out of venues and opportunities fast.

The problem for us was the guitar player, Barry Newhook, was a student at a rival high school. One we would actually be competing against at the drama festival. The lead singer was a guy named Clark Hancock; he also was not a student at PWC. In fact, he wasn't a student anywhere. He had been kicked out of virtually every school in the city and was now an official dropout rock star. He was a brilliant front man. Girls loved him. He would go on to make his fortune in oil and gas.

Eventually someone, despite knowing the answer, asked Lois the obvious questions. "Are we allowed to have students from other schools in the show?" and "Do you have to actually attend school to be in the drama festival?"

Lois thought about it and said, "I'm pretty sure a lot of people would get upset if they found out we had a student from another school in the play and a student who wasn't actually in school at all . . . so we better not tell anybody."

We cheered! Miss Brown could be punk rock too.

She added, "Also—don't tell anyone what WAFUT stands for. I'd be killed."

Ten days later the Prince of Wales Drama Club performed the world premiere of *The Twenty Minute Psychiatric Workout* featuring WAFUT.

Students were shocked when the show started. It was actually funny. This was no *commedia*. Andrew and Ashley were brilliant as the spy and the assassin. And when Donna and I were onstage hosting the TV show and the calls came in from rival schools, the pandering worked like a charm. My jokes were killing.

And when the band appeared a few kids stood up and screamed, much to the faculty's dismay, "*What a Fucking Ugly Truck!*"

We got a standing ovation. I had never seen that happen in the school gym before. Not even for the country musician who lectured us on the evils of addiction while severely inebriated.

Our principal, impressed that the drama club did something that the school actually liked, never inquired as to why he didn't recognize two members of the cast.

And now we were taking our creation to the Avalon East High School Drama Festival. I couldn't wait.

This was also new to me. I had never represented my school in any capacity. There were no basketball trophies or hockey tournaments in my past. In fact, looking through the list of everyone involved in the show's cast and crew, I am pretty sure the same could be said for every single one of us. None of us were what you would call joiners. Now we were joined at the hip.

Within days the show's flats, props and costumes were loaded into a small bus for the long drive to the drama festival. We were hitting the road. Seven minutes later we arrived at Bishop Feild Elementary School in downtown St. John's.

Bishop Feild elementary. If you can make it there, you can move on to grade seven in the fall.

As we unloaded our gear from the bus, kids on the playground looked on. I could tell they were impressed by the drum kit and the guitars. We were an eighties version of those "hippies in a van," except we were punks on a short bus. Especially Clark. He had given himself a new mohawk.

The school might have been just a few kilometres away from ours, but compared to any school I'd attended it might as well have been New York. On entering, our jaws hit the floor. This school had a theatre—a dedicated auditorium for concerts and plays. I had never seen such a thing in a school. The schools I attended were modern, so there was no real place for arts or culture. Stages were an afterthought added to the arse end of the gymnasium. In every school I'd attended the stage had two distinct purposes. It was a place where the principal could stand during assemblies and it was a place for the gym teacher to store volleyballs and hockey nets.

This actual auditorium in a school for small children was like the big time. There was an ornate proscenium arch with a coat of arms at its peak. In our school that's where the basketball net was. It had marble columns, not climbing ropes. It had beautiful acoustics. There was no incessant sound of sneakers squeaking on hardwood and no irritating hum from the fluorescent lights.

Over the next few days, we watched many plays. Some intimidated me because they were slicker than ours. But there was little attempt at humour. When our time came to hit the stage it was evident that we were, to put it mildly, something completely different.

From the very beginning the audience was ours. Local reference after local reference landed and killed. The idea that international assassins were running around St. John's was absurd and far-fetched but also inherently funny.

We weren't as well-rehearsed as some of the acts, but the local references made up for it. This was exactly the kind of thing I wanted to do. I wanted to do what the *Grand Band* did. Marry music and comedy. And thanks to WAFUT, that's exactly what we were doing.

Twenty minutes after walking out on stage, we had our curtain call. Not a full standing ovation but a kind reaction for sure.

At the end of the two-day festival, representatives from each show were told to gather in the auditorium. The actors, crew members and friends, along with a smattering of people who apparently enjoy amateur theatre performed by adolescents, were about to hear the results from the adjudicator. Andrew, Ashley and I were front and centre.

The adjudicator was a fellow named Terry Goldie. He was tall and handsome and extremely well dressed. I could see girls swoon for him. The head of the festival who introduced him informed us that Dr. Goldie was a professional theatre critic who had a PhD in English and whose dissertation was on Canadian drama, specifically from 1919 through 1939.

Immediately I disliked everything about the guy, right down to his jaunty scarf. How, I thought, could an academic who studied Canadian theatre from the dark ages understand what we were doing?

Ten minutes later, Dr. Goldie concluded his wrap-up of the festival by saying that our show was the most exciting, inventive thing he'd seen on a stage in a very long time. He praised the direction, the script and the acting. He said he was thrilled to award us first prize and wished us well on our upcoming performance at the province-wide festival in Gander. He summed up by predicting that he would be watching many of us on stages across Canada for many years to come.

As I'd suspected from the moment I clapped eyes on the man, Terry Goldie was a genius. A man who knew what was what.

When he came down into the audience and shook our hands he said, "Have fun in Gander and do exactly what you did here."

It would be many years before I saw Terry Goldie again. I was performing a one-man show at the Factory Theatre in Toronto when he came backstage after, as he'd predicted, having watched me perform.

I would have recognized him anywhere, despite the eyeshadow, high heels and fetching dress.

I love show business.

7

A Troupe Is Born

To say we were cocky heading to the Provincial High School Drama Festival in Gander would be a substantial understatement. When playing the "If you could go back in time would you kill Hitler?" game, my answer is, "Yes, most certainly, I'd be happy to go back and kill Hitler, but only if I get to stop in the late eighties and slap myself in the head."

In Gander we set up camp at the Albatross Hotel. Andrew and I shared a room with all of the props and flats for the play. We discovered that our days were to be filled not only with shows but with workshops and lectures. We decided that we would sign up for as many as possible. We were just starting to talk about the notion of becoming professional actors and we were sponges. So we gave it the college try.

And we really did. In our first workshop, surrounded by kids from all over the province, we did the prerequisite warm-up. We shook our arms and rolled our heads back and forth. What this had to do with theatre we had no idea, but we were fully committed. We were learning.

Then there was a vocal warm-up. Much clucking and howling. And then we were instructed to breathe from our diaphragm. Apparently we had been breathing wrong our entire lives. The instructor wandered around the room placing his hand on each student's lower stomach while intoning, "Lower, lower, lower." It was hard to see what he was more passionate about, the performing arts or the opportunity to touch young male abdomens.

Eventually we were lying all over the floor in a zigzag pattern with our heads on each other's stomachs. A guy from Labrador was instructed to place his head on my stomach to judge my breathing. The fellow told me his name and informed me he went to Goose High. We had heard Goose High was the school to look out for. Their show was so popular they had actually run it in the local arts and culture centre and had half a dozen sold-out audiences.

I asked him what made his show so popular and he said proudly, "It has a lot of audience participation in it. It's designed to be a winner." Being a neophyte to the performing arts, I had no idea what "audience participation" was, but it sounded awful. I made a mental note that if I went to see his show I'd make sure I was as far away from the stage and the actors as humanly possible. Perhaps armed.

Our paths would cross again. He went on to study theatre in university but never worked as a professional actor. Instead, he hosted *Canada AM* and became a bit of an institution on the CTV network. Later, tired of the early mornings, he changed hats and became a senior cabinet minister in Justin Trudeau's government, where his theatrical training has served him well. Seamus O'Regan and I are friends to this day. We have similar tastes when it comes to theatre, but we still disagree on audience participation. I maintain that in the theatre it is an abomination.

Very quickly Andrew and I decided that we were done with the workshops. Instead, we just sat around in our room and talked about how much we liked the entire process of writing the play. I tentatively told Andrew a few ideas I had for next year's collective and he said, "Why do we have to wait until next year? Let's just do our own."

And it was then that we started writing. And we didn't stop for about three years.

For our first comedy sketch we took inspiration from one of the canvas flats from the show that was resting against our wall. It was a painting of a giant white mug and on it were painted the words "Coffee with Chuck."

I played Chuck, a morning TV show host who was interviewing Andrew, a botanist, on the proper care of begonias. (As luck would have it, the lobby of the Albatross Hotel had plastic begonias, another "found prop.") Long story short, it is revealed that the plant expert recently had a lobotomy and has a vocabulary of only six words. Also, Andrew seemed to have a romantic attachment to the plant.

As far as sketches go, I can report that this one had a beginning, a middle and an end. We felt it was reminiscent of the famous "Dead Parrot" sketch by Monty Python. It was not. Not even in the ballpark. Not even on the continent. It was, looking back, juvenile theatre of cruelty.

But as I said—a beginning, a middle and an end. We had words on a page.

Our first audience was eleven of our closest friends jammed into a hotel room, chain-smoking in order to appear cool. Smoke so thick it looked like a German cabaret.

And then, in search of new audiences, we decided to do it in the lobby. We carried the flat to the check-in area, pushed some chairs to one side and started doing the sketch over and over again. Our audience was people checking into the hotel and kids who were coming and going to the workshops. Sometimes the kids would stick around and watch it a second or third time, so we would make it different by changing the ending.

Our largest audience was a tour bus of seniors from the United States who clapped appreciably. Afterwards some of them approached and laid change and American dollar bills on the floor in front of us like we were buskers. It was like crack. We were addicted.

Later, the guy who ran the breathing workshop came up to us and told us he liked our performance. He even offered to give us notes on it, "later tonight, over drinks in my room." He leaned in and whispered, "415."

"Will there be tequila?" Andrew asked.

The breathing instructor winked and walked away. We were naive, but we weren't that naive.

And then it was time to get to the theatre. We had a show to do.

The performance of *The Twenty Minute Psychiatric Workout* at the provincial championship was a memorable one. And for all the wrong reasons.

When Terry Goldie had congratulated us for winning, he said we should do in Gander exactly what we had done in St. John's. We did the opposite.

Being onstage when everything works is an exhilarating feeling. When you are new to the game it's especially gratifying. But being inexperienced carries with it inherent risks. It's a bit like being a new driver. Yes, it's exciting to be speeding along in total control of a five-thousand-pound beast, but inevitably things will get tangly. You will hydroplane on water or hit some black ice and spin out of control. If you're lucky it might just sort itself out. It might just be a brief skid that scares you into slowing down and paying more attention. Or you could lose control and end up in the ditch. Or plunge off a cliff into the cold Atlantic Ocean.

When the curtain went up in Gander, something was different. If I had to put my finger on it, I would say the main difference was the lack of laughs. Yes, silence was the difference.

Being a rookie, I choose to panic. I hit the gas and went faster. Which made Donna go faster. Which made everyone go faster. We shaved seven minutes off a twenty-two-minute show. We didn't plunge off the cliff, but we did end up at the bottom of the bank with a dented car and bruised egos.

The most important obvious lesson I learned by bombing is that you have to know who your audience is. You have to know who you are writing for. When we created the show, we knew our audience was going to be people from St. John's. It was loaded with St. John's references. Never once did we think, "Would this reference work for an audience of people not from St. John's?" or "Will they even know what the hell we are talking about?"

Also, St. John's is the big city. The capital. Newfoundland and Labrador is made up of two groups, baymen and townies. Baymen are from rural Newfoundland and townies are from town. Between the factions there exists a rivalry not unlike the one that exists between Calgary and Edmonton, or the entire country and Toronto.

Did the baymen like the townies talking ad nauseam about themselves and acting like they were cooler than everyone else? Not even a little bit.

This revelation only dawned on me when I got off the stage. I was infuriated. How could I have not anticipated that happening?

The lesson carried through for my entire career. At the *Mercer Report* a cardinal rule was to avoid being Toronto-centric. No talk of the subway system, no talk of how varied and wonderful the restaurants are, and for god sakes no mention of the Leafs. Nobody in the rest of the country cares.

Later that night at the awards ceremony, Best Play went to Labrador West. Best actor went to the yet-to-be-Honourable Seamus O'Regan.

Afterwards all of the young actors from across Newfoundland and Labrador ended up in our neck of the hotel. I have great memories of our room being so full that not a single extra body could enter. Dozens of other kids were lying on the floor out in the hallway. I remember the bathroom in our room held the entire cast of a period production set during World War Two. All were in full wardrobe, some of them in the tub, power-drinking cherry coolers, a relatively new alcoholic beverage designed to appeal to toddlers.

We had all found our tribe.

The hotel was not so accommodating for this great rite of passage. With the aid of the local constabulary we were shut down at one a.m.

Afterwards, Andrew and I, still wide awake, high on adrenalin, were bemoaning that somehow the room was void of adult beverages.

"This blows," I said. "*Saturday Night Live* is almost on."

Andrew said, "I know where there's tequila."

A minute or so after knocking on room 415 there was a giant crash on the other side of the door. Loud enough to make us jump. It seems that the resident of room 415 misjudged his trajectory when approaching the peephole and slammed face first into the door jamb. Eventually he recovered and the door opened. For a breathing instructor he was looking pretty winded.

"Gentlemen!" he announced. "How good to see you." He was over-enunciating every word. And judging from the way his eyes were attempting to focus, he was addressing at least four of us, if not eight. Between bobs and weaves I could see behind him on the table an incredible amount of alcohol. The variety was impressive. Never mind the two of us, there was enough booze in there to contribute to the delinquency of twenty minors.

"We thought we would pop by," I said. "*Saturday Night Live* is on soon."

"Gentlemen," he said, "how good to see you. Come in."

He turned and navigated the treacherous twelve feet from the doorway to the closest double bed. He crawled up on the bed, managed to flip himself over, and settled in. He was asleep in under a minute. With him out of the way, we poured cocktails, flipped on the TV and perched on the other bed.

Saturday Night Live should have been rebranded "Early Sunday Morning" in my province. Because of the time difference in Newfoundland, the live broadcast started not at 11.30, as it did in the US and central Canada, but at 1:00 a.m. They would say goodnight at 2:30. God forbid if you were both a comedy fan and a churchgoer.

The guest hosts that night were Penn and Teller. They were comedians and magicians. We, like most of North America at the time, were not that familiar with the act. What they did in that particular episode launched them into the stratosphere.

Sitting at a news desk, they announced that not only could they do card tricks but they could defy gravity. What followed was literally mind-blowing. They delivered on their promise and defied gravity!

Inanimate objects began to fly straight up in the air. They showed there was no use of strings. It was astounding. Our minds were blown to the extent that we were suddenly, incredibly stone cold sober.

"How are they doing that?" "Holy crap!" It was like nothing we had ever seen. "Is it mirrors? Some new TV effect?" We were shouting so loudly we even woke up the breathing instructor.

"Gentlemen," he said, "how good to see you," and then went back to sleep.

When the sketch was over, neither Andrew nor I nor anyone else in North America could figure out how they had done it.

Then there was an astounding reveal. The camera pulled out and then flipped over 180 degrees. Penn and Teller had performed the entire sketch upside down, strapped into their chairs. So when Teller took out a deck of cards and dropped them, they looked like they were flying straight up into the air. It was brilliant. How could they be so innovative? "What," I thought, "must it feel like to do something so brilliant on TV?"

Twenty-plus years later I found myself, on a shoot for the *Mercer Report*, in the cockpit of a Canadian Forces Tutor jet operated by the Snowbirds, our military's world-renowned Air Demonstration Squadron. They are an iconic Canadian institution. It was a huge opportunity, and it was an incredible thrill. Obviously there's no room for a camera operator in the small jet, so a pencil camera was firmly fixed on the dashboard pointing at my face.

Every move in the plane was thrilling. From the ground the planes look like they are flying close to one another, but in the air they seem even closer. The precision of the moves is astounding. We were almost through a series of manoeuvres when my pilot asked the question I had been waiting for my entire life: "Are you ready to go upside down?"

"Yes," I answered. "Yes!" It was a pinch-me moment like no other.

And with that he went full *Top Gun* and flipped the plane completely upside down. My adrenalin surged but it simultaneously dawned on me that viewers at home would have no idea what was happening. This was exactly like the Penn and Teller sketch before the reveal. Everything just looks normal.

I looked into the camera and shouted, "I'm really upside down! Look!" And then I removed my gloves, waved them around and let them go. They shot to the ceiling and stayed there. I did it again and again. I was defying gravity on national TV.

I got mail from people who said they stood up and screamed when my gloves shot to the ceiling.

After we landed, I showed the pilot the footage. "That's amazing," he said. "Nobody can ever tell on camera when we're upside down. How did you come up with that?"

I told him I owed it all to Penn, Teller and an alcoholic predator from my high school days.

When we got back from Gander, Andrew and I continued to talk and daydream about doing our own shows. Eventually Ashley Billard joined us. And then with Lois Brown's encouragement we approached Christine Taylor, a student who had recently shown up from Calgary.

Having done nothing, we decided we were now a bona fide comedy troupe. What that meant or what the next steps would be, we just weren't sure.

Lois's advice was that if we were serious about doing our own shows, it made no sense to do them at the school. In her opinion we needed a proper theatre. She said she would arrange for us to meet the people who ran the Resource Centre for the Arts. They owned a theatre, the LSPU Hall.

I reminded Lois that we were kids and we had no money to rent a theatre. She told us that the Resource Centre for the Arts was just that, a resource for artists. We should talk to them.

We had been called a lot of things in our life, but never artists.

We agreed to the meeting. "How exciting," I thought. "We have a meeting!"

8

A Shining Paradise

The LSPU Hall is located in the heart of downtown St. John's at the bottom of a very steep dead-end residential street. A few feet from the front doors, a treacherous set of concrete steps takes you down to the street below. It doesn't make a lot of sense; but that can be said of much of the downtown core. Eighteenth-century cows were the city planners and civil engineers of St. John's.

Originally the hall was the home of the Longshoremen's Protective Union, or the LSPU. In its heyday the union had thirty-four gangs representing 3,500 men who worked the harbourfront loading and unloading ships by hand. For hundreds of years history poured non-stop through the entrance of St. John's Harbour. It came from France, England and Ireland, from the Caribbean, Portugal and Spain. Burly longshoremen would haul cargo off ships and drag it up the hill to the people. The union hall was ground zero not only for the longshoremen but for the entire labour movement in Newfoundland and Labrador, the site of many strike votes, historic debates and bare-knuckle brawls.

In 1975 local theatre director Chris Brooks wandered into the building on a whim. He was looking for a place to rehearse a play and was curious about the building's interior. At the time, the inevitable modernization of the shipping industry had reduced the union's membership and slowed activity in the building. And so, in theory, the place was available.

That said, one look at Chris and the union men rightly assumed he would be a poor income stream. Out of pity, or perhaps curiosity, they agreed to rent their hall to the arts crowd for the grand sum of five dollars a day.

The space worked perfectly for rehearsals. Longshoremen would sit at the back and watch with what one can only assume was bewilderment as long-haired actors with holes in their pants stood around improvising a play about the history of the east end of St. John's. The actors liked the building so much they approached the union about using it as an actual performance space. The price on show nights, when it was filled with paying customers, jumped to twenty-five dollars.

An unlikely relationship between the union members and the theatre company began. A second show was staged in the building— a collective creation that told the story of a ground-breaking strike in the lumber woods of central Newfoundland in 1959. It was an ugly tale of union-busting by the provincial government. The labour movement was thrilled that this dark period in Newfoundland's history was finally being documented and preserved. Their story was being told.

Four days into the run, with crowds lined up in the street, inspectors from the city showed up minutes before showtime and shut the building down, citing a new regulation, inspired by the play's run, that required sprinkler systems to be installed in buildings of a certain size. Like the strike in the lumber woods, the play was brought to a halt by powerful outside forces.

Backing onto the LSPU Hall was a large stone mansion that housed the downtown branch of the Bank of Montreal. When the bank heard that their neighbours of sixty-plus years were in need of a sprinkler system, they did what any good neighbour would do— they offered the union a lowball "take it or leave it" price for the entire place. They wanted to tear it down to make room for six parking spots for the bank's executives.

The union leadership weighed their options. Knowing they could no longer afford to maintain the building, they told the bank to shove their offer up their cash flow. Members voted to sell the building to the gaggle of long-haired lefties for $45,000.

The parking places for the Bank of Montreal would not come to be. The LSPU Hall remained in place, it kept its name, and it became the home base for a cultural revolution that was sweeping the province and making waves in the rest of Canada. Strike votes may have come to an end, but debates and brawls of an artistic nature would carry on indefinitely.

By the time we showed up in 1987 the gentrification of the downtown was approaching full bore, driven in no small part by a vibrant arts community. Rainbows of row houses formed a united front, designed to combat the grey winter days and to attract the summer tourists who came in search of something they call Jellybean Row.

Compared with these row houses, "the Hall" is an imposing structure. But as far as theatres go it's fairly impractical. But impractical is hardly uncommon. Newfoundland itself is impractical. The very definition of impractical is a group of actors, writers, dancers and musicians deciding that they would build a professional arts community on a rock in the middle of the North Atlantic.

Foremost among the Hall's challenges is its size. Or lack thereof. In show business, size matters, but as in life, you have no choice but to make do with what God gave you. Upon entering the theatre, you found a cramped box office that was also used for administration. Across the way was a bar the size of a passenger van. The small lobby was used as an art gallery, reception space and, late at night, a performance venue that was zoned to hold sixty or so people—that is, if they were malnourished and jammed in like cordwood.

At the top of a winding staircase was a simple black box theatre. No bells, no whistles. A series of risers could accommodate 150 chairs. There was little in the way of backstage space, and the wings were shallow. No flats could fly to the ceiling, no curtain could rise and fall.

The dressing room for both performance venues was exactly that. A single, solitary cell on the ground floor. In there on any given night you could find up to fifteen actors and musicians in various stages of undress. A tight-knit community in both a figurative and literal sense, it was cheek to jowl and boob to bum. There is very little dignity in the arts in Canada and there certainly was next to none in that dressing room.

But to me it was a shining paradise, a green clapboard jewel in need of a paint job. It was a dream home. I never wanted to leave.

It was all there. Practically free for the asking. The arts community that came before me built it all. They wanted to create and perform, but in order to do so they had to find a building and acquire it. They had to fight city hall. They had to beg, borrow and steal every light and every riser. They had to hold a bake sale to buy the greasepaint if they wanted to hear the roar of the crowd.

For us it was a very different story. We wanted to do a show and all we had to do was take the metro bus downtown and walk through the front door. Which is exactly what we did.

Andrew and I met with the artistic animateur of Resource Centre for the Arts. To this day RCA has an "animateur" rather than a "director." This makes the theatre perhaps unique in North America. All professional theatres have artistic directors except for the Hall. Artistic directors generally have all the power. They call the shots, and their vision is what moulds a theatre company. At RCA it is the artists themselves who collectively make all the decisions. Instead of a single director with a vision, there is a Kafkaesque system of committees and a labyrinth of internal politics.

Like socialism, on paper it looks perfect. In practice, it's challenging. But somehow it works. The legacy speaks for itself.

Our ask was pretty simple. We had a comedy troupe, we wanted to perform a show and we needed a theatre. Also, we had no money.

As luck would have it, they were used to people with no money. They said the downstairs performance space was available and for a short run they could waive the fee and instead would split the box office. They said the split was 60/40.

We didn't know anything about negotiating but we had sense enough to ask for more, so we suggested that 50/50 was a better deal.

They told us that the 60/40 split would be in favour of the artist.

So we, hardened negotiators with minutes of experience under our belt, asked for 80/20.

They said yes. We got 80 percent of the box and no expenses up front. To this day, it's the best deal I have ever signed. It was that kind of place. God love them.

After we had our deal, we left the Hall and made our way a few blocks west to a six-storey asbestos-filled office building that housed the offices of Memorial University Extension Services. Again thanks to Lois, we had an appointment with Mrs. Mina Hickey.

MUN Extension was a downtown community outreach program run by the university. Their mandate was to support and encourage the arts community. Citizens could go there and take drawing lessons, use a dark room or roll around on the floor in a movement class. The classrooms were available to theatre companies as meeting rooms and rehearsal space. There was a nominal fee. I can't remember the numbers, but it was a deal even by broke-high-school-student standards.

Mina was a classic Newfoundland lady, an Irish Catholic from the Southern Shore, not to be trifled with. She was the gatekeeper. She scared the hell out of us on first sight. She laid down the rules, and there were many. But she did say we were more than welcome to work there.

Eventually we learned that all those rules she laid out were theoretical. Over the next few years MUN Extension became our clubhouse. Mina became our champion.

It was here that the four of us gathered for the first meeting of the terribly named Corey and Wade's Playhouse. Why we named our theatre company after two hash dealers, I have no logical explanation. I blame, obviously, the hash.

Immediately an amazing thing happened to us at MUN Extension. We realized that the adjoining room was being used as a rehearsal and writing space by none other than Tommy Sexton and Greg Malone, they of *The Wonderful Grand Band*. We were next-door neighbours to comedy legends. Imagine if you were just learning to play guitar and had yet to write a song and you found yourself in a studio next door to Lennon and McCartney or the Everly Brothers.

Oddly, I don't remember feeling intimidated. I allowed myself to imagine a life in which I could make a living by indulging in creative endeavours. I knew it was theoretically possible. After all, it was being done fifteen feet away on the other side of a door.

From that moment on, every day after school and on Saturdays we gathered there and we wrote. Eventually we began to do the same on Fridays and often Mondays. Priorities.

We would get on our feet and improv; we would throw suggestions around like mad people. We didn't know what we were doing but we did it anyway.

Christine was brilliant with improvisational comedy. She had a character called Ginger Taylor, a fierce feminist who was the host of *Ginger Taylor's Talk Show*. It was an incredible thing to watch her create. I'll never forget when she said, "Hang on, I want to try something new." She whipped off her shirt, tossed aside her bra and said with bare-breasted bravado, "Hello, and welcome to *Ginger Taylor's Topless Talk Show*. I'm Ginger Taylor."

Christine clearly did not have the characteristic shyness that so many girls in grade ten suffer from. We applauded her idea and her breasts. Apparently, our show was going to have nudity. Good thing we went to the Hall. We were clearly not creating a show that could be done in a school auditorium.

I came in one day fuming about the bank's refusal to give me one of those newfangled debit cards. Andrew suggested that it was an entire piece. It became my first rant.

Andrew and Ashley created a pair of skateboarders who spoke Californian bafflegab about life in St. John's. Ashley, in the powder blue tuxedo his brother had been married in, created TV evangelist FatherBrotherSisterMother. Andrew and I spoofed a much-loved local cable sports show and became brothers Huey and Dewy

Fitzgerald. Christine (on Andrew's shoulders) became the nine-foot Jewish nun.

We brought in musicians Sean Panting and Bob Earle. With guitar and piano they created musical stings to go between the sketches.

I played a cowboy singing about his first sexual experience with a cowgirl. (This was fiction, and looking back on the lyrics I think this was evident to all—or at least to anyone who had ever had sex with a woman.)

And of course we had "Coffee with Chuck."

We plastered the school with posters. "Corey and Wade's Playhouse presents Hardly a Sensible Evening! A late-night comedy cabaret, live at the LSPU Hall. April 30 to May 3. Thursday to Sunday, admission five dollars." Curtain was at 11:00 p.m.

Our principal hit the roof. He pulled me into the office. The posters that had been on the walls were now on his desk. "You can't tell kids to go downtown at eleven o'clock on a school night," he said. "Or any night, for that matter. It's *downtown*! Do you know what goes on down there? There are hoodlums down there!"

It seemed like every time I turned around, I was having to remind the school principal it was a free country. As fast as he took the posters down, we put them up again.

On opening night we were jammed to the rafters. School nights be damned. By ten that night we had sold eighty tickets, breaking every by-law known to man. The crowd overflowed into the bar and the hallway.

The rumour that the bar at the Hall wasn't particularly picky about IDs in those days proved to be a great ticket sales incentive. The rumours that Christine was to be topless didn't hurt either. That turned out to be quasi-true. She appeared naked from the waist up with a long, thin piece of black cardboard duct-taped to her nipples. The word "censored" was emblazoned across her breasts.

Ten minutes before we went onstage, Tommy Sexton and Greg Malone, having listened to us rehearse for weeks, walked in and stood at the back. It was a coronation.

And the most amazing thing happened. It all worked! Well, other than my cowboy song. It would be the first and only time I dipped my toe into musical theatre. Sad, as it is actually my greatest love.

We were a hit. And the kids kept coming. Every night we blocked the joint. And then we held over.

The following Friday, John Holmes, theatre critic for the St. John's *Evening Telegram*, wrote a column with the headline "Two Shows Worth Seeing." Our very first bit of ink. The majority of the column was devoted to a glowing review of a new production by the Longside Club, an amateur theatre company who produced plays starring young actors with physical and/or mental disabilities.

But in the last few paragraphs of his column, he switched gears and turned to us. He wrote "Hardly a Sensible Evening presented by Corey and Wade's Playhouse is very funny. It's raw and a bit crude and needs polish and discipline to hone its wit, but there can be no doubt of this group's insight, energy and dedication to the traditions of CODCO."

Raw? Crude? That's what we were going for! And he mentioned CODCO! From that moment on I was laser-focused on writing and acting. Everything else moved to the foggy periphery.

Hi-diddle-dee-dee—it's an actor's life for me!

9

Joining the Circus

Because the end of the school year was fast approaching, we were ostensibly supposed to buckle down and start cramming for exams. Or at least that's what anyone with a brain would do.

Yes, a brain. The seat of intelligence, the interpreter of the senses and controller of behaviour. The most complex part of the human body. Or so they say. Complex or not, my brain was far too busy processing that we now had a comedy troupe. We had been seen by a paying audience; we had been seen by the dudes from *The Wonderful Grand Band*. I was completely unable to think about anything else. It was humanly impossible.

Exams were always a strange experience for me. In the period leading up to exams I always felt like I was a visitor from another planet. Everyone around me would be overcome with stress. It started in grade seven or eight and increased incrementally year after year. By high school, in the lead-up to finals, great swaths of the student population would become shells of their former selves and they would spend every waking minute with their face in a textbook or studying copies of exams from previous years. They were hysterical about the future.

I couldn't for the life of me understand why these kids were losing sleep at night. Now of course I know. Those stressed-out students of yesterday are the successful and stressed-out professionals of today.

And besides, we had momentum now, and clearly the worst thing to do would be to ignore momentum. That was a scientific fact. So while others hit the library, we headed back to the LSPU Hall and booked more dates for early in the summer—we wanted to create *Hardly a Sensible Evening: Volume 2*.

If the others struggled with this decision I certainly didn't. Andrew was a naturally gifted student; his solid and impressive 65 percent average was a testament to that.

Christine, no matter what she did or didn't do in school, was pushed ahead in every course she took. She had something that was called dyslexia. This was a new buzzword at the time. The school had no real method of dealing with dyslexia other than to pass her in each class she took regardless of her effort or lack thereof. She seemed to pass classes as if by magic. The rest of us were under the impression that she had pulled off some sort of great, long con. If anything, we were somewhat bitter that we hadn't got in on this action. Why couldn't we get the dyslexic treatment? Seemed like the perfect crime.

Turns out that Christine was not faking her condition. She was not, as we suspected, simply too lazy to write words on a page. She is actually profoundly dyslexic. She hid the severity of her condition from everyone, including us. She wasn't a kid who read slow or who saw certain letters backwards; she was for the most part completely illiterate. She would go on to have a successful career as a writer, performance artist and academic. She has a PhD and lectures at universities, but still to this day, if you gave her a hundred dollars she could not easily read a column in the *Toronto Sun*. Neither can I, but for different reasons.

Ashley? Nobody paid much attention to Ashley, other than Lois. And I think she was just glad he was with us and not in the back of a squad car.

And me? I crunched the numbers and realized that at this point in the academic year I was formally screwed. Up until this point in my life I could go through the motions and somehow pull a 50 percent out of my back passage. Things changed near the end of grade eleven. One glance at what my classmates on the bus were studying and it was evident that 50 percent plus one was not in my future. Especially in math. There were mathematical formulas and symbols I had never even seen before. Since when did hieroglyphics enter the picture?

It was my own fault. In algebraic terms I was not even 100 percent sure I could pick my math teacher out of a lineup two out of three times. Also, how could I possibly cram for an exam when I didn't even know where my textbook was? A further complication was that I couldn't remember the combination for my locker.

If memory serves me correctly, my teacher was a Mr. Leonard. At least he was the one who, around this time, cornered me in the hallway and informed me that I was in need of some straight talk. Without math, he said, I would become a hobo selling newspapers on Water Street. He became quite animated, informing me that he had gone to school with a fellow just like me and that was his fate. He told me the last he heard of him, he was swallowing pickled wieners for drinks in dingy bars on George Street. "That," he said "is where you are headed!"

"So," I thought, "this gentleman who reminds you of me, he ended up in the entertainment business as well?"

He told me my only salvation was summer school. He lost me at *salvation.*

I am loath to say I completely ignored his advice. God, how dim was I. A few weeks' work and things might have been very different. But to me, show business was everything. And I knew in my heart of hearts that math would never make sense to me.

It would be years before I figured out how wrong I was on that front. Once dollar signs became attached to the numbers, math made all the sense in the world.

Being in a comedy troupe changed everything. It may sound corny, but suddenly we all belonged to something. There was a vision. It was like being in a band. Or at least it felt that way. Of course, being in a band requires the ability to play an instrument. That requires forethought. Or parents who have the inside track.

When I was a kid, playing an instrument was decidedly not cool. In my school, if you were going to get on the bus with a trombone case, it might have been a wise move to wear a helmet. And if you were a boy who sang in the school choir without a court order, you might as well draw a pair of balls on your forehead and get it over with. That is bravery.

But then suddenly—in grade ten or eleven—that kid from the classical music competition? His skin clears up, he gets himself a DX7 synthesizer, he places a call to his choir buddy who can sing Depeche Mode and before you know it they're sitting around coming up with band names. Once they settle on something really cool like Parental GuiDANCE or ME2YOU, they find themselves a guitarist and they are off to the races.

Because even if you're in a shitty band (and at that age, covering Depeche Mode, you're bound to be), the other kids are jealous. Of course they are, because they were too stupid or lazy to learn guitar and now, because you put in the long hours, there is a small chance that somehow you, weird guy in the blouse singing a rock ballad in the school gym, will be a rock star.

Best job on the planet.

And rock stars, even budding rock stars, of the male variety get the girls in this exact order: singer, guitarist, bass player, piano, sound guy, manager, friend of singer and then finally drummer. I have known many professional musicians in my life, and every single one of them admits that their impetus for being in a band was to attract the opposite sex. The only exception to that rule is gay and lesbian musicians, whose impetus was to attract the same sex.

So being in a comedy troupe was very much akin to being in a band. Except the sexy part. There's absolutely nothing sexy about being in a comedy group. In fact, it's anti-sexy. Almost all men and women say a sense of humour is attractive, but that's something that kicks in during adulthood. As a young person, being in comedy does not make you attractive. The only occupation less attractive is that of puppeteer.

Soon after our first show, Andrew and I marched down to the Bank of Montreal and opened a commercial chequing account. "Who are Corey and Wade?" the lady asked. "Associates of ours," I replied.

Again, why we didn't take that moment to change our name to something half-sensible, I have no idea. Instead, we persevered, and we ordered a chequebook with the name of the troupe emblazoned across the top of each cheque.

When the cheques eventually arrived, we couldn't believe it was true. Unlike a personal chequebook, these cheques came in a genuine pleather binder with two cheques to a page separated by a perforated line. This was the big time. We were now a professional company with real cheques, much like General Motors or Monsanto. The difference being, our chequebook was attached to an account with a balance in the low two figures. But it was what it represented that mattered. In many ways a blank cheque is not unlike a blank page or a blank stage. It is filled with unlimited promise.

And so as the two members of the troupe entrusted with signing power we did what any sensible young artistic entrepreneurs would do. We wrote each other cheques for the sum of $1 million.

I still have mine.

With that chequebook, Corey and Wade's Playhouse was born as a professional theatre company.

Having chosen not to attend summer school after grade eleven, I showed up in grade twelve and was confronted with a schedule that had me not only repeating grade eleven math but also taking grade twelve math at the same time. Sometimes on the same day in reverse order.

This was not a plan for success, this was Dieppe. Nobody could survive. Knowing this, I did what those young men on that beach never had the chance to do. I surrendered.

I didn't bail entirely. I enjoyed the social aspect of school, so I continued to pop by on occasion. But the academic part ceased to be a feature. I was mostly interested in the theatre. At the beginning of the year Andrew and I launched a political party to run candidates in the student council elections. This was pure performance art.

We formed the Neurotic Party. I was the Neurotic candidate in grade twelve, and he was the Neurotic candidate in grade eleven. The Neurotic candidate in grade ten was a kid by the name of Zach Kellum, whose father just happened to have been the CBC producer for *The Wonderful Grand Band*. That meant Zach was like royalty.

All the Neurotic candidates got elected and somehow I ended up as student council president. Eventually I earned the nickname President In-Absentia, which is Latin for "Didn't come to school again today."

My attendance at the Duckworth Lunch, however, was exemplary. This was a small café and bagel joint that overlooked the war memorial in downtown St. John's. It was a great arts community hangout and I began to spend hours there every day. I would drink coffee, smoke cigarettes and write in a journal. I read Jack Kerouac's *On the Road* in that café and absolutely everything by Hunter S. Thompson. My uniform consisted of an army jacket, converse sneakers and an earring from which dangled a menacing silver skull. I drove a used Honda 450 Nighthawk motorcycle. How I didn't end up on the cover of *Cliché Teen*, I have no idea.

And I was always planning, or rather daydreaming, about what Corey and Wade's Playhouse would do next. My great friend Dana Warren waited tables at the Duck and she always made sure my cup was filled and I was never charged. She would sneak me an errant tuna melt for lunch. Eventually with Dana's help I began to pick up shifts there.

Grade twelve was also the year in which I finally took theatre as a subject. But even that didn't seize my attention. Lois and I continued to get along famously everywhere but theatre class. She told me straight up if I was bored and not interested in learning about Shakespearean sonnets I shouldn't bother to show up at all. So, no hard feelings, I stopped going.

And then in the middle of the school year I took a job touring Newfoundland with a clown by the name of Beni Malone.

Beni, Newfoundland's only professional clown, was a graduate of the Barnum and Bailey circus school in Florida. He had a theatre company called Wonderbolt Circus. He would travel all over the province, including to some of our most isolated communities, to do one-man shows at schools and community centres. And he could do a hell of a show. In his latest creation he played a deranged scientist, an inventor of robots, who would teach the kids about science. Along the way he would walk on his hands, walk on stilts, ride a twelve-foot-tall unicycle, juggle every flaming toy imaginable and try not to burn the school down.

I begged him to take me with him, and god love him, Beni said yes. And so, in grade twelve, just before mid-terms, I ran away and joined the circus.

For a month we drove around the province in a Pontiac station wagon filled with props and smelling of kerosene. We did two shows a day. My job was to hide behind the flat that doubled as the mad scientist's laboratory and pass him props as he needed them. I dunked the various torches in accelerant as required. I was also in charge of manning the fire extinguisher that was standing by in case the flaming devil sticks came into contact with the gym curtains. On most days I remembered to bring it in from the station wagon.

I would distract the kids in the audience during a big costume change by appearing as Bucky the out-of-control roller-skating robot. Appearing out of control came naturally, as I could not roller skate and the helmet was not designed for me so I could barely see a thing and had no peripheral vision at all. One day I lost it completely and skated off the edge of the stage. Suddenly I was airborne. I felt like I had been thrown out of a plane. Everything went silent and I hit hard on my feet and somehow I kept my balance, arms flailing. The kids went wild.

Over the next few years I went out on the road with Beni pretty regularly. Beni was a machine. Nobody worked harder. And any time he toured he always offered me a spot. We toured the coast of Labrador and did shows that were in communities that were only accessible by boat.

He's such a good guy. Beni, at his own expense, brought theatre to places that had never seen it. Yes, he toured to make a living, but he also toured with a missionary zeal. Bigger shows would subsidize his going to an isolated community. There are thousands of adults in Newfoundland who can say their first or only live show of any kind they saw as a kid was a Wonderbolt Theatre production. I took this mission very seriously as well. I only had to see the enthusiasm and hear the screams of the kids to be transported back to grade three when I was lucky enough to see those hippies in a van.

Back in St. John's, when the tour was over, Corey and Wade's Playhouse managed to do more shows. They were becoming better, we were becoming bigger, and the runs were getting longer.

As the end of the school year approached, I didn't sprint through the tape so much as stagger towards it. Without math credits Christ himself couldn't graduate from high school, let alone get into any post-secondary institute. I came very close to not showing up to get my final report card of failure, but for some reason I did. As expected, it was a washout.

Surprisingly, despite not attending, I actually did pass theatre in grade twelve, with a D minus, or exactly 50 percent. I remember thanking Lois for passing me, and she told me that it had nothing to do with our friendship. She said, "I have no problem failing you for a class you didn't bother to attend, but what I am not going to do is give you the satisfaction of being able to tell the *Globe and Mail* in a few years that your drama teacher failed you in grade twelve."

Lois was always in my corner, even when giving me a D minus.

I've been very fortunate in my life. I have had the career that I wanted, I have had jobs that I have adored. I realize how incredibly lucky this makes me. I don't even like saying it out loud or putting it in writing because I realize how very rare that is. I am also fortunate that I have had few regrets. But I do have one major regret. And that is how I treated school from day one to closing night.

What I know now, which I never understood then, is that education is one of the greatest privileges that can be afforded an individual.

A free education like we have in Canada should be cherished and taken advantage of in every possible way.

I was, for some reason, convinced in my heart of hearts that I was a bad student. This had nothing to do with teachers. In fact, I can remember so many teachers telling me I could do better if I just applied myself. I heard it so much I came to believe it was something they say that means nothing. Now I realize they were right. I am blessed. I had every advantage that could have been afforded me, I do not have a learning disability, I did not grow up with a stressful home life. I have no excuse. I was a bad student because I was lazy and for some reason convinced I couldn't do it.

While I was in a classroom, for some reason I never figured it out. But when I went to work it became crystal clear. Wherever I worked, with Corey and Wade's Playhouse or with 22 Minutes, I was a model student. I wasn't the best or the smartest, but I worked the hardest. What a revelation: hard work equals success. Had I known then what I know now, school would have been a much better experience. And I would have had the option to further my studies.

Regrets? I've had a few, and that's the biggest one of them all. Stay in school, kids. Without a post-secondary education or a trade, it only goes two ways: against all odds you win the lotto and knock it out of the park, or you end up broke and swallowing pickled wieners for drinks.

Think about that, then do your homework.

10

Living the Dream

With my academic career behind me, I moved downtown and began to enjoy the most creative years of my life. A madcap period of house parties and after-hours clubs. A time when fifteen dollars in your pocket felt like a small fortune. If I had enough money for a pack of Player's Light and a jar of peanut butter, all was right with the world.

While friends were at Memorial University or on the mainland studying, I was spending every waking hour creating and learning. There was success and spectacular failure.

Corey and Wade's Playhouse were no longer a late-night act—we were a mainstage act at the LSPU Hall. And we were no longer drawing an audience that was exclusively our own age. We had a buzz about us. It was exciting. We had fans.

Coincidentally, this was the same time that Lois left her job as an English and theatre teacher at PWC and began her life as a full-time artist. She began to direct our shows, which paid off immensely. They became slicker and more professional.

We still had to beg, borrow or steal all of our props and costumes, though. A roommate of mine had a job at Mary Brown's Chicken.

With the job she was given two uniforms. Andrew and I became the Mary Brown's Girls. Andrew's mother was kind enough to make us brown miniskirts to show off our legs. I remember Andrew saying, "Mom, can you make them shorter?"

Everyone involved became an expert at pulling off shows with no money. In one show we had a family scene that required a bouquet of flowers to be stomped on. Every night Geoff Seymour, our stage manager, would arrive with the flowers. I never asked any questions and assumed he was purchasing them out of our very limited budget. When the run was over and he was submitting receipts for expenses, I asked him, "What about the flowers?" He said, "There's no receipts for flowers. I had to cut through the graveyard on my way to the Hall anyway."

We also began to grow our audience by playing venues that had never seen comedy before. In those days there was a giant dance bar and live music venue called the Cornerstone at the end of the fabled bar strip, George Street. The owner, Doug Warren, hired Andrew and me to sit high on top of the shooter bar in character as two brothers, Lar and Gar. We would do comedy bits and introduce music videos, give out prizes and promote cheap shooters. Lar and Gar were essentially drunken Newfoundland versions of Bob and Doug McKenzie. We were heckled relentlessly, but we had the microphones so we always won. Often we would stay in the bar long after it closed, convinced that the hecklers were outside waiting, as promised, to beat the face clean off us.

Corey and Wade would also perform shows with bands at the Cornerstone. More than once we would be onstage doing a sketch and a person would wander up to us, tap one of us on the shoulder and drunkenly ask, "When is the band coming back on?" or "Where is the washroom?"

Bounder's Lounge was much more our speed. It was a live venue that hosted alternative bands. Punk bands. This was our crowd, and we put on many successful shows there. When Bounder's was on wheels it was something to see. If you were downstairs and the band was playing upstairs and the kids were dancing, the ceiling would

My handsome father Ken, my glamorous mother Pat and a pudgy me, distracted by something shiny, perhaps an errant blasting cap.

In preparation for my performance as the Roly Poly Teddy Bear at the Christmas concert, I wore my costume around the house for a week. Seen here with my older brother Gilbert (he is on the right).

Starring in *The Twenty Minute Psychiatric Workout*, the show that changed my life. Donna Pinhorn played Dr. Feelgood. I was Dr. Feltgood. Here we are, pandering shamelessly to a townie crowd.

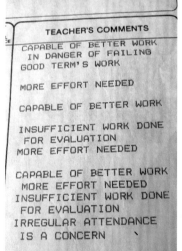

TEACHER'S COMMENTS

CAPABLE OF BETTER WORK
IN DANGER OF FAILING
GOOD TERM'S WORK

MORE EFFORT NEEDED

CAPABLE OF BETTER WORK

INSUFFICIENT WORK DONE
FOR EVALUATION
MORE EFFORT NEEDED

CAPABLE OF BETTER WORK
MORE EFFORT NEEDED
INSUFFICIENT WORK DONE
FOR EVALUATION
IRREGULAR ATTENDANCE
IS A CONCERN

Grade 11 midterm results. I'm sensing a pattern. Why my mother saved these I have no idea.

The Wonderful Grand Band

The greatest TV show ever. A CBC Newfoundland and Labrador production.

Introducing Corey and Wade's Playhouse: Ashley Billard, Christine Taylor,
Andrew Younghusband and me.

Andrew and me shooting a commercial for the annual Peace-A-Chord. This
picture was taken moments before I was nearly electrocuted. Good times.

In the William D. MacGillivray movie *The Vacant Lot*. Here I am channelling my punk-rock idols. Unfortunately I can't sing, even by punk-rock standards.

Before it was the cover of this book it was the poster for the one-man show that brought me across Canada.

Gerald and I were tempting fate in every way with the title of our second show.

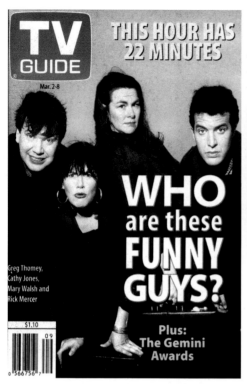

Gerald Lunz, creative producer and showrunner for *This Hour Has 22 Minutes*. Though I've been surrounded by comedians all my life, nobody has made me laugh like he does.

There was a time when *TV Guide* was the biggest magazine in the country. And there was a time when Mary Walsh and I secretly stalked supermarkets, staring at this issue by the cash registers.

The poster for the After-the-Rehab Reunion and World Tour.

move up and down an easy six inches. When I cut through the downstairs on the way to the bathroom I would instinctively walk against the wall, my rationale being that when the floor above me collapsed, taking a hundred teenagers with it, I might survive if near a support column.

But I had to look beyond Corey and Wade's Playhouse. Not because I wasn't fully committed but because I was a year older than the rest of them. I was out of school and they were still in their last year. And they, being wiser than me, did things like attend class on a regular basis and study for exams.

And so it was during this time that I was hired for the first time as a professional actor and appeared in a number of plays. In those days an actor would make about $300 a week. Which is what I was paid by the Newfoundland Shakespeare Company to take on the role of the Duke of Cornwall in Mike Wade's *King Lear*, to this day the scariest thing I have ever done in my life. The upside was night after night I got to pluck a man's eye out of his head with my thumb.

CBC Radio did actual radio plays in those days and I ended up in a few. In a short time, I got to know and had worked with most of the actors in town.

I was picking up shifts as a dishwasher in a trendy spot called the Continental Café. Customers would have to walk past me to get to the tables. I found out that one of the regulars was a CBC Radio producer by the name of Glen Tilley. Apparently he was the guy who booked political commentaries on the morning show. Every time he walked by I would say, "Glen, I heard so-and-so on the show this morning. That commentary? It made no sense. You should give me a shot." Or I would say, "Why does CBC Radio still have Rex Murphy doing commentaries? He's like a hundred. Do you have to be a geriatric to get on the radio in this town?" Of course, Rex was probably only forty at the time, but still, in my eyes . . .

The owner told me over and over, "Do not talk to the customers and definitely do not tell them how to do their jobs. Shut up and wash the dishes." I wasn't there to wash dishes. I was there to relentlessly harangue people into getting me a gig.

Eventually Glen relented and said I could have a shot but there was no guarantee it would go to air.

And so I recorded my first political commentary for CBC Radio. The audio technician remembered me from a recording I'd done the previous year. Alison Gzowski was a CBC Radio producer who'd been in town from Toronto. She came to one of the Corey and Wade shows and asked me to come in and record my bank rant for a show she was working on. The rant was spiked and it never aired, but I did receive a cheque for forty-six dollars (which I photocopied). The tech asked me how old I was. When I told him he said, "You're lucky you don't sound eighteen. Nobody wants political commentary from an eighteen-year-old, what the hell do *they* know?" It went to air and became a quasi-regular gig.

One trajectory-changing job I did land that year, and for which I am eternally grateful, was working backstage for Cathy Jones in her one-woman show *Wedding in Texas*. It was a pretty simple job interview. My friend Sebastian Spence—another young actor banging around downtown doing whatever he could to make ends meet— and I were sitting at a table at the Ship Inn and Cathy wandered over and asked us if we'd like to "help out with stuff" on her show.

I was thrilled to be on board. This was legendary. *Wedding in Texas* had run in St. John's the previous year and went on to have a very short run in Toronto. Now it was being remounted and heading out on tour. A real tour. A national tour. It would play the LSPU Hall for an extended run with a built-in holdover and then it was heading west with stops in Halifax and Ottawa before an extended run in Toronto and then on to Vancouver.

The idea of touring the entire country like that was a dream come true. This was the big time. Of course we were only being hired for the St. John's portion, but a guy could dream.

I can't tell you how funny this show was. To this day it's one of the best things I have ever seen in a theatre. Cathy Jones is a brilliant character comedian and she easily played a dozen characters in this production, every one of them charming as hell and hysterically funny. She played sexy women and sleazy men. She sang and she danced. It was a tour de force. As far as a play goes it was stuck together with Scotch tape, but that didn't matter. It was a showcase for a comic actor at the top of her game. I had seen the production in its original run and I had never witnessed anything like it. From start to finish the full houses were screaming with laughter. There were moments when the entire theatre was gasping for breath.

This tour was Cathy's chance to show the country just how brilliant she was. Because of that, CODCO's manager, Mary White, was leaving nothing to chance. Nobody called her Mary. She went by the single name White. Like Cher. White hired an Ottawa-based producer by the name of Gerald Lunz to mount the show in St. John's and drag Cathy and her set across the country.

White had met Gerald the previous year at a CODCO show in Ottawa, a fundraiser for post-production on the first feature film ever made in Newfoundland, *The Adventures of Faustus Bidgood*, written by Andy Jones and Michael Jones and starring CODCO and every actor who ever breathed a breath in the province. White was impressed with Gerald's organizational skills and his ability to wrangle the notoriously distractible theatre company.

The touring version of Cathy's show was designed to be compact. And while it had all the bells and whistles of the original show, the production could be pulled off in each city by hiring two technicians in each location—as long as they were experienced and good at multi-tasking.

That's where Sebastian and I came in. And that's when Gerald's head nearly came off.

To be clear, it was Cathy and Cathy alone who hired us to be those two experienced theatre technicians. She hired us before Gerald's boots hit the island. She hired me because she liked my comedy troupe and she thought I was funny. She hired Sebastian because he is an awesome guy and she knew his mother, Janice—a well-known local actor and director. And while I am sure this had nothing to do with it, I should also note that Sebastian was, and is, insanely good-looking. Sebastian was so good-looking it was like he was from another planet. A planet where Brad Pitt could have a baby with James Dean.

I used to wonder, why does Sebastian stick around in St. John's? He should just go to Vancouver or LA and become a star, or at least get paid to stand around shirtless. Eventually his movie-star looks did take him to Vancouver and Los Angeles, where he has had an extremely long career playing handsome cops, handsome teachers, handsome alien hunters and handsome perps.

Cathy also hired us because she knew that we both needed the money badly.

This was true. We were the proverbial starving actors. Now, while Cathy's gesture was certainly admirable from a humanitarian per-spective, it was exactly the wrong reason to hire people to work on a professional theatrical production.

Cathy is a brilliant comic actress, but having worked with her for over a decade, it amazes me how someone in her position could have such little understanding of actual production. That said, I'm kind of glad, because if she had understood anything about production Sebastian and I would have been the last people she would have hired. Or at least, I can say that about myself with great certainty.

Gerald was not amused.

The tasks I had were not exactly unskilled. I had to run two follow spots during musical numbers and had a dozen other lighting cues to orchestrate. I was also the projectionist.

The show included a music video entitled "Outport Lesbian" pro-jected onto a large screen at the back of the stage. It told the story of a young lesbian in rural Newfoundland who is rescued from her job as a waitress in a fish and chip restaurant by a carload of townie les-bians. Very funny and a catchy tune.

Outport lesbian
Working in the takeout,
Outport lesbian

Let me take you home.

Outport lesbian

Is there any reason that it's so late in the season

and you're all alone?

It has a happy ending; the townie lesbian lands the fish. Cathy is seen in bed with, of all people, my old theatre teacher Lois. Small town.

This and another short film allowed for costume and set changes. Brilliant idea. It was my job to project and swap out the two reels. Also, I had to sync a music track to one of the films based on a visual cue. When Gerald explained my duties, I stood there and nodded with great conviction—despite having no idea what the hell he was talking about.

When Gerald learned that I had done exactly none of those things before, he hit the roof. Of course I had never operated a film projector. It was hard enough to find the courage to join the drama club. I wasn't going to go all in and join the audiovisual brigade.

I heard him arguing with Cathy, saying that it was his job to ensure the show was tight and slick and ran like clockwork. He needed professionals to do this; this was important. He said the plan was to go to Toronto and blow their minds, but in order to do that they needed good people with experience. "You just can't hire people who have never done anything before. What," he asked, "are you going to do if there's a problem with the projection and he doesn't know how to fix it?" Cathy, god love her, wouldn't budge. He was stuck with us.

He did make her promise that she wouldn't hire any more strays in any other cities.

For the record I did learn how to use the film projector. A good friend of Cathy's, film director Nigel Markham, came in to give me a lesson. He was very intense and was lecturing me about the importance of wearing gloves while handling the print. He was obsessive about any dust coming in contact with the precious film. I was so bloody nervous that no sooner were these words out of his mouth than I dropped the canister, it popped open, and the precious film unravelled all over the dusty LSPU Hall floor.

Nigel looked like a man who was watching an orphanage burn.

Later I could hear him saying to Cathy in the dressing room that there were a dozen young people in town better qualified to do the job than me. Apparently, everyone who knew what they were doing wanted me gone. I was the weakest link. Thankfully I had Cathy in my corner. I was not let go.

Eventually, during rehearsals, I muddled through. I got to the point where I never missed my cues and thank god the projector never faltered.

As we got closer to opening night I was becoming reluctantly in awe of Gerald. He really ran the production like a fine-tuned machine. It was like nothing I had seen before. Everything was scheduled properly. It was a level of professionalism that was foreign to me. We were all connected with walkie-talkies. He made us rehearse cues over and over again. The set changes became flawless. Everything about this show was head and shoulders above anything I had ever been involved in.

I was also quite taken with Gerald. He was funny. "He's handsome," I said to Cathy. "And he carries a briefcase!"

"Don't be fooled," she said. "The only thing in there is a *Rolling Stone* magazine and a package of Zig-Zag Whites."

The run itself was a sensation. I was used to being in or watching shows at the LSPU Hall that did well, but they did well with a certain audience—an audience that was made up almost entirely of the downtown arts community. Cathy's show was mainstream. They were coming from all over. I had teachers from grade ten calling me and saying, "My sister says your name is in Cathy's program. Can you get us tickets?"

It was a fantastic sold-out run. I couldn't wait for the end-of-show party. But on closing night, there was a snowstorm. The roads were treacherous. There was talk of the show being cancelled. But in the tradition of the theatre, pre-pandemic at least, the show must go on. So we prepared as usual. Not a single person failed to show up. That's how hot this ticket was.

After the show Cathy went to the Ship Inn to celebrate. Gerald announced, however, that we would have to wait. Because of the snow, we needed to get the show loaded into the cube van immediately. He didn't want the van stuck next to the theatre in the morning, as it had to be on the road at daybreak in order to cross the island and catch the ferry to the mainland.

This was not part of the deal. We were supposed to be wrapped. He was supposed to load the show the next morning with another crew. Reluctantly, all three of us started to load the props and flats into the van in a blinding blizzard. It was the worst work I had ever done. I felt like I was a member of the crew of HMS *Erebus* after they'd found themselves trapped in the Arctic ice 150 years earlier. I lost my will to live.

My lack of enthusiasm, general lethargic pace and terrible attitude eventually brought Gerald to the breaking point. If memory serves, he screamed something to the effect that I was the laziest SOB he ever had the misfortune to work with. At least I think that's what he said. It was hard to tell over the gale-force howl.

In any event it was three hours later when the van was loaded, and he said goodbye to the both of us, hopped in the cube van and drove away. We watched it make its way up the steep hill, wheels spinning, quickly disappearing into a whiteout. I didn't see the guy again for eighteen months.

Sebastian looked at me and said, "He wanted you fired so bad."

We had a laugh about that and then we headed downtown looking for something, anything, that was still open.

And that's how I met the man I ended up spending the rest of my life with. Gerald, not Sebastian.

11

Onward and Upward and Down Again

Meanwhile, I was still washing dishes to pay the bills. On Saturday mornings I taught theatre to kids. Corralling a gaggle of screaming six-year-olds at nine in the morning on no sleep illustrated a true commitment to the life of a starving artist.

At MUN Extension I picked up the odd job as a still-life model for art classes. Fifteen bucks an hour in one's underwear, twenty-five if you posed nude. My bird has been scrutinized and sketched by more middle-aged ladies in search of a hobby than you can possibly imagine.

And there was, on occasion, acting work. At one point I was able to draw on my experience playing that pirate in grade three. I was hired to dress as a swashbuckler and deliver small wooden boxes filled with sand and chocolate gold coins to every big wheel in St. John's: the premier of the province, the leader of the Opposition, the lieutenant-governor and every rich lawyer we had. I stood in their offices while their staff gathered; I would reach into the box and pull out a scroll and say something to the effect of "Aye, Matey, I've come ashore to announce that you are being shanghaied. You and your lovely wife/husband are to report to the Cabot Club in the Hotel

Newfoundland for a New Year's Eve you will never forget. Music by 12 Gauge, tickets seventy-five dollars per couple." Dreadful, yes, but it was still show business. Kind of.

Quite unexpectedly, in 1988 I was cast in a one-off TV show called *My Brother Larry*, a thirty-minute drama that was being produced independently in Halifax but would air on the CBC. I played Larry, a developmentally delayed boy who spends all his time tending to his chickens. In fact, almost all of my dialogue was directed at chickens. I had one pivotal scene with a rooster.

I shot the audition in my kitchen using a bleach bottle as a stand-in for the bird. I caressed the bottle and said, "I love my chicken, you're a good chicken," over and over again. Apparently I nailed it. I got the part, was flown to Halifax and was put up in a bed and breakfast.

When the shoot was over, a CBC producer from Toronto pulled me aside and asked me what my plans were. I told him that I was an actor living in Newfoundland and that I had a comedy troupe. He said to me, "Kid, if you're getting on a plane you shouldn't be heading east. There's nothing for you there and there is nothing for you here. You need to go to Toronto."

He then went on to tell me I should forget comedy. I should focus on doing what I had just done. He said, "With your talent, you could corner the market on playing developmentally delayed men in Canada or even in the United States." He added, "There's nothing wrong with being typecast as long as it pays the bills." Of course, he used the R word.

My first impression of CBC brass wasn't a good one.

The next day I headed east.

The TV gig led to some film gigs. The director of *My Brother Larry* was Bill McGillivray and he cast me in his film *The Vacant Lot*. He was so enamoured with my ability to act like I had an intellectual disability that he assumed I could pull off being a lead singer in a punk band. Unfortunately, carrying a tune is above my pay grade. Somehow I muddled through. Bill, bless him, continued to cast me whenever he had a project. In *The Vacant Lot* my credit was "And introducing Rick Mercer." Thank you, Bill.

Back in Newfoundland I landed a part in a feature film called *Boat in the Grass*. Written and directed by Ken Pittman, it was a very personal family drama. In a strange development, I persuaded my father to audition for the part of the father. He nailed it and played my father. I didn't see that coming. The complete story eludes me at the moment but a boat in the grass was pivotal, although it ended up being a boat in the snow because budget delays forced the film to shoot in winter.

Corey and Wade's Playhouse began to make short films of our own to play during our shows. We went to NIFCO—the Newfoundland Independent Filmmakers Co-operative—and found out that they had a mandate to help anyone who wanted to make a film. That would be us.

I wrote a short film called *Father Loves Us*. It featured a boys' choir singing about abusive priests—angelic voices making shocking allegations against the church. The lyrics parodied the hymn "Jesus Loves Me." It was a classic young comedy group's attempt to be over the top and outrageous. Which we were. And it rhymed. I thank god my grandmother never had the opportunity to see it. *Father Loves Us* won Best Short Film at the 1989 Halifax Film Festival.

The film was produced two years before Newfoundland was rocked by perhaps the most traumatizing scandal in our history, a scandal that saw the infamous Mount Cashel Orphanage in St. John's permanently close its doors after decades of abuse and cover-ups by the church and the government.

I loved everything about the business of film and television. Being on a TV or film set was far more intoxicating than the theatre. And with the short Corey and Wade films we were in charge, and that was exciting. It didn't have to be a huge film set to get me excited. Any set, no matter how small, did the trick.

Andrew felt the same way. Together he and I created a series of commercials for the Peace-A-Chord. Andrew played a homemaker (he loved dressing like the ladies) baking in her kitchen while I did a voice-over listing all the great bands and poets that would appear at that year's festival. The gag was that near the end of the commercial the homemaker opens her fridge and finds me inside.

Take after take, we shot this thing. I actually was in the fridge the entire time. As time went on, I found it harder and harder to breathe. We had to light the inside of the fridge with small film lights, so it was becoming excruciatingly hot, and I was getting soaked as the ice from the freezer began to melt and pool around my ankles.

When we were finally done, I remember Andrew opening the door and extending a hand to me to help me out. He pulled me up and I stepped out of the pool of water into the kitchen. Immediately, with the door still open, the interior of the fridge exploded, and arcs of 220-volt electricity bounced around against the walls like something out of Frankenstein's lair. When it was over black electrical burns scarred the inside of the fridge. Being the age we were, we laughed until our sides hurt at this near-death experience. Now the thought of being electrocuted in a dark, wet box surrounded by ketchup and leftover chicken fills me with dread. It's all fun and games until an actor is fried to a crisp.

But still, even this set was my happy place.

I began to do rudimentary research on film and television schools in Canada. "Rudimentary" because on paper I was barely qualified to get into driving school, let alone a film school. As much as I liked to fantasize about the notion, a post-secondary education was not in the cards.

The absolute best time I spent on a set was in the summer of 1992. I landed what was my biggest film job yet, a part in Edward Riche's *Secret Nation*. Directed by Mike Jones and produced by Paul Pope, it was a feature film that was both political thriller and comedy. It explored the notion that the 1948 Newfoundland referendum had been rigged. In that referendum 52 percent of Newfoundlanders voted to join Canada and 48 percent voted to remain an independent nation. The results were absurdly close. The anti-confederate crowd never truly accepted the results. They were just too clever by half. Or in this case too clever by 4 percent. The angry young Newfoundland nationalist inside me was desperate to be part of this project. As luck would have it, Ed wrote a part with me in mind.

This film was different from anything I had been part of before. Up until then, the films I was involved with were for the most part serious, earnest affairs; films that comfortably wore the mantle of "Canadian cinema," a genre that was big on landscapes, less so on lighting and completely void of anything that might smack of a joke. Compared with that, this was rock and roll.

Edward Riche is a sharp, funny writer, one of my favourites. His books are hysterical, and he is a master of the tall tale. Cathy Jones played the lead, I played her younger brother and Mary Walsh played our mother. At the time it was the biggest set I had been on, and Mary and Cathy were bona fide stars. It was exhilarating. That said, despite the impression of grandeur (to me, at least), it was very much an independent film with a shoestring budget.

But what I loved about it was how it was flying in the face of what I saw as standard Canadian fare at the time. Lots of producers in Canada were making projects that were very successful at home and abroad, but they would employ a series of tricks. They were essentially creating Canadian content that operated like the TV or film equivalent of a stealth bomber. They would create content that was Canadian, but yet they would never show Canadian money, they would avoid the licence plates, hide the flag, ignore the Mounties and never do a courtroom scene because in Canada, unlike the States, lawyers wear robes. So essentially, they would do everything in their power to ensure that the finished product was completely sanitized of anything that might make a viewer in Texas confused. You didn't want potential viewers suddenly confronted with questions like "Why is their money purple? Am I having a stroke? And why are those police officers dressed like fancy waiters on horseback? And why is there a picture of an old lady on the wall in the hockey rink?"

Secret Nation was the opposite of that. If was a thriller set so firmly in Newfoundland that nobody ever could think it was anything other than 100 percent Canadian. It was glorious.

I couldn't help but notice that there was a broadcaster attached. The Canadian Broadcasting Corporation. I was starting to like them more and more.

Corey and Wade's Playhouse continued to create shows, but things were getting complicated. The rest of the troupe finally graduated from high school, but that didn't make things easier for us. Andrew was accepted to Memorial University and may have attended one class before the largest theatre company in Newfoundland, Rising Tide Theatre, came calling.

Rising Tide had decided to get into the theatre-for-young-people business. They created a young person's company that would tour the province with a show about teen issues. To do so they hired a half-dozen young actors, two of whom were Andrew and Ashley. It was good, solid work, but it took them out of the Corey and Wade business for a substantial amount of time.

We did manage to get together in August of that year, and Lois directed Andrew, Ashley and Christine in a play I wrote called *The Beatles Play Bishop's Falls*, based loosely on my cousin Paul, from Bishop's Falls, who was a Beatles fanatic. He played in a band, was a brilliant singer, did brilliant harmonies with best friend Wayne and played only Beatles covers. Eccentric.

It was in essence a musical. We had a full band and we ran for ten days. The reviews were, well, reviews. The headline in the *Evening Telegram* screamed "FEW ACCOLADES FOR 'THE BEATLES PLAY BISHOP'S FALLS'" John Holmes wrote: "This is not so much a play as an excuse to belt out some very, very loud Beatles music with an ear-splitting drum accompaniment by Louis Thomas." This whole "not so much a play" thing was beginning to be a pattern in my reviews.

He continued: "The dialogue that connects these wild forays into the Beatles canon is depressing, not very original and abounding with vernacular language."

And then my favourite part: "The show opened to a packed sticky house and was received with tumultuous applause, whistles and yells.

It is too loud, too crude and too long, but the audience was in the mood to be blasted out of their seats and laugh at anything so if that's your choice go to it." Andrew's performance was hailed as "believable" and Ashley's as "consistent." Christine was noted for having a "large body." Happy International Women's Day.

But hey, we sold out. And at that point in our lives the fact that the critics were complaining about how loud the band was? That was music to our ears. The 1988 equivalent of "two thumbs up."

Fifteen years later I happened to find myself standing outside of a restaurant in Nassau, in the Bahamas. I was on a small footbridge that went over a lily pond, waiting for Gerald, who was settling up inside. A little girl walked up to me and pointed to the lily pads and said, "There are no fish in the pond."

I could see a fairly large orange koi hiding behind a rock. I said, "Look over there. Do you see the orange tail? That's a fish right there. I think the rest are sleeping."

The girl moved a little way down the railing so she could see the fish and proclaimed, "You're right, the fish is sleeping." And then she said to her father, "Daddy, there's fish in the pond. This man showed me where the fish are. The rest are sleeping."

And then I heard a voice so distinctive that it is perhaps more recognizable than the Queen's. It said, "Well, that man must be very smart indeed." I looked up, but I need not have. It was Paul freaking McCartney.

I assumed this is when every person on the planet says, "OH MY GOD, I'M SUCH A FAN," so that's exactly what I did, but I added: "Mr. McCartney, when I was nineteen I wrote a play called *The Beatles Play Bishop's Falls*. It had six Beatles songs, a full musical, I know you're not supposed to do that but we were kids and we didn't know about rights. It was set in Bishop's Falls, Newfoundland, and got terrible reviews but we sold out every single night."

To which Sir Paul said, "Oh, I'm sorry I missed that one," like it was the most normal thing in the world.

"I'm sorry I missed that one"? How incredibly polite and patently absurd is that! Imagine if Paul McCartney had showed up at the

LSPU Hall on a hot August night. Had I known he was interested I would have left tickets at the door. If we ever stage a remount, I shall do just that.

After the Beatles debacle, our next foray into a mainstage theatrical production was a show with the ridiculously long and improbable title of *We Have No Pity for the Pseudo-Downtrodden*. What that title means? I have no idea. But this show was huge. In fact, the largest show budget-wise that Resource Centre for the Arts ever produced.

Corey and Wade's Playhouse was used to selling out the theatre, but everything we did was on our own dime and on a shoestring budget. It was starting to bug us that there was a professional theatre company at the Hall that was supposedly artist run but they only produced shows by the older arts community. They were, we accused them, very establishment. We went to the wall and argued that the time had come for generational change, that we should have a shot with a properly funded collective.

We persevered, and a new collective starring the young up-and-coming arts crowd was added to the season. This was our shot.

Lois and I put together a cast that was, in our eyes, insanely impressive. Corey and Wade's Playhouse was the nucleus, but we added four other actors and writers. And in an attempt to recapture lightning in a bottle from our high school days, we hired a band. Not WAFUT but a trio by the name of Dead Reckoning. They were the hottest band in town. You would not see them in any room that wasn't packed. They were my favourite.

Unfortunately, they had no interest in being in the show, other than that it paid a weekly salary. They had zero interest in acting and very little in doing anything other than agreeing to play a few of their hits. Also, the drummer was afraid of elevators, so he refused to rehearse at MUN Extension and just showed up on show nights.

Throw in the fact that we had no real impetus for the show and no real creative vision or even a subject matter in mind. We were in serious trouble.

What I think we agreed on was a meandering exploration of what it meant for our generation to grow up middle-class in St. John's. I know—can you think of anything worse?

Eventually we ended up with a big-budget show groaning under excess production values. At some point a snowmobile was driven across the stage, threatening to asphyxiate the audience. Why that happened? I would have to dig into the archives and look at a script. I am not that strong.

I will say that I distinctly remember Lois begging me, actually begging me, to cut the script down, claiming I was the only one who could do it. I studied the script for days and came to the conclusion that no, there was simply nowhere to cut. Every word was that important.

On opening night, *We Have No Pity* ran for three hours and thirty minutes, a scant eighteen minutes shorter than *Gone with the Wind*. But they had two intermissions.

It was a giant failure. It quickly earned the nickname "We Have No Pity for the Audience." The number of walkouts was incredible. While scenes were happening onstage I would be peering out from the wings watching the theatre empty. It was like someone pulled a fire alarm and everyone except the cast could hear it. A giant blow to the ego. I had nobody to blame but myself. It was a collective, but I was the de facto head writer.

I was if anything mortally embarrassed.

Around this time the CODCO cast were back in town writing their new TV season. And with them was none other than Gerald, the one who had wanted me oh so fired from *Wedding in Texas*.

While I was busy writing *No Pity*, I would see Gerald and the CODCO cast at the Ship Inn and we had become friendly. Clearly we got on much better when I wasn't working for him and I wasn't expected to partake in heavy lifting. And he had seen Corey and Wade in some comedy cabarets and liked our stuff. In fact we seemed to be going out of our way to bump into one another. We both became adept at the coincidental run-in.

In hindsight it did strike me as a little odd on opening night of *No Pity* that he left me a card wishing me well and suggesting I was a great talent. Seemed a bit over the top. I wrote it off as a mainland Canada thing.

And after that opening night? Two things happened. I had to deal with the soul-crushing feeling of being in a show that nobody liked night after night, and I began to spend more time with Gerald. As in days and nights.

Being in the closet as a young man was not that hard for me. If you meet someone you want to spend your nights with, it's actually not that difficult to pull off. Just takes a bit of sneaking around. Likewise, if you meet someone you'd like to spend your days with, that too is easy. The problems occur when you meet someone you want to spend your days *and* your nights with. That's when being in the closet becomes entirely unsustainable. That's when you need to make some serious decisions.

And if that person makes you laugh—which Gerald never ceased to do—then you better make the right decision.

When you are on the down-low or in the closet, for lack of a better term, you are always susceptible to distorted thoughts. The big one is "What will people think?" The answer in most circles is "People don't give a shit."

When you're in the closet you think coming out publicly will change everything. Honestly, most people are lucky if they become a twenty-four-hour news story among friends. After that they move on to more pressing issues, like rent and food and any number of imminent environmental catastrophes.

But yet there I was, living and working in a liberal arts community in a liberal city, essentially a bubble inside a bubble, and I was sneaking around, hiding who I was, trying not to be seen too much with the one person I actually wanted to spend all my time with.

What a completely ridiculous way to live your life.

So we stopped giving a shit. By osmosis people seemed to come to the conclusion that we were now together. The world did not come to an end. Our earth-shattering news was mostly met with a collective shrug.

12

A Two-Man Show

Unbeknownst to me, Gerald had a side hustle that had nothing to do with CODCO. The National Arts Centre in Ottawa had asked him to bring in a show from the East Coast.

Gerald had worked at the NAC both as an actor and a producer, and they knew he was in Newfoundland working with CODCO. Gerald had always been one of the voices at the NAC who chided them for being an "Ottawa" arts centre more than a "national" arts centre.

The programmer for English Theatre was an expat Brit by the name of Gil Osborne. She basically called Gerald's bluff. She told him the NAC had some money for three cabarets that they were going to run as a series. Two were from Ottawa. She asked Gerald to work with someone from Newfoundland to create the third.

Eventually he told me about this opportunity. He was taking it very seriously. He was seeing literally everything that was being done in St. John's. He had come to *No Pity* five times. I thought that was because he just liked me that much, but really he was familiarizing himself with the cast, wondering who among them had a show in them. I should have realized as much; no amount of attraction would justify sitting through that show five times.

Having me do the one-person show was never in the cards. We both saw that. Our relationship was in its early days. The optics would be terrible. And besides, everyone knows it's a bad idea to work with someone you are involved with—it always ends badly. Ask Sid or Nancy.

Eventually Gerald approached Ashley and asked him if he would be up for creating a one-man show with Lois on board as a dramaturge. Good call. Ashley's solo works—his monologues in the Corey and Wade shows—were always audience favourites. But Ashley said no. He had his work with Rising Tide Theatre, and that was a huge contract. They would tour for months on end. It was as good as it got when it came to gigs in the theatre.

Gerald then asked Greg Thomey if he wanted to go to Ottawa. Also a good call. Thomey is a comedy genius. Thomey said no.

So I was neither Gerald's first nor second choice. He was getting turned down all over town. I was lucky number three. Whether he wanted to ask me from the beginning or whether I was just the last palatable option, I have no idea. All I know is that one night, while staying over at the house Gerald was renting, I was partaking in my favourite pastime, which was yelling at the TV about Brian Mulroney and ranting about Ottawa.

Now to be clear, when I say "Ottawa" I never mean the people of Ottawa or the city of Ottawa. Ottawa is a city with a population of about 980,000 people, all of whom have to put up with Canadians talking trash about their hometown. When I say "Ottawa" I am, like every other Canadian, talking about those few souls who are elected to run the country and are fortunate enough to do so out of those stunning buildings that stand guard on the shores of the river that bears that city's name.

And when I say I was "ranting about Ottawa" I was more likely ranting about the raw deal that I felt Newfoundland had received under the administration of Brian Mulroney. There was a long list of grievances. For me, chief among them was that this was the government that took away our trains. When it was suggested that trains running through the pristine Newfoundland wilderness and along our rugged coastline would be a tourism gold mine in the years to come, we were laughed at. No trains for you!

Through my lens, we were always getting screwed.

I had a chip on my shoulder. For my entire life I had lived in the poorest province in Canada. People called us an economic basket case. The editorial board of the *Globe and Mail* routinely made fun of us. We talked funny. We were referred to in many official capacities not as Newfoundlanders but as "Newfies." It was not perceived as a term of endearment.

When we joined Canada in 1949, we surrendered control over our fishery. Decisions concerning what countries in the world could fish in our waters were made in Ottawa. And decisions were made. Lots of them. If you were a country with giant boats and a penchant for raping a natural resource, Canada had a deal for you. Bureaucrats in Ottawa who had never once in their lives smelled salt water controlled the industry that made up the heart and soul of the province.

Many voices in Newfoundland, in politics and academia, felt that confederation was a bad deal for the people of Newfoundland. Whether they were right or wrong, they certainly found an eager audience with me.

I was aggrieved.

My entire life I would hear good news on *The National* delivered with what I call the Newfoundland caveat. The anchor would give us the good news—"Unemployment is down in Canada for the second quarter in a row"—and then would add, "EXCEPT IN NEWFOUND-LAND where it is up 2 percentage points." "The cost of living in Canada decreased this year, EXCEPT IN NEWFOUNDLAND where they are charging four dollars for a tomato."

And so, one night while I was in full blather about Brian Mulroney and his either real or imagined disdain for my province, Gerald interrupted me long enough to say, "Why don't you go to Ottawa and say that? Come to Ottawa with me and do a one-man show. Instead of whining and complaining down here, go up there and tell them to their faces."

How could I say no to an offer like that?

Gerald has always had a way of saying exactly the right thing at exactly the right time. He was waving a flag in front of a bull.

Had I known then what I know now, I never would have agreed to the offer. I didn't know anything about writing a one-person show. And I certainly didn't know anything about performing onstage alone. I had no idea what I was in for. Ah, the youth. Too stunned to know any better.

Even now, having worked in show business for three decades, the idea of walking out on a stage alone and staying there for eighty minutes is a daunting, terrifying notion. I would rather jump out of a plane or be tasered. And yes, I have done both.

I was all in, but I was still very nervous. The only one-person show I was familiar with was *Wedding in Texas*. That was brilliant, in no small measure because Cathy was such a brilliant character actor. I knew that was not me. I am not a chameleon. If I was going to play the Pope followed by a banker followed by a grandmother, they were all going to sound suspiciously like Rick Mercer.

Luckily, out of the gate, Gerald said, "Write what you know, and write a character that is a version of yourself."

And what did I know? Well, I was an angry young man. Even today my Twitter biography says, "Anger is my cardio." But that is more an homage to my younger self. I am decidedly not an angry middle-aged man. How could I be? I drive a Volvo.

As luck would have it, at the time I was attempting to put pen to paper, weird machinations were afoot in the nation's capital. Canada was about to go through a political upheaval that would plunge the country into a constitutional crisis that would threaten the very existence of the union. But nobody really knew that at the time, or saw it coming.

In the waning days of the 1980s, Brian Mulroney was working diligently behind the scenes on an agreement between all of Canada's provinces and Ottawa. He was quietly negotiating a series of constitutional amendments that would put an end to some of the grievances Quebec had with the Confederation of Canada. The ultimate goal was getting Quebec to finally sign on to the 1982 agreement that repatriated our Constitution from the UK. It was to be called the Meech Lake Accord.

I know—can you bear the intrigue?

I'll stop boring you now with details because yes, constitutional amendments are the domain of a very small and dry community. And yet Meech Lake became my muse.

Meech Lake, in order to work, needed the consent of all ten provincial premiers. And Mulroney did indeed have the approval of all ten. It must have taken a tremendous amount of thankless work. Public opinion was favourable to the accord, but truthfully few people knew anything about it. The vast majority of the public thought the Meech Lake Accord was a hatchback from the Ford Motor Company. It was under the radar.

But if Mulroney could pull this off, it would be his crowning achievement. Bringing Quebec into the Constitution would be an act of nation building, all the more impressive for being achieved by a federalist leader from that province.

With all the premiers on board, Mulroney must have been spending his days imagining the glory. And then it all began to go sideways.

Former prime minister Pierre Elliott Trudeau emerged from his art deco mansion in Montreal, walked up to the shores of Meech Lake and took a leak from the highest rock. Trudeau didn't like the agreement. The accord acknowledged that Quebec was "a distinct society"—this, he claimed, could lead to all sorts of special treatment for Quebec.

Quebec being declared a distinct society seems downright quaint today, mainly because they clearly are. But when Trudeau started saying that Meech would lead to special treatment for Quebec, it was a dog whistle heard around the country. Pierre Trudeau didn't just dig up the corpse of the strained relationship between Quebec and English Canada—he danced it around the room.

Now at this point I wasn't particularly interested in the Meech Lake Accord. If anything, it sounded fine to me. And I was of the opinion that Quebec already was a distinct society. I went to Quebec on an exchange program when I was fifteen and when I walked in the door of my host family's apartment, they poured me a glass of wine. The next morning, they gave the kid I was with (who was also my age) the keys to the car. Throw in the fact they spoke French and they were sure as hell distinct as far as I could see.

But some people didn't feel that way. Cowboys in Alberta declared that they were distinct too. As did fishermen in Newfoundland and WASPs in Ontario. And of course they were all right. We are all distinct.

But Mulroney didn't need the cowboys, the fishermen or the accountants, he just needed the premiers.

And then the premiers began to go down in defeat. Three Conservative premiers were tossed out in general elections. Two of them were replaced with Liberals. Taking their cue from Trudeau, they began to pump the brakes on Meech. But nobody pumped the brakes with such gusto as Newfoundland.

The new premier of Newfoundland and Labrador was proving to be a real problem for Mulroney. Clyde Wells knew his stuff. He was and is a constitutional lawyer. He reads constitutions for fun. He had severe ideological issues with the accord. His able right-hand advisor, Deborah Coyne, was also a constitutional lawyer. Both seemed to be taking cues from Trudeau.

To say Coyne was a fan of Trudeau's would be fair comment. She gave birth to his youngest child two years later.

Again, none of this was really capturing the attention of the Newfoundland people, but if it upset Quebec, then Newfoundlanders were on board. The historical grievance between Quebec and Newfoundland is deep and severe. In 1969 Newfoundland signed the worst deal in the history of mankind, one that allowed Quebec to buy most of the electricity produced by a dam in Labrador. The result is that Quebec has made literally billions of dollars off this natural Newfoundland resource and we pull in something like nine dollars a year. It's our own fault—we signed a terrible deal. But to add insult to injury, maps produced by the Government of Quebec showed Labrador as part of Quebec. Upsetting Quebec was an entirely pleasurable pastime for Newfoundlanders and an easy sell.

But still, Meech was not exactly dinner table talk.

And then Charles Lynch wrote a column. And the *Evening Telegram* in St. John's ran it.

Charles Lynch was a very big deal in Canadian journalism. He had been a war correspondent, he was the former head of the Southam News network, he was the author of many books. He was a shit disturber of the highest order. In his retirement he wrote a regular column that touched on many things: some weeks it was politics, other weeks it was the ongoing battle he was having with the beaver that was flooding his creek. That week he wrote about Newfoundland.

In his column he said that bringing Quebec into the Constitution was imperative, but in order for that to happen, all provinces had to agree to the terms. He said, and I'm paraphrasing here, that if Newfoundland was the lone holdout, then Canada should recognize that Quebec was more important than Newfoundland and kick Newfoundland out of Confederation. We were, he said, not equal and not important. *Vive le Québec.*

If he wanted a reaction, he got it. He might as well have attached booster cables to my ears and run every drop of power generated in Labrador through my cerebral cortex.

You could say I took the bait.

The column was literally in my hand the day Gerald informed me that we had reached a deadline. We were contractually obliged to inform the National Arts Centre what the title of this unwritten show was. They needed it for promotional purposes. Up until that moment we had both agreed that the title of the show would be "Show Me the Button: I'll Push It."

Gerald said, "Are you okay with that?"

I said, "How about 'Show Me the Button: I'll Push It—or Charles Lynch Must Die'?"

Gerald said, "Well, that will certainly get their attention."

And it did.

When the National Arts Centre got Gerald's fax with the title they hit the roof. For two reasons. First, they thought the "Charles Lynch Must Die" part was way over the top. As did their excitable lawyers.

Gerald argued it was satire. Somehow, he won. Andis Celms, the man who ran the entire English Theatre operation, overrode the lawyers and decided that he would not censor the title.

And second, unbeknownst to me Gerald had put my name above the title. So the full title was now *Rick Mercer's Show Me the Button: I'll Push It—or Charles Lynch Must Die.*

This was a no-no. Gerald knew very well that the NAC had a policy against putting an actor or an author's name above the title. It just wasn't done. At least not for anyone alive. William Shakespeare might get his name above *Hamlet* but even that would be an exception. And let's face it, I was no Shakespeare. I had never written a one-person show and nobody knew who I was and there would be no name above the title. When pushed on this Gerald responded with, "His name is not above the title, his name is *in* the title."

Again, Andis made an exception for this kid from Newfoundland that he had yet to clap his eyes on.

My name would be above the title! If I was taken with the guy before, I was all in at this point. Gerald was passionate about this. He felt that if you wanted anything resembling a star system in Canada, you had to at least promote the actors and writers by name.

This, by the way, is not something that has ever changed. If you walk down Broadway in New York City you will always see the names of actors on every poster and on the billboard. But at the Shaw Festival in Canada, one of the largest and most prestigious festivals in North America, there is rarely if ever an actor's name on a poster. You are expected to come because you like the play, not because you like any of the actors.

This weird reluctance to promote individual actors or performers is systemic in this country. Years later I would learn that some brass at CBC Radio deeply resented that the radio program *Morningside* was referred to all over the country simply as "Gzowski." They wanted the program to be the attraction, not the host's personality. It's *The Nature of Things*, damn it, stop calling it "David Suzuki"! There were forces inside the CBC that simply wanted all names dropped from all titles.

It certainly makes show business in Canada unique. Ever since that first one-man show I have done everything to buck the trend. Not because of ego. *I* don't need to see my name in the title. I need it there because it builds a brand that helps sell the tickets and hope- fully, these days, the books. By the way, thank you for purchasing.

When I began to write this one-man show I had no clue where to start. So far all I had was the longest title in theatrical history. I had a blank page and an opening night six weeks away. If that sounds like a lot of time, believe me, it is not.

So, harkening back to those early days with Lois, I just started writing and wouldn't stop. Pages and pages. Not knowing where I was going or why. I just wrote. Eventually, miraculously, I found a voice.

The show was starting to appear, not so much as a play as a list of grievances. I played the character of Roy, a young man who spends far too much time in a bar complaining about life. The first words out of Roy's mouth were: "I woke up this morning sucking the mois- ture out of a PantSaver car mat in the back of a Gulliver's cab." After that it was "That's the reason I drink here, it's the only bar I know where you say that and a guy will say, 'Oh yeah, big deal, I got so drunk last New Year's, I woke up in a burn unit. Ninety percent of my skin gone, and the guy I was with? Sure, he was killed altogether.'"

On paper, looking back now at least, the character was an odd choice. Not someone you might want to spend seventy minutes with. But Roy was full of opinions. He talked about growing up, going to school, teachers he had, relatives he loved. He railed against author- ity figures, banks and of course Ottawa.

And Meech. Or at least Charles Lynch's reaction to our position on Meech.

The words came fairly easily. Apparently I had a lot to say. The hard part was the structure and the editing. Gerald announced from on high that this show would not be too long. My penchant for long- windedness was going to end. The play would be exactly seventy minutes, the premium length. There would be no repeats of my pre- vious epics, when critics and some audience members practically fainted from exhaustion at the sheer length of the work. Gerald was pretty firm on this.

Every segment I wrote, Gerald attacked with a red pen. He edited, I felt, to the bone. But gradually, as the thing got tighter and tighter, I began to see that the jokes-per-minute ratio was higher than anything I had done before. This was no meandering monologue. This was being armed with a verbal machine gun.

This was the debut of what is perhaps the most important element in our professional relationship. Gerald and his red pen. He would not only edit this play and the next and the one after that, he would go on to edit every rant I would perform over the next twenty-five years.

Once I had a script, I never stopped repeating it. I was constantly memorizing it. I wanted to know the words as well as people know the Lord's Prayer. When I wasn't saying the words out loud, I was repeating them in my head. It was how I fell asleep at night and it was how I woke up in the morning. I had the work ethic of a Mennonite.

By the time we headed to the bright lights of the National Arts Centre in October 1990, the script was locked, and I was well on my way to having it memorized.

Anyone who is familiar with the nation's capital is familiar with its arts centre. It is a stone's throw from Parliament Hill. You cannot miss it. When the CBC broadcasts from the National War Memorial on Remembrance Day, it is there, lurking in the background.

Recently its exterior underwent a much-needed renovation, but when I showed up and locked eyes on it for the first time, it looked exactly the same as it did the day it opened in 1969. Its exterior was a textbook example of intimidating brutalist architecture. It was a massive monolith. It didn't look like a theatre; it looked like the kind of place Soviet dissidents would go to find out they had been sentenced to life in Siberia.

In other words, it was intimidating.

This was no clapboard union hall in downtown St. John's. This was the big time.

Gerald had worked here before and he knew his way around. The first place he took me was the Southam concert hall. He walked me down a backstage corridor, into the bowels of the building. All along the hallowed route my eyes drifted over the hundreds of photos of artists, including many forbiddingly big names, who had graced the NAC stage. And then we were through a final curtain and in the big room.

If the exterior of the building combined with the photos was intimidating, the view from centre stage of the concert hall was even more so: 2,065 royal red seats fill the room, red carpets line the aisles, four levels of balconies are garnished with gold. It is a majestic, soaring room designed to stand with the great theatres of the world, designed to wow the audience and the performers.

And it has.

But first there was the issue of the union tech who was yelling at us to get the hell off the stage. "Nobody is supposed to be in here!" Seems I was to play the arts centre but not this hall.

The guided tour continued. We visited the two other performance spaces in the centre. Each one was decidedly smaller than the previous. There was a cozy and elegant 897-seat venue, followed by a 300-seat studio. I felt good standing on this stage. I told Gerald, "This is awesome. I can't wait to play this room."

He said, "We're not playing this room."

And then we went for a walk. We left the concrete building and strolled across the Rideau Canal, into the Byward Market, a groovy, gentrified market filled with restaurants, cafés and food vendors. But then we turned down a busy street, past a series of low-rise industrial buildings and came to a stop at 333 King Edward Avenue.

The building stood out from its rundown neighbours only because it had a bright yellow paint job. The small window in the front was plastered with posters that would not look out of place on a telephone pole in St. John's: alternative dance shows, late-night cabarets and lost dogs. If it wasn't for the paint and the posters, the building would have looked exactly like what it had previously been, an abandoned gas station and garage.

This was the National Arts Centre's Atelier—*atelier* being French for "not quite the big time."

We cut through the small lobby and went down a hallway. Double doors led to an area I assumed was once a series of garage bays. The walls and ceilings were painted black. Stacks of folding chairs and mismatched government office chairs were pushed to the side. A few lights hung from the ceiling and were pointed towards a small stage. The City of Ottawa had zoned it for eighty-five seats.

I loved it instantly. The smell of the greasepaint competed with the smell of ten thousand oil changes. It was my kind of room.

We immediately went to work. And boy, did I have a lot of work to do. I had never been on a stage alone for any length of time. I'd almost always been with the gang. This was a whole other ballgame. I realized, or rather Gerald realized, that I didn't actually know how to stand on a stage alone. I had a tendency to look to the left when talking, or even worse, at my feet. In a narrow room, this meant I would be addressing a blank wall instead of the audience. The audience would be staring at the side or the top of my head. During every rehearsal Gerald was constantly yelling, "WHERE ARE YOU LOOKING?"

My voice started giving me trouble. Seventy minutes is a long time to talk under any circumstances; it is an impossibly long time to yell, which I had a tendency to do. So when Gerald was not asking "Where are you looking?" he would be saying "WHY ARE YOU YELLING?"

My other fault was that I would speed up as I went along. Which is why the third most common note Gerald gave me (and something he still tells me to this day) is "SLOW DOWN!"

"SLOW DOWN! WHERE ARE YOU LOOKING? WHY ARE YOU YELLING?" I don't think Laurence Olivier's director had to say that more than once.

But gradually, as the opening approached, his entreaties started to sink in and I began to get the script under control. I started telling the story instead of yelling the story. I started to have fun with the delivery instead of trying to say it as fast as I could.

And then a week before opening night, all hell broke loose. Or rather, Charles Lynch broke loose. He found out about the play and he came at me with everything he had. I didn't quite know what hit me.

Out of the blue Lynch wrote a special column for the *Ottawa Citizen*, one that was syndicated across the country. With his tongue firmly in cheek, he declared that he was now the Salman Rushdie of Newfoundland. His life was in danger. An angry young man had declared a fatwa on his head for the blasphemy of insulting New-foundland. His life would never be the same. That said, Lynch vowed to be a champion of free speech. He would not, like Rushdie, go into hiding. No, he would attend opening night, front row centre. Let's see, he said, if the kid has the guts to say it to my face.

Well, it was Gerald who had said a month earlier, "Why don't you go to Ottawa and say that?"

The column ran next to a very large picture of our poster. A picture is worth a thousand words, and we suddenly had a great big ad in the biggest paper in town. Everyone in the Ottawa press gallery was now aware that a one-man show about Meech Lake would be running at this small theatre they had never heard of.

This was at a time when the press gallery was exhausted from writing about the arcane details of Meech. And readers were fatigued as well. Now they had a new angle and a new story. The show was getting mentioned in actual news stories. To the great surprise of the folks at the National Arts Centre, we had buzz. They were not used to buzz about the Atelier.

Lynch alerted the folks at the *Hill Times*. By mainstream Canadian standards the *Hill Times* is fairly obscure, but on Parliament Hill it is an organ of record. It is essentially the school newspaper for the Hill. Everyone on the Hill, from the prime minister to the janitors, reads the paper.

The *Hill Times* asked me to come in for an interview. They had Charles Lynch's side of the story; now they wanted mine. It would be at their offices and there would be a photographer. So off I went to the offices of the *Hill Times*.

I had certainly experienced the occasional awkward social situation before, but none quite so awkward as that day. I entered a small waiting room in their nondescript office to find myself face to face, and alone, with the Canadian journalistic icon I had threatened to kill.

"Hello," he said, "I'm Charles Lynch."

It was an ambush.

I had not been expecting this. I was already having nightmares that he would follow through on this threat to show up on opening night. I had no idea how I would deal with that.

He shoved out his hand and said, "I love the title." I am not sure everyone would be as gracious.

Eventually the reporter and the photographer showed up. We were posed back to back, arms crossed, like two boxers promoting a prize fight.

In the interview, Lynch picked up where his column had left off. He was taking the Salman Rushdie ball and running with it. He railed against Newfoundland. He acknowledged we were "allegedly hospitable" but, clearly, to anyone other than him.

I reached into the script of the play and had a few choice words for the "wizened old hack" who didn't understand modern Canada. If I didn't know better, I could have sworn we were creating an act.

When the interview was over, we found ourselves together on the sidewalk. Lynch wished me well on the show and assured me that despite his pledge he would not show up on opening night if it caused me any consternation at all. "I don't want to upstage you on your big night," he said, "or make you nervous."

I assured him that nothing could make me more nervous than I already was. There would be, I told him, two tickets waiting for him at the box office.

Show Me the Button was a huge game changer for me, in no small part because of Charles Lynch. We could never have afforded the publicity his faux outrage delivered to us.

Opening night was a circus. It was impossible to get a ticket. There were scalpers.

It was an eclectic crowd. It seemed like every Newfoundlander who worked in politics was there, along with half the press gallery. The one thing everyone had in common was that they all seemed to be enjoying the complimentary miniature bottle of Newfoundland Screech that we had taped to each seat. We were nothing if not shameless. The number of seats, by the way, had miraculously doubled in number when nobody was looking. Gerald had a catering company deliver them to the side door.

A terrified building manager asked Gerald what he would do if the city showed up and closed the show because of overcrowding.

"Send out a press release?" he said. "I might even call them myself."

And now it was really happening. It was showtime. Gerald came to the dressing room to walk me to the wings. If he was nervous, he didn't show it. But he had to be. This was his town; these were his people at the National Arts Centre. If this show was going to stink out the joint, it would be on him, not me.

He told me all the things a director tells a young guy about to go onstage in a one-man show for the first time. He told me I had this. He said I was prepared. He said he hadn't seen anyone be as prepared. He assured me I knew the words and the words were good. He also told me the play was funny. Funny as hell, he said—any actor would kill to say those words. Now do the work, he said.

Whether he was telling me the truth I have no idea, but I chose to believe him. If he had faith in me, then I had faith in him.

I headed for the wings to wait for the music cue that would start the show.

Gerald's experience with *Wedding in Texas* had impressed on him that a set could be a show's undoing. *Wedding in Texas* was a brilliant showcase for Cathy Jones, but it required as a major plot point a life-sized model of a car onstage. A car that actually blew apart during a comically dramatic crash. The show relied on bells and whistles.

Gerald wasn't the producer of *Wedding in Texas*, and he didn't own the show, so he had no say in such matters, but he always felt that the show could have played more rooms for longer runs had it not been saddled with that set.

He also thought that because of its universal themes, it was the CODCO show that should have played New York. He had seen Whoopi Goldberg's show in New York and thought it was brilliant, but he thought Cathy's show was better. That it never had a shot in New York drove Gerald to distraction. "Cathy," Gerald would say, "was meant to play the big rooms, she was built to play New York." If she had created a show that could be performed out of a suitcase, it could have happened. As it was, it wasn't in the cards.

My show was obviously not destined for New York. My theme was as far away from universal as you could imagine. I was worried that only people who actually went to Bar None on a regular basis would understand any of it. But that aside, Gerald insisted there be no set.

And so we created a show that did not need a truck. Far from it, the entire thing could fit in a glove compartment. My only prop was a bottle of Jockey Club beer.

In the wings I was having one of those moments where you are asking yourself how you got to where you happened to be standing at that very moment. The place was on wheels. It sounded like a party, not an audience waiting for a play. Music was blasting, people were shouting. And then we went to a blackout. And the crowd went quiet.

Dead Reckoning, still my favourite St. John's band despite the *No Pity* debacle, had recorded a song that opened with a searing version of Beethoven's *Ode to Joy*. As it started to play, the screen at the back of the stage flashed pink, white and green lights. Eventually all three colours came together to form the Pink, White and Green—the flag of an independent Newfoundland and Labrador. The Newfoundlanders in the crowd, the ones who knew the flag and had felt the sting of Charles Lynch and so many others, went crazy.

A spotlight found me standing there with a hand-held microphone. Under the instrumental opening of the song, I delivered a sixty-second poem that set the stage. "It's 3:45 a.m., the middle of the night, early in the morning, St. John's, Newfoundland." And suddenly on the screen an image of a dark, rainy St. John's street appeared—black-and-white film cut to the music of Dead Reckoning. The camera moves through a side alley and comes to a stop at an unmarked door. It opens. The camera goes inside and up a back staircase into a raucous, bar. It moves though a crowd of people of all ages engaged in all sorts of debauchery. The camera finally comes to a stop in the far corner. In the shadows sits a man at a table with a single bottle of beer. It is Roy. Fade to black.

At that point the lights would come up on centre stage. And there I was, at the same table we just saw in the film. It was as if I'd been transported from the film to the stage, or better yet, the audience had been transported from the theatre to the late-night St. John's bar. And then I started talking and didn't shut up for seventy minutes.

And the greatest thing happened. Every joke worked.

Seventy minutes later Charles Lynch was on his feet, hands clapping above his head. I guess that meant the show was over.

And just like that we were off.

Within a few days CBC Radio's theatre reviewer revealed with great fanfare that he hated the show. Thankfully it turned out he was in the minority. Over the next few days of our run, every media outlet in town reviewed the show and we got raves.

Gerald took out a congratulatory ad in the St. John's *Telegram*. Borrowing the National Arts Centre logo and image, the ad proclaimed, "The National Arts Centre of Canada congratulates Rick Mercer on the success of *Show Me the Button: I'll Push It—or Charles Lynch Must Die*." Then there were blurbs from every Ottawa media outlet barring CBC Radio. (This was before the internet, so some of those quotes may have been embellished.)

The National Arts Centre didn't place the ad and were unaware it even existed. This ad served one purpose: to sell the show in Newfoundland. It would not be the last time I was in awe of Gerald's ability to promote. This was Gerald in full hype mode. We had not even announced a St. John's run yet and he was building hype for one. We did have the main stage of the Hall booked for two weeks with a week-long holdover.

Within days of the ad's appearance the province of Newfoundland got in touch with us, and we began planning a tour of the arts and culture centres across Newfoundland and Labrador. If the show was a hit at the National Arts Centre and it was about Newfoundland, Newfoundlanders wanted to see it.

Also, we never mentioned the Atelier. If people wanted to think I was playing in one of the fancy rooms at the National Arts Centre, so be it. I never once let on that all this hype was for a show in a theatre one-third the size of the LSPU Hall. In fact, when the CBC supper-hour show in St. John's wanted to do an interview with me, we didn't do it at the Atelier. Instead we did it inside the three-hundred-seat theatre in the main arts centre. I was sitting in the audience surrounded by luxurious red chairs. If people jumped to the conclusion that this was the theatre I was selling out every night, so be it. Smoke and mirrors.

Gerald seemed to love this part of show business more than he did creating or directing the show.

And then we got an incredible break courtesy of my friend Alison Gzowski—the radio producer who had first hired me at CBC Radio and who happened to be the daughter of CBC Radio legend Peter Gzowski. Alison did something that she had never done before: she persuaded her father to have a friend of hers on the show.

At the time *Morningside* was the biggest show in Canada. For Gzowski to have a young playwright on was like being anointed by Canadian arts royalty. I don't know how Alison made it happen, but god love her she did. Gzowski's people wanted a bio of me, and Gerald faxed them exactly one sentence: "Rick Mercer is Newfoundland's fastest-rising comedian." When Gzowski used the line on the air, Gerald was triumphant.

The interview itself was dodgy at best. I had no idea how to sell back then. And when Peter asked me what the show was about, I refused to answer. I didn't want to give anything away. I had yet to wrap my head around the fact that Gzowski's audience of millions was more important than the people we were packing into an old garage night after night in Ottawa.

That the interview was unconventional didn't matter. Gerald had his quote: "'Newfoundland's fastest rising comedian'—Peter Gzowski." From then on it was splattered across every print ad and poster for the show. People trusted Gzowski, a cutline from him was golden, and Gerald felt that using Gzowski in our promotional material was a message to the CBC. And Gerald was laser-focused on the CBC.

At CBC Television there was a light news and entertainment show that aired every day at noon called *Midday*. I had done a few commentaries for them already, so they were familiar with my work. Somehow Gerald convinced them that myself and Charles Lynch debating Meech Lake would make for good TV, and we got booked.

Charles and I picked up right where we'd left off. We both yelled at each other and feigned outrage. The sight of a twenty-year-old and a seventy-year-old yelling at each other over national unity was peak CBC. The executives were ecstatic. At this point we had done more than a few radio spots together and we had our act down pat, except now Charles not only called me a menace but he started throwing the term "boy genius" around and said the show was a riot.

It was becoming clear to me that Charles had as much of a vested interest in the show's success as I did. It meant that he was still very much relevant. He was one of the great shit disturbers and he was going to do just that to get this show noticed.

Meanwhile, Gerald was constantly wooing George Anthony from the CBC to come see the show. Gerald was a huge fan of George. He felt he was one of the good guys. George was in charge of comedy at the CBC. He was the network guy in charge of *CODCO* and *Kids in the Hall*. In fact, George was in charge of, it seemed, everything. He had all the awards shows, the arts programming, the skating specials and the science shows. He was a champion of, and the executive in charge of, *The Nature of Things* despite never having set foot in nature.

George loves show business. He is the proverbial man who has forgotten more about show business than most people will ever learn, and he was impressed with the buzz around a show in, of all places, Ottawa. I know George couldn't care less about Meech Lake or Newfoundland's position in Confederation, but he did love hype. He confirmed his attendance.

I didn't know George then, but for Gerald you would swear the Pope himself had said he was coming to town.

It was also a big deal for me. A CBC executive at my show?

Nerves got the best of me the night George attended. I shaved ten minutes off the run time. By the time I got to the end I was talking like an auctioneer on a coke jag.

But maybe it didn't matter. Backstage, George told me he didn't know where or how but someday I would be in the CBC business and the CBC would be in the Rick Mercer business. On the way out the door he added, "But maybe slow down a little bit next time." It was not the last time I would receive wise counsel from Mr. Anthony.

I was ecstatic. An executive from Toronto said he wanted to be in the Rick Mercer business! And I didn't have to pretend to be developmentally delayed in order to make it happen. This was turning into a fever dream.

But now what?

13

Lucky

To have a successful career in show business you need a lot of things. You need a modicum of talent and you need a healthy dose of discipline. You need to be fearless, but you also need to be lucky. Luck plays a big part in it. Ask any professional actor or singer or musician how they got to where they are, and if they are honest, they will admit that, in part, it took luck. And not just any garden-variety luck. You need big stupid luck.

Luck gives you your start. It's up to you what you do after that.

This is why show business is such a dumb career move. It is a mad gamble. Nursing is not a gamble. Engineering is not a gamble. Teachers' college is not a gamble. You graduate from teachers' college, you apply for jobs and eventually, barring being on an offenders list, you will land a position and get those coveted summers off. Show business is not like that at all.

If a person asks me advice on which theatre school their son or daughter should apply to, I wonder what it is they have against their children. Why would they want to doom their kids to a lifetime of penury? Why encourage them to enter a field that is marked by constant rejection?

My advice is always the same: Is there *anything* else your son, daughter or non-binary offspring can imagine doing? If so, they should do that, and dabble in amateur theatre on the side. Show business is a road that should be avoided by anyone with other options or a clue.

As a young man I had neither. I could imagine no other life. And with my academic background I had basically nowhere else to go. I was operating without a net.

Fortunately, I have had my share of big stupid luck. So much so that I have fully expected a Mike Edwards–style end to it all for most of my life.

For those not familiar, Mike Edwards was the former cello player for Electric Light Orchestra. When you pick up the cello, there is no reasonable expectation that you will become rock and roll royalty. That takes more than just talent on the cello. That takes luck.

In 2010, Mike, now retired, was driving through the English countryside, whistling a tune, when a thirteen-hundred-pound round bale of hay rolled down a nearby picturesque hillside, picked up terrific speed, struck an ancient rock wall, became airborne and landed on the roof of his van. Driver's side. It was flattened like an empty Coke can under André the Giant's boot.

Luck can go both ways.

For me, my good luck came in the form of a break that can only be described as lotto worthy.

There was no doubt our little show did extremely well in Ottawa. I felt like I was tasting the big time, but I was not. It was a very small theatre. And yes, we got some great ink, an interview on Gzowski and a spot on *Midday*. But those things create buzz for a short period of time.

I knew the show was going to do well in St. John's. And Gerald was doing everything to ensure that every single seat would be sold out. He didn't just want a good run; he wanted to set a box office record for the Hall. And then he wanted to move the show uptown to the Arts and Culture Centre. The fancy room that could seat a thousand people.

But even if all that came to pass, it would not change anything in the grand scheme of things. I would still be right back where I started. Doing shows at the Hall in St. John's.

What did change everything was another actor, in another show, in another province, who was experiencing a bit of bad luck.

At the same time that we opened in Ottawa, another show was opening elsewhere in the country. It was by all accounts an excellent script written by a seasoned playwright. It was a one-man show starring a great actor. Many people had very high hopes for this show. It was also, because of technical reasons, incredibly ambitious and complicated for a single actor to perform.

This show, like mine, opened in a small theatre outside of a major city. The difference was, I opened with a finished product. This other production was opening discreetly so they could work out the kinks before a major Canadian tour. Unfortunately, come opening night it was clear that the production had more kinks than a Tory caucus. The technical complexity proved too much. Within days the show was closed.

To be clear: this kind of thing happens every day in the theatre, in dance, in music, in art. There is no crystal ball. There is no foolproof formula for success. A show not working is part of the DNA of show business. The history of Broadway is littered with shows created and performed by some of the most talented people in the world closing within days of opening. This was just one of those shows.

And what did its closure have to do with me? The show had a lot of backers. It was a co-production between the Factory Theatre in Toronto and the Great Canadian Theatre Company in Ottawa. It was also developed with the assistance of the Vancouver East Cultural Centre. Three major Canadian theatres had booked this show for substantial runs as part of their seasons. Three major Canadian theatres in three major markets suddenly had huge holes in their schedules. They needed a one-person show and they needed one fast. They all had a very big problem on their hands. And Gerald had the solution.

Gerald had worked with Factory Theatre before and made sure that the artistic director at the time, Jackie Maxwell, was well aware of our little production. He had kept her informed of the progress, and she had her eye on every bit of ink and buzz we created. Gerald called Jackie, and Jackie bought the show. Ottawa followed suit and then Vancouver. And just like that I had a major national tour.

But first we had the supreme pleasure of taking the show home. The crowd in Newfoundland went bananas. The show sold out immediately.

Honestly, I thought that was the way it was supposed to happen. My dream was that the show would be a hit. And it was. So it made sense to me that immediately I would go on tour. I just assumed that's how these things happened.

Nothing could be further from the truth. Theatres are booked well over a year in advance. No theatre in their right mind was going to buy a show about Meech Lake and mount it a year down the road. Topical shows don't really tour in theatres for this very reason.

That three theatres would suddenly need a show and need it now was unheard of. This was my break. Another show died so mine could live. That's brutal survival-of-the-fittest-on-the-Serengeti shit.

And so, after a record-breaking run at the LSPU Hall and an unprecedented move uptown to the Arts and Culture Centre, we headed back to Canada. Or at least I did. Gerald went to Halifax to work on the new season of CODCO while I went on tour.

First up it was the big smoke. I headed to Toronto for a month-long run at Factory Theatre, complete with a two-week holdover if we sold well. We sold better than well; we literally filled the place every single night. This in a real theatre, with real seats and no smell of gasoline.

From there the show moved back to Ottawa for a month at the Great Canadian Theatre Company. Young performers on Broadway often talk about how overwhelming their first show on the Great White Way is, in part because of that New York tradition of famous actors and Hollywood royalty dropping in backstage afterwards. Well, Ottawa was my Broadway because the political class came in droves and the press gallery kept talking about it. It seemed like every night people from the world of politics and journalism were popping backstage. It was mind-blowing.

Again, I owed thanks to Charles Lynch. He and I had appeared together on radio a number of times carrying on the dog-and-pony show we'd developed to sell tickets. But as the Toronto run was coming to a close, he once again wrote a column that mentioned the show. This column too received a lot of attention, but for very different reasons.

Charles and his daughters had recently taken a cruise off the east coast of Canada. He was practising that age-old show-business tradition of singing for his supper, or rather giving lectures in return for a cabin. It was off the Eastern Seaboard that he encountered a medical problem so serious that he needed to be medevaced to a surgeon. He was given two options: helicopter to St. John's or a small commercial flight to Halifax. He opted for Halifax.

In his column he said he had made that call because St. John's was "home to the boy genius playwright who had penned a work titled *Charles Lynch Must Die.*" He mentioned that I, along with Prime Minister Brian Mulroney, showed some class by sending flowers to the hospital. He wrapped up the column by saying he was planning on living a long time because "as long as I am alive, the play can keep running and Mercer can go on bringing in the cash. If I croak that little frigger is finished."

But this time it was the column's byline that caused the stir. It read, "Charles Lynch, former chief of Southam News Service, is recovering from cancer surgery in Halifax." I heard through the grapevine that once he was back in Ottawa, Lynch's spirits were high but that his cancer was very serious.

I placed a call to him to give him my best wishes, and for the first time I truly angered him.

"We're dropping the subtitle for the Vancouver run," I told him. "It's just *Show Me the Button* now."

"Why would you do that?" he demanded.

"Well, no offence, but if you die you'll be on the front page of every paper in the country and I'll have posters all over Vancouver saying, 'Charles Lynch Must Die.' I think that's probably in bad taste."

"How long is your run in Vancouver?" he asked. I told him five weeks. "Fine," he said. "I won't die until you're finished. But don't you dare take my name off that damned poster." He slammed down the phone.

And so we went to Vancouver, title intact. And true to his word, he lived.

In the end, *Show Me the Button* was performed over 150 times around the country. In what seemed like the blink of an eye I was making a living as an actor. On paper, at least, it almost looked like I had a full-time job. I would never have a real job ever again. No more dish-washing, no more waiting tables, no more standing around naked while holding an apple. If anyone asked my occupation, I could honestly say it was that of actor.

Unless of course I was entering the United States. As a young person, if you tell the American border authorities that you are an actor or, god forbid, a comedian, you might as well tell them your last name is bin Laden.

The show changed everything for Gerald and me. It put us on the radar in Toronto, both in the theatre community and at the CBC. People suddenly knew who we were, and more importantly, they knew we could sell tickets. Shortly after *Button* wrapped up its tour, the National Arts Centre commissioned a new one-man show for the following season. And all the theatres that had booked *Button* wanted us too.

I leapt at the chance to do the second show. It was a mad act of youthful hubris. Once again, if I knew then what I know now, I might have acted differently.

Doing a second show is like recording a second album. The internet is filled with thousands of chat rooms devoted solely to debating and ranking the most disastrous follow-up albums ever. So many bands who knock it out of the park with their first album stink out the joint with their second. In fact in show business, second albums are generally considered cursed from the outset. The same is true for second novels and second plays. It's called the sophomore slump. It makes sense. You have an entire life to make the first record or to write that first novel. Comparably speaking, you have five minutes to complete the follow-up.

But what did I know? I signed on the dotted line.

Once the contract was signed, the tyranny of the blank page returned. Suddenly the gargantuan task ahead of me came into focus. I couldn't for the life of me get started. It felt like someone had chased my muse up the street with an axe and it was never coming back. All I could think of was the past year. The success of *Button* was real, but was it a fluke?

I had to admit, for my first time out the planets had totally lined up in my favour. I not only had a constitutional crisis in my favour; I had a cantankerous old press hound who leveraged his sizable reputation to sell tickets. I couldn't count on that happening again. Also, part of the buzz we created was because I was unknown. I had come out of nowhere. Now I was a guy who had to prove that buzz was warranted. Even before the first word was on the page, I wondered if I had a giant target on my back.

I knew enough about the Canadian psyche to know that some of the same critics who raved about the first show would have their knives out the second time around. Yes, the critics love a hit, but they can enjoy a miss almost as much.

Eventually the time came to provide a title to the National Arts Centre. They had an upcoming season to promote. All I had was a blank page and a crisis of confidence.

"I don't know what the title is," I said to Gerald. "How about 'His First Show Killed, This One Not So Much'?"

"Or," Gerald said, "'I've Killed Before, I'll Kill Again.'"

It hung in the air. If we wanted to be cocky, that title would do it. How bold would it be to give that name to the follow-up to a hit show? The Stone Roses called their second album *Second Coming*. This was even saucier.

It would be tempting the gods of failure. It would be giving the middle finger to the sophomore slump. I said, "I like it."

So, we had a title. And from the title grew a notion and then an idea and eventually a premise. I played Billy Baggs, judge, jury and

High Lord Executioner of Newfoundland in a post-apocalyptic world ten years in the future. A future in which millions of Canadians had flocked to the island of Newfoundland after an explosion at the Pickering nuclear power plant made Central Canada uninhabitable.

It was here, on a wooden gallows, high above the city of St. John's, that the executioner passed judgment on an extraordinary list of Canadian icons. Everyone from Sharon, Lois and Bram (who, with the aid of Greenpeace, accidentally caused the explosion in Pickering) to Burton Cummings to the entire cast of *Front Page Challenge* were judged.

It was a seventy-five-minute examination and evisceration of every sacred Canadian cow I could think of. I was merciless. I even had a go at the Friendly Giant. If the fifty-year-old me had existed back then, I would have had a field day at my own expense.

Again we incorporated film in the show. At one point my character, after a failed conversation with God, was sucked through the trap door of the gallows and sent to the fiery pits of hell. It was there that I came face to face with Satan on film. Greg Thomey played him with a maniacal glee. How much fun it was to lie under the stage and listen to the audience killing themselves with laughter at Thomey's performance.

For Gerald and me the pressure was immense. We were again opening in an old garage in Ottawa but the stakes couldn't have been higher. An entire tour was on the line and there would be critics for days. If there was ever a time to put on the big-boy pants, this was it. We both worked harder than we had before. During rehearsals we ran the entire show three times a day.

I won't go so far as to say I had confidence at the outset, because the theatre doesn't work that way. It's entirely natural to be racked with fear, and I was certainly that. The difference being, this time around I knew, in theory, that what we were attempting was possible.

And on opening night, which should really only be referred to by its Christian name, Judgment Day, an amazing thing happened. We killed.

We'd killed before; we killed again. The hard work paid off. This show was tighter, slicker and funnier than the first one. And the audience didn't need an interest in arcane constitutional wrangling to get the jokes. Everything landed exactly the way it was supposed to.

If there is a greater feeling, I have no idea what it is.

Every theatre that bought the first show bought the second, and it would go on to tour the country and Newfoundland and Labrador. Gerald and I were a two-man cottage industry. Bona fide show folk.

I love the theatre more than anything. From that day in grade three when Andy Jones showed up as Uncle Val, it has been a love affair like no other. There is nothing better than being in the audience when the lights go down. At that moment anything is possible. If you are lucky the entire universe may just unfold before your eyes. Some of the greatest moments of my life have occurred sitting in a cramped theatre chair. That said, the theatre, like the Greek playwrights that invented it, can go both ways. For every performance that you hope will never end, there is one that you wish had never started.

As an actor I'd like to think I have been responsible for creating some good memories for folks sitting in a theatre. It's a privilege to have people show up and pay good money to see something you have created. If they walk away happy, that's a good day at the office. The National Arts Centre allowed me to do that on a national scale, and I will always be grateful.

The following year I would return to the NAC for a third one-man show, this one called *A Good Place to Hide*. It was the most fun I ever had creating a show. I played a pirate radio operator who was hiding in an abandoned Newfoundland community called Lots for Sale. "The sign went up decades ago. The lots never sold but the name stuck." The show featured cameos from all the great CBC Radio voices: Peter Gzowski, Michael Enright, Bob Oxley and Mary Lou Finlay. It was a bit of a love fest for the Mother Corp.

We hauled out the stops this third time out. Gerald fulfilled a life-long dream and we had actual interior fireworks in the show. Pyrotechnics! We figuratively and literally blew up our set every single night. What a thrill it was to stand on the stage and see the light from the pyrotechnics illuminate the audience. All of them sitting in the royal red chairs in the actual National Arts Centre main building.

This was no gas station. This was the big house.

The large set and the technical complexity of the show was a departure for us. We had always avoided any element that would make touring difficult or costly. But this time was different. We knew that despite an offer that would have seen this show tour more theatres than we had before, it wasn't going to happen. In fact we wouldn't even have a chance to mount it in Newfoundland. We were getting a shot at TV. The idiot box was calling.

One of the first people I'd called with the news was Charles Lynch. He said, "That's the best news I've heard since being told I was in remission."

Charles Lynch passed away in July 1994. By that point, my time treading the boards as a touring actor was in the rear-view mirror. I was working in television and living in Halifax.

Soon after his death, an envelope arrived for me in the mail. Inside was the program from his funeral. Attached was a yellow Post-it note. On it, Charles Lynch had written in his own hand:

Dear Rick,
For your Files
Regards,
Charles Lynch

He had written it days before his death. He gave it to his son with instructions to attach it to the church program and mail it to me. Years later I bumped into his son on the street in Vancouver and he told me that Charles was very frail when he passed over the note, but was chuckling the entire time. He thought it was very funny.

And it was.

If I had to write his epitaph, it would say: "Charles Lynch—he got the last laugh."

I owe him very much.

Thanks, Charlie.

14

Eight Episodes

In 1992 the *CODCO* TV series came to an end after delivering 62 groundbreaking, hysterical half-hours to the country. Andy Jones was already long gone, having quit halfway through the run over a censorship issue. And Tommy Sexton, he of *The Wonderful Grand Band*, my first TV crush, was battling HIV/AIDS. CODCO didn't agree to wrap the show up—they simply imploded in the way that only dysfunctional families can.

Mary went one way; Cathy went the other. And Greg joined Tommy, who wanted to devote his remaining time and boundless energy to making a movie he had written about his life: *Adult Children of Alcoholics: The Movie.* Still the greatest movie title I have ever heard.

In Halifax, Michael Donovan and Salter Street Films were desperately looking for a show to replace it. They had been the ones who invented the CBC co-production model, and they wanted the relationship to continue, if for no other reason than it kept the lights on and the bank at bay.

Ivan Fecan, in charge of CBC's English-language programming, agreed to meet with Michael and receive a pitch. Fecan was a huge fan of *CODCO* and before that *The Wonderful Grand Band*. In fact, when *Grand Band* was the biggest show in Newfoundland and Fecan was running CBC Toronto, he would air the Newfoundland-centric regional program in Toronto after midnight once a week.

Michael worked long and hard developing a show with an actor and writer in Nova Scotia who shall remain nameless. I think perhaps it was a classic sitcom, but I cannot be sure. But there were scripts, a production plan and a full proposal.

Legend has it, or Michael has it, that the day before meeting with Fecan, Mary Walsh called him and said she wanted to do a show "about the news" and was he interested? Michael filed this away in his mind, along with conversations he had had with George Anthony and Gerald and me about doing a series of TV shows that were based on my one-man shows. They would have a rapid turnaround. They would be "about the news."

As the story goes, Michael entered Ivan Fecan's office in Toronto with a briefcase filled with copies of the sitcom he was prepared to pitch. But instead of the planned pitch he said, "We would like to do a show, weekly, with a live audience, with Mary Walsh and Cathy Jones and this young actor and writer, Rick Mercer." And then he added, "And Andy Jones."

Nobody knew much more than that, because there was nothing to know.

And then we all waited.

Eventually, days or perhaps weeks later, I do not know, Michael called Mary with the news. We had the green light. We had a TV show.

Ten minutes later she burst through the backyard gate of the tiny clapboard house Gerald and I had just purchased in St. John's and shouted "We've got eight episodes!" Those were the best words I had ever heard. Doctors go their entire lives without delivering such welcome news. A show was born!

At that point I would have taken eight episodes even if it meant I'd have just eight years to live. Clearly I would not be negotiating from a position of strength.

The three of us formed a huddle, hugged it out and danced in a circle. We celebrated like nobody's business. We actually began to sing "We've got a TV show hey! We've got a TV show hey." I don't think anyone has ever been happier.

Cathy lived a stone's throw from our house. Together we cut through the alley, found her in her kitchen and gave her the news. She immediately burst into tears. These were not tears of joy. She was the opposite of elated. She was inconsolable. "I hate the news," Cathy sobbed. "Nobody likes the news." She continued, "Why can't we do a *fun* show, with characters, and all our cool friends, something really wild and funny? Why does it have to be a news show?"

This was a refrain that Mary and I would hear for many years to come. This is a refrain that whoever is currently within shouting distance of Cathy has heard twice today so far. Someday there will be a judicial inquiry that will look into why Cathy was forced, against her will, to do a comedy show about the news for twenty-eight years when she didn't even like the news.

For days afterwards, I was walking around on an insane high. But eventually the elation turned to trepidation. Now what? The only thing worse than not getting a TV show is getting the go-ahead to create one.

In any creative process there is nothing quite so awful as the blank page. When you're staring at the blank page, anything is possible. Yes, you could write a play that people will applaud or you could create one so poorly written it will bring you nothing but shame and humiliation. I had a passing familiarity with the former and an intimate relationship with the latter.

The tyranny of the blank page is what keeps me awake at night. Did then, does now.

Although in this instance it turned out a blank page was the least of my worries. Because, it was soon revealed, the page was anything but blank. A four-page follow-up proposal went to Ivan Fecan fleshing out the notion of the show. It described in great detail what this show would be. It was written by Michael Donovan and *CODCO* producer Jack Kellum and was based on conversations with Mary. Conversations I had no part in. A document I had never seen. Why should I be surprised? I was the low one on the totem pole.

It's not that the show being described was bad. It just wasn't the show I had envisioned. Finding out that this document existed was a bit like being told you can build your dream home as long as you follow these plans for an A-frame. You don't know much about dream homes, but you do know you are not fussy about A-frames.

According to this document, each episode would be anchored by a guest host à la *Saturday Night Live*. The host would not, however, do an opening monologue. The opening monologue would be a task shared by Cathy and me. This was news to me, and terrifying. Two people side by side doing an opening monologue has, to the best of my knowledge, never been done on a network series. And for the same reasons that home surgery has not caught on. It would be both awkward and painful.

The only time you see two folks standing side by side doing jokes is during awards shows. Or I should say the only time you see two folks standing side by side is during everyone's least favourite part of awards shows.

After the monologue there would be a sketch featuring recurring characters with the addition of the guest host. When I read that I felt like I had been thrown off a building. Cathy and Mary are great sketch comedians. Their ability to do characters is extraordinary. Nobody can touch Cathy when it comes to versatility. I just didn't feel I had what it took to dance with these two this way. I felt like a hobbyist boxer being asked to step into the ring with Mike Tyson.

Also surprising was the addition of a musical guest. It was yet to be determined whether this would be a Canadian music star performing a new single or a musician hired to perform a song ripped from the headlines. My initial reaction to a song ripped from the headlines was that I would prefer the home surgery.

Puppets were mentioned. I remember this making me dizzy.

The whole thing would wrap up with something called "comedy minute grabbers 'Laugh-In' style." I didn't know what this meant.

Not only was this a show I could not pull off, it was a show I would not watch.

The cast listed in the document was Mary, Cathy and Andy Jones and myself. Three members of *CODCO* plus me. How I ended up in such company I have no idea. It was like Ringo dropped out of the Beatles and I got the call.

Immediately Andy quit the project. Turns out he had told Mary she could use his name as long as he didn't have to do it.

To replace Andy, Mary chose Greg Thomey. This was an obvious call for Mary. She had always wanted Greg to be part of the *CODCO* TV series, but the rest of the gang wouldn't have it. It's safe to say that while Greg was an unknown entity in Canada at the time, he was a comedy legend in downtown St. John's. I was a huge fan. I remember being at a house party when Greg started mopping the kitchen floor as a performance piece. It was a brilliant comedy routine that had the entire room crying with laughter. The next day, when trying to explain why it was so funny, all I was left with was, "But it was the *way* he was mopping the floor." I once saw Greg eat a bowl of cereal onstage for ten minutes. To this day it's probably the funniest ten minutes I've spent in the theatre. Again, it was the *way* he ate cereal.

Eventually we got word that the cast would gather with Michael, Jack and Gerald and plot a way forward.

Gerald's advice to me was to not be shy. He said I would have to fight to carve out a part of the show I felt good about. He said the problem with a collective was that "he who shouts the loudest wins the day." He warned me, "Walsh can shout louder than anyone. Don't be intimidated."

Great advice. Don't be intimidated by the comedy legend with the TV track record. Remember you created a stage show that is firmly embedded as a semi-significant footnote in regional Canadian theatre.

Gerald kept reminding me that I was supposed to be in that room. And, he reminded me, George Anthony wanted me in the room and, end of the day, that's all that mattered.

Before we even met, things began to get complicated. Mary envisioned a very large tent. She wanted there to be room for everyone.

Other people began to come out of the woodwork and tell me in confidence that they were going to be part of Mary's new show.

Ron Hynes, now my neighbour and great friend, told me he might be doing a song a week on the show and writing the theme song.

Lois told me she was going to be on one of the episodes as a special guest. In those days Lois spent much of her time wearing a wedding dress and reciting spoken word poems about loss and despair. There were also elements of modern dance. I love Lois, but how she would fit in a show about news, I had no idea.

Likewise, Andrew Younghusband told me that Mary might be adding him to the company. This was welcome news, except based on the proposal I had seen, I knew that wouldn't be in the cards. This was one of the most awkward moments of my life.

I think I know where Mary was coming from. In those days, there would be regular cabaret shows at the LSPU Hall. They were more often than not a fundraiser for a pressing cause. A comedian could be followed by a country singer, followed by a fiddle player, a dancer, a poet, an activist or a classically trained Bulgarian cellist. Wonderful, memorable eclectic nights. Art and politics intersecting. Established artists mixing with new. So many times, I sat in the audience or stood in the wings at these shows knowing I was witnessing something truly brilliant. And if you didn't like any part of it? Wait five minutes and Andy Jones would come out and do something extraordinary.

If what Mary envisioned was a variety show, I think she wanted to capture that magic and put it in a bottle. Or rather capture that magic and put it on TV. Or maybe she was just thinking out loud while Lois and the Bulgarian cellist were in the room.

When we finally got together with Michael and Jack, I was relieved to get the sense that no single element of the proposal was set in stone. Other than the live audience.

Michael was consistent about two things. One, anything is possible, and two, there was no money. These struck me as two mutually exclusive notions. Order whatever you want on the menu but be aware that we have very little money for food.

Mary and I were on the same page about one significant element. The show had to be about the news. How this would be achieved we didn't know, but whatever was on the front page of the *Globe and Mail* or was the lead story on *The National* would have to be in the show.

I knew from both of the one-man shows that Canadian audiences were starved for topical, ripped-from-the-headlines satire. I also knew the more topical the theme was, the more forgiving the audience would be.

How the news would be presented and satirized was where we began to disagree. Mary loves sketch. Every biting point she had made in her career up until then had been in character. All great sketch comedians are comfortable when they are immersed in characters. Mary wanted to be in character and dissecting the news. I wanted to dissect the news, but I wanted to do it as myself at a news desk. I actually had no interest in sketch, and in fact was intimidated by the idea.

I didn't want a desk like *Saturday Night Live*; I wanted a real news desk. I wanted a news desk that looked like a real supper-hour news desk. I wanted a desk like the one I had seen on *This Just In*, a failed CBS comedy pilot that nobody except me was familiar with.

I never mentioned this show to anyone but it was on my mind constantly. A friend of mine had given me a collection of bootleg videotapes that featured the greatest TV shows ever made, some that aired and some that did not. The tapes included great cult classics like *Fernwood 2Night* and *The Tracey Ullman Show*. One tape featured "the best shows never aired," which included the pilot episode of *This Just In*. On the surface it was a standard sitcom that was set in a TV newsroom. That wasn't entirely new, but what was astounding was that the news anchors were delivering jokes from the headlines and they were throwing to real news footage that had been edited for comedic effect. I had never seen that before. They had footage of presidential candidate Ross Perot sitting on-camera, clearly before an interview and unaware that he was being recorded. How this was possible, I had no idea, but it blew my mind.

Naturally the more we talked about the news, the more Cathy cried. Eventually she decided she would do something called the "good news fairy" and only talk about news that didn't make her sad.

Thomey kept saying things like "I will do the business news for people who don't know what the stock market is."

Jack produced full-colour photographs of elaborate puppets in the likeness of current political characters such as Brian Mulroney, Kim Campbell and Jean Chrétien. They were based on the puppets of the hit British TV series *Spitting Image*. The show was a huge hit in the UK, and a Canadian version had been produced as a pilot. The consensus was that the puppets were great but the jokes weren't. The CBC wanted us to use these puppets.

None of us were keen on the idea, and my guess is because none of us are impersonators. Also, none of us were interested in giving screen time to Styrofoam.

Thomey held up a picture of the Brian Mulroney puppet and said, "Can we catch them on fire?"

"God no," said Jack. "They are very expensive."

"Then I vote no," Thomey said.

Ever since we'd got the go-ahead, I kept telling myself not to think beyond eight episodes. It was sound advice that I would give to anyone auditioning for a part in a movie or recording their first album. Concentrate on the task at hand, and don't envision yourself getting the part and then winning an Oscar or having a number one album. Don't sit around and play "what if." Just get the job done. And for god's sake don't start spending money in your head that you don't actually have.

Of course I didn't really pay attention to my own advice. For a whole month, when I wasn't pinching myself, I was thinking about what it would be like if it turned into a regular series. What if, like *CODCO*, it ran for five years. Because of TV, *CODCO* members had actual cars and mortgages! By Newfoundland arts community standards they were rich! They had freedom. They were working artists. What a gift that would be.

And now I was in a room listening to so many different visions of the show, I began to think that the chance of this going past eight episodes was remote at best.

Mary was actually of the opinion that doing just eight episodes was fine with her. To me this was the most insane thing I had ever heard. Who would get a TV show and let it run its course after eight episodes? Of course, Mary was ahead of her time. Now people do limited series all the time. But back then it was unheard of.

Days of meetings in St. John's delivered few if any concrete conceits.

Michael seemed to love every idea. When Mary mused that the famous Canadian author Timothy Findley could write us a series of sketches satirizing the wealthy Toronto enclave of Rosedale, Michael thought it was a fantastic idea. "We must do it!" he would say. All I could think was, "Who will I play?" I had never been to Rosedale and I was pretty sure I didn't sound like anyone from Rosedale. Maybe they could have a driver from Newfoundland who liked to talk about the news.

Grand discussions never brought us a single step closer to conceiving what this show would look like. Nobody seemed concerned. I chalked it up to my having no experience in television and almost everyone else being veterans.

And then suddenly I found myself in the uncomfortable position of siding with the network against my castmates. The issue was Geoff D'Eon.

Michael dropped an aside on the room one day as we were wrapping up. "Oh, and by the way, there's another producer on the show now. A fellow named Geoff D'Eon. He works for the CBC."

Mary hit the roof. Where did this producer come from? What was he going to be doing exactly? Was he a babysitter? Would he be answering to Toronto?

Michael answered, "I believe he grew up in England. He's never worked in comedy or theatre. He worked in news. He ran the supper hour in Halifax."

This was the exact worst thing he could have said. In fact, it might have set a world record for worst answer ever. He could have saved himself a lot of time and just doused the room in gasoline and waited for the sparks from the electrical fire in Mary's head to ignite the entire building.

Cathy, taking her cue from Mary, also hit the roof. "They want him on the show because they think he can tell us about the news!" This coming from someone who insisted she hadn't actually watched the news in a decade.

Mary's natural instinct was that this unknown CBC producer was a threat. Mary knew Michael and Jack and Gerald, and they had not just professional relationships but friendships. Mary and Gerald had worked together on *CODCO* and stage productions. They'd toured Labrador together. She was comfortable with all the producers involved. On *CODCO* there was no extra CBC producer kicking around. Mary was concerned about how much power this guy would have and who he would be answering to. This reaction was 100 percent due to Mary's insecurity. Show me any great talent who oozes confidence and I assure you that beneath the surface there is seething insecurity.

My reaction to this issue was the exact opposite. When I heard that an actual news producer would be on the show, I felt like a drowning man who was being thrown a rope. And my reaction was also 100 percent due to my own insecurity.

Mary was worried this unknown British news wanker would be judging her comedy. I didn't care about that. I was terrified of what lay ahead. All I could think was that maybe this unknown, unfunny British news wanker might know how to get this supposed news show off the ground. Also he might know how to get his hands on news footage we could use in the show. Also he could teach me how to sound like a reporter.

It was the first time Mary and I were at opposite ends of a creative argument. We both stuck to our guns. In hindsight it was a huge error on my part because it was a done deal that Geoff was assigned to the show. This decision came from on high. Neither Mary's position nor mine was relevant. We just burned up equity arguing over something that neither of us could control.

Within a few weeks the whole lot of us decamped to Halifax with a vision for a new TV show that was as clear as the newly released NDP economic platform.

The only real thing that was accomplished during the St. John's meetings was that we agreed on a name for the show.

There was much debate over this, naturally. No different than a group of kids sitting around and instead of jamming just talking about what they're going to call their band. A perfect way to pass the hours. If only we had a cool name for the band, surely the next step would be Massey Hall.

Mary made the point that while she didn't necessarily agree with the notion, she couldn't help but notice that many hit shows in America had a star's name in the title: Roseanne, Seinfeld, Arsenio and so forth. Cathy began to hyperventilate. She did not want to be in a show called *Mary*.

I had kind of expected Mary to float that balloon. After all, the show was sold on her back, not ours. It never came to a vote, and honestly, if it had, I probably would have accepted *Mary* as the title. It was not a hill I was going to die on. I was in no position to. I was the one who was "lucky to be in the room." I would have signed on to appear in a show called *Adolf*.

The title, *This Hour Has 22 Minutes*, was Michael Donovan's idea. In a discussion about great titles that summed up a show perfectly, we ran through the usual suspects. The greatest titles, we agreed, were *That Was the Week That Was* and *This Hour Has Seven Days*. *Seven Days* was a legendary Canadian TV news show that changed television forever. It only ran for just two years but it's considered the template for all the tabloid TV programs that came afterwards. Shows like *60 Minutes* owe it all to this scrappy Canadian offering. The hosts voiced their own opinions, which was unheard of in those days. Also, a key signature of the show was that it allowed satire a place on a real news program. It also featured, I was sorry to hear, songs based on the headlines. It was wildly popular and also subversive, so much so that in 1966 it was cancelled, allegedly on orders from the Prime Minister's Office. This led to a huge scandal over political interference and the CBC. There were protests on Parliament Hill when it was shuttered.

God, how I wanted to be on a show that the Prime Minister's Office would want cancelled. I wanted to be on a show that would make politicians in Ottawa kick their TVs in.

And so, while we mulled over titles and ruminated on the efficiency of the title *This Hour Has Seven Days*, it was Michael who said, "This Hour Has 22 Minutes"—twenty-two minutes being the length of a half-hour of television at the time. Twenty-two minutes of content and eight minutes of commercials.

Consensus was quick. I agreed that it was smart, but privately I was worried. Yes, *This Hour Has Seven Days* may have changed television forever, but it was cancelled three years before I was born. That meant there were a lot of people walking around who had no memory of the show—a lot of people who would not get the joke or the reference. But I kept my concerns to myself. There were worse things than being on a show with a smart title. And it was certainly better than *Adolf*.

Eventually I grew to love the title *This Hour Has 22 Minutes*, going so far as to have it translated into a single Chinese character, which I had tattooed on my lower back.

Not really, but I would have. It's that good.

15

Countdown

Once we were in Halifax it became clear that Michael Donovan had been brutally honest about one thing. There really was no money.

Michael had sold the show to the CBC at a bargain-basement price. He had literally a fifth of the budget of *CODCO*.

Also, and we did not know this at the time, the contract was actually for twenty episodes, with a clause saying the CBC could cancel us after eight. This tidbit was kept from us. Allegedly, it was thought that if we'd known, we wouldn't work as hard.

This notion of a shoestring budget was particularly hard for Mary and Cathy to comprehend. *CODCO* would shoot three sketches a day on elaborate sets. If Mary wanted to play the Queen at Buckingham Palace, an elaborate set was created. If Cathy wanted a courtroom filled with extras, it happened. It was pretty clear that with this show we would be lucky to afford the Queen's garden shed.

CODCO also employed Bev Schechtman and Judi Cooper-Sealy. They were hair and makeup legends who'd come from *SCTV*. They were the best and therefore the most expensive team in North America.

They were experts in prosthetics and came with a legendary wig collection. Give them the time and the budget, they could make Joe Clark look like Dolly Parton.

Mary and Cathy just assumed that Bev and Judi would be on the show. Instead, they were told there would be one local person doing both hair and makeup. There were two wigs in storage at CBC, which we were free to borrow.

I can see how this was upsetting to them. They had always done shows with adequate resources. They knew this wasn't up to scratch. I didn't know any better. One local makeup person sounded good enough for me. But what did I know?

The next problem, and this was insurmountable, was our producers' insistence on having a live audience. This was a deal-breaker. The feeling was that with a live audience the cast would avoid doing take after take after take, something that had rankled the producers of *CODCO*.

But the Halifax studio was, by any standards, small. If you had all the money in the world it would be physically impossible to fit multiple sets and a musical guest in that studio. So very quickly the notion of a musical guest disappeared. Corey Hart would never sing "Never Surrender" in the second act. Gordon Lightfoot would never get a chance to premiere a new song about a scandal involving a cabinet minister and a case of tainted tuna.

Everyone was busy pitching ideas for sketches and concepts for the show. I didn't pitch much, but I did pitch the idea of a rant—which I called a streeter. The streeter would be a one-and-a-half-minute commentary in my voice, not in character. It was very close to what I was doing on *Midday* except there would be no edit point. It would be a single rant shot in one take only. Secretly my rationale was that when this show crashed up against the rocks in eight weeks, I would have tape of me ranting about Canadian politics and perhaps I could use that to pitch another show or land a regular spot on an existing news program.

Turns out the producers loved the idea.

I realize now that they didn't love the idea because they had any faith in my editorial prowess or ability to make news funny. They loved it because what I was pitching was essentially the cheapest minute and a half in Canadian TV history.

It was a great lesson. If you embrace your budget or lack thereof and only pitch things that are affordable, more often than not you will win. It was with this in mind that I became a consistent advocate for the simple news desk.

Mary had no problem with a news desk that could be used as a portable set, but she didn't like the idea of it being the central element of the show. I wanted a set that looked exactly like any national or local news program. A set that would confuse the viewers when they saw it for the first time.

It was in the midst of this exciting and tumultuous creative debate that a terrible thing happened to Mary. Her back went out. And not in the sense that her back was sore, or her back was causing her problems. Her back completely stopped working. She was racked with pain. She was suddenly bedridden in a Halifax hotel room, far from home and far from the room where the show was being invented.

Also "bedridden" is not entirely accurate. She was actually lying on a single thick piece of plywood laid on top of the mattress. It was quickly determined that she would need serious surgery. Back surgery is always a gamble. It was a very hard time for her.

It would not be wrong to say she was angry. And understandably so. Chronic pain is a terrible thing. To be felled like that a month before opening a new TV show that was sold on her name must have been crushing.

Initially we would all traipse to Mary's hotel room and gather around the bed and talk about what we had discussed or decided earlier in the day. This proved disastrous. Mary felt like decisions were being made behind her back. Technically that was true, but only because she was incapacitated. Mary, from her bed, revealed a new character she wanted to do. It was a worm who loved Canadian books. She envisioned a segment of the show called "Bookworm" that would highlight Canadian literature, discuss bestsellers and champion underdogs—again before her time, long before Oprah's Book Club.

Mary was passionate about the idea, and I knew why. She is the most voracious reader I know. And her idols since she was a very small child have been fiction writers. Mary would in fact go on to create a show devoted to Canadian literature and as a result sold a lot of books for a lot of writers. I also know that of all the great things she has done in her career, writing a novel is the one she is proudest of.

But in the end the producers didn't go for the idea of a bookworm being a regular segment, claiming they didn't have the resources to create a worm costume and set. From what I could tell, *CODCO* hadn't had producers calling the shots this way.

This was a blow to Mary, who literally couldn't lift a finger or shoulder in defence of her idea.

In the end the most defining voice in the creation of *This Hour Has 22 Minutes* did not belong to Mary or me or anyone else. The two greatest contributors to the final product were the absurdly small budget and our ridiculously tiny studio. The powers that be crunched the numbers and the space and determined there was only room for one set, and it had to be small and affordable—a.k.a. a news desk.

Once again I could have kept my mouth shut.

Before *22 Minutes* launched, my gut told me that the great advantage of having a show that covered the news was that the news was always happening. It's not likely the country was ever going to run out. We would always have subjects to discuss, dissect and satirize. "No matter what the headline," I prophesied, "we will provide the punchline."

After a lifetime in this racket, I now realize I was only half-right. True, there is always news, but some weeks there is only bad news. Sometimes the news is unrelenting and unkind. Try sitting around in a writers' room attempting to pound out jokes when the entire news cycle is dominated by heartbreaking testimony from a national inquiry investigating how thousands of Canadians contracted HIV from the nation's blood supply. It's days like that when you regret having a career that relies on making jokes out of headlines. It's days like that when you think, "Cathy Jones was right. The news *is* awful."

Fortunately, it would be quite a while before I learned that lesson. Because the first three episodes of our show aired, entirely by coincidence, during the absolute best possible time to be in the news business—during a federal election. And not just any election. One of the most fascinating federal elections in our history. The political climate in Canada was about to change dramatically, and so were Monday nights on CBC.

It was in many ways an election defined by one man. A man who was in fact absent. Brian Mulroney had been elected eight years previously with the largest Conservative majority in Canadian history. He was young, handsome and telegenic. He had a beautiful wife and an adorable young family. A son of Quebec and of Irish decent, he could make a speech and tell a joke in both official languages.

When he resigned as prime minister shortly before the election in 1993, he had been rebranded. Surrounded by scandal, he was the least popular leader in the history of polling in Canada. On the day he tendered his resignation, polio had higher approval numbers.

Mulroney, love or loathe him, was a polarizing figure. He was a leader who did big things: a free trade agreement, the GST, two failed attempts at ratifying the Constitution. He believed in rolling the dice. He was a fan of the grand gesture.

Immediately after his resignation, most of Mulroney's cabinet took a look at the entrails and ran off to receive their just rewards in the afterlife of the private sector. None of the old boys entered the race to succeed him. A cabinet rookie and relative newcomer became his successor. And in that way, history was made. Heading into the election, the governing Progressive Conservative Party was led by our first female prime minister, the Right Honourable Kim Campbell.

Campbell was always a long shot. The Conservative brand was bloodied and bowed. But if anyone could salvage the party it was her. She represented generational change, and she represented gender change. She was from British Columbia, and she was bilingual. When she was justice minister, she posed for a portrait, ostensibly nude, holding a judge's robes in front of her breasts, her milky white shoulders exposed for all the country to see. She was sassy.

The Liberals too had a new leader in Jean Chrétien, although *new* was not the first word you would use to describe the man. Though he had spent the last few years hiding out in a law firm, he was first elected in 1963. The gargoyles on the Parliament Buildings seemed fresh by comparison.

The NDP were led by Audrey McLaughlin, the first Canadian woman to lead a national party, and the first leader from the Yukon. She took over the NDP in 1989, at the height of its popularity. By the time the election rolled around, a series of unfortunate events, namely wildly unpopular NDP governments in Ontario and BC, had rendered her party *personae non gratae* in the majority of Canada. Even before the writ was dropped, the party carried with them the air of defeat.

Normally in Canada that would be the entire picture. Elections were always a fight between the Liberals and the Tories and, to a much lesser extent, the NDP. But this election was unique. This election had wild cards. Wild and crazy cards.

Conservatives in the West were so disenchanted with the leadership of the Progressive Conservative Party that they actively supported a breakaway movement called the Reform Party. Reform had just one seat in the House of Commons, held by political pioneer Deborah Grey. She was a down-to-earth, plain-spoken Albertan. She was constantly tailed by her keen young parliamentary assistant, a no-nonsense policy wonk by the name of Stephen Harper.

The Reform Party was led by the profoundly unilingual Preston Manning: son of a preacher man, deeply religious and conservative to his core. As the leader of a protest party, he spent most of his time promising everyone lower taxes and assuring the rest of the country that his party was not a haven for western separatists and white supremacists.

Conservatives in the vote-rich province of Quebec also abandoned the party of Mulroney. Mulroney's Quebec lieutenant and former best friend, Lucien Bouchard, had departed the Conservatives to become the leader of the separatist Bloc Québécois. He spent all of his time assuring the country that yes, his party was indeed a haven for sovereigntists who wanted to break up Canada.

And wait, there is more.

The early 1990s saw a huge proliferation of parties that fell firmly in the category of fringe or "other." In total an unheard-of fourteen registered political parties contested the election. Chief among them were the Green Party of Canada, who were pro-Earth; the Christian Heritage Party of Canada, who were anti-abortion; and the Libertarian Party of Canada, who just wanted to be left alone. Always the bridesmaid and never the bride, the Marxist-Leninist Party of Canada were hoping this might be their lucky year.

Had I not been about to embark on a life as a non-partisan political commentator, I might well have endorsed yet another party that appeared to be on the verge of a breakthrough: the Natural Law Party of Canada. For a fringe party they were running an astonishing 231 candidates across the country, all of whom were followers of East Indian transcendental meditation guru Maharishi Mahesh Yogi.

Also, they had a legitimate star candidate in the person of magician and escape artist Doug Henning. Henning was a Broadway star and a fixture on the biggest American talk shows. He had a healthy pile of Emmy nominations, a Tony Award and a house full of disappearing rabbits. How would a Natural Law government deal with the pressing issues of the day such as high unemployment. The party's platform suggested yogic flying as a solution. It really doesn't get much better than that.

The idea that we could all fly caused great excitement nationwide, but when footage of the actual yogic flying was released, it looked not like flying at all but like a bunch of imbeciles bouncing up and down with their legs crossed. It looked terribly hard on the knees, so the practice failed to take off—either as a way to tackle the deficit or as a fitness trend.

A sad footnote: Henning retired from politics soon after the election and passed away seven years later at the age of fifty-two. He lost a battle with cancer that he fought valiantly, refusing conventional treatment and choosing instead a strict diet of nuts and berries. He provided us great material in the early days, and he will be missed. I like to think he didn't so much die as escape.

And so, it was against this backdrop that *This Hour Has 22 Minutes* was birthed. The political landscape was fertile ground. In fact, there was manure as far as the eye could see.

But before we could get busy with covering the election, some decisions had to be made. First among them, we needed a show opener.

I can't stress enough how important the opening credits of a TV show are. The opening sets the tone. It tells the audience what to expect. It alerts everyone in the household that the show is about to start. Also, if you are lucky and your show is a hit, people will be watching the opener for years to come. You want it to be something they enjoy. In other words, nailing the opening for a show is imperative. As they say, you only get one chance to make a first impression.

Right out of the gate we blew it.

For most of its life *22 Minutes* has had an opener that looked and felt like a supper-hour newscast with a twist. It's always worked because it's the obvious choice. In the beginning we did not make the obvious choice.

I honestly cannot remember how it happened, but somehow we decided that when it came to the opener we would think outside of the box. And then for good measure we took a hatchet to the box, chopped it into a thousand pieces and used it as kindling to start a dumpster fire. If you were sitting in your living room on the night that *This Hour Has 22 Minutes* premiered, you would be forgiven if you weren't entirely sure what it was that you were watching.

It was essentially an eerie montage of pivotal moments in news history. It was completely washed out, with a yellowish sepia-toned treatment. Some of the footage was generic angry wallpaper—cars burning and people protesting in the streets, chaos. Some of it was more recognizable: the crash of the *Hindenburg*, an atomic bomb exploding. In the background a children's choir was singing a slow and creepy version of "The Happier We Will Be."

At some point you would see that the alleged stars of this show had their heads superimposed on the bodies of people in the footage. Cathy Jones's head was superimposed on Barbra Streisand's body standing next to Pierre Trudeau. Greg's head was on Lee Harvey Oswald in the famous photo taken at the moment he was shot by Jack Ruby. My head was superimposed on the body of a little boy who was standing next to Iranian dictator Saddam Hussein. The image of Saddam patting the little boy on the head was beyond cringe-worthy. Luckily the boy and his family were released soon after the footage was shot, and they returned safely to England. Putting my head on the body of a terrified child was in terrible taste.

But if medals were being given out for lack of taste, I would have won the silver because the gold (or perhaps the award of excellence) went to Mary. Mary chose one of the most famous images of the Vietnam War: photojournalist Eddie Adams's photograph of a Viet Cong squad leader being executed during the chaos of the Tet Offensive. Walsh's head was on the shoulders of a man being shot at point-black range.

If you are keeping score, the show's opening featured two cast members being executed and one being inappropriately touched by a Middle Eastern dictator. Did I mention this was a comedy show?

Gerald, in his role as creative producer, hated the opener. But somehow the majority got the best of him and it went to air. It was the kind of creative decision that could get you cancelled before you leave the gate. It was certainly the type of decision that seemed designed to make people reach for the remote and switch over to *Destiny Ridge* on Global.

How we started with a bleak sepia-toned hellscape accompanied by the haunting voices of sad children lost in purgatory, I have no idea. How we survived it is a mystery.

I'll chalk it up to the fact that out of the gate we were a late-night show. Audiences at that hour are traditionally harder to horrify.

Despite the intense debates over what the show was going to look and feel like, we had, as a cast, one big advantage over comedy shows that came before us. Namely, we had never existed as a comedy troupe. Cathy and Mary had been in a comedy group together, but for the most part we were four individuals in four silos working on one show.

And the great advantage of not being a troupe was that we didn't come with the baggage that all of them acquire over time. Comedy troupes are no different from rock and roll bands. A group of musicians who theoretically have similar tastes get together and start jamming in someone's garage. They get better over time, but from the moment they produce their first notes, time is running out. By the time that first record is produced there is a lot of water under the bridge. All sorts of rock and roll shenanigans have occurred; members have slept with each other or, better yet, each other's significant others. They have formed alliances and have partaken in betrayals. They have seen each other at their very best and very worst.

They have spent hundreds of hours jammed in a van and they all know who has sleep apnea. Throw in addiction issues, weird food habits and natural competitiveness and you have all the makings of a great big horrible dysfunctional marriage. A marriage where everyone agrees to stay together, not for the kids, but because they have a record contract or a TV show.

Oh, and let's not forget the lawyers. Bands and comedy troupes are not just like-minded individuals pursuing an artistic passion. They are business partners as well. So, with any modicum of success there are lawyers. Lots of lawyers.

Seriously, if you are thinking of starting a band or a comedy troupe, why not just go to the hardware store, buy a hammer and start driving galvanized nails into your forehead.

Keeping the band together is the hardest thing in the world. Not that long ago ABBA turned down $1 billion to reunite and go on tour. Those historical grievances must be pretty intense to turn down a thousand million dollars. This is everywhere in the music business. As of writing, you couldn't get all of the original members of Great Big Sea in the same kitchen party supposing Yo-Yo Ma was shaking a jar of lentils.

22 Minutes didn't come with historical baggage. We had the luxury of investing in and inventing new baggage as we went. That gave us a lot of runway.

And one thing we all had in common was that we all wanted to work. Except for Cathy, who was still struggling with the notion that the show was going to be about the news.

16

Showtime

From the moment I arrived in Halifax in 1993, despite the revelations about the budget and the internal struggles about the tone and style of the show, I was in a constant state of elation. It was almost too much to bear.

As far as I was concerned, every single problem, no matter how big or small, was a good problem to have. I wasn't washing dishes.

The show had no money? I didn't care. All I cared about was that we had a TV show! There was no room for us inside the CBC building, so we camped out in three used construction trailers in the back parking lot. To me this was a luxury.

I felt like I had been given the keys to a kingdom. I loved every single moment.

A week before we launched, I walked into the studio and saw, sitting in the corner, under plastic, a news desk that looked like any supper-hour news desk in the country. Victory. I could not have been happier if there was a brand-new Lamborghini under that sheet, or Sting on an ant hill.

Behind the desk were three chairs for three news anchors. Mary's chair was in storage. I was counting the days to our premiere; she was counting the days to a risky surgery. Our heads were in distinctly different places.

When I sat at the news desk I felt entirely at home. This was a place I could picture myself being for a very long time. Everything about it felt right.

The feeling was short-lived. I quickly found myself on the losing side of a battle that I never quite anticipated and never accepted.

Once it was clear that the show would feature all of us at a news desk, there was suddenly a robust discussion about what our names and characters would be.

I felt like I had slipped through the looking glass.

The whole advantage of a news desk, in my opinion, was that we could be free to be ourselves. It seems that nobody shared that opinion.

Cathy, Greg and Mary all wanted to play characters, with character names, when sitting at the desk. It was as if they'd never considered appearing as themselves. I do understand this. Mary and Cathy are brilliant character comedians. It's what they do. They find freedom in character. Greg was much the same way.

I was the opposite. I glanced over from the desk and saw the makings of a small set that would be used for a sketch. I thought I would throw up. That terrified me. I never for a second thought I belonged over there. Sketch was Cathy and Mary's domain, maybe Greg's, but certainly not mine. They could wear the funny hats and fight over the two existing wigs; I was happy wearing a suit and being the straight man.

I wanted to sit at the desk and say, "Good evening, I am Rick Mercer," in much the same way that Barbara Frum, Peter Mansbridge, Knowlton Nash and Lloyd Robertson had. No such luck. We were to use *noms de plume*.

Interestingly enough, the person who was most insistent that nobody use their real name was Michael Donovan. I had never seen him so serious about an issue before, and it was a long time before I would see him so serious again. He looked at me and said with complete authority, "You will never use your real name on this show."

You can't win them all, and so Mary became Molly McGuire (named after a secret Irish republican gang), Cathy became Sydney Dubizzenchyk (a play on the name of the CBC broadcaster Tina Srebotnjak, a brilliant TV interviewer whose name WASPs allegedly found hard to pronounce), Greg became Tim MacMillan, and I reluctantly became J.B. Dickson (a name roughly inspired by CTV news anchor J.D. Roberts, now John Roberts of Fox News).

One area where the lack of money and physical space paid off was our location work. We had no room or money for sets, so we shot on location more than most sketch shows did. This had a huge bearing on the tone of the show. The great outdoors was our set. When we went on location, which we did often, our show looked incredible. Halifax was a TV producer's dream. You could find whatever you were looking for within minutes of the CBC building. And everyone in the city was more than eager to open their doors and let us shoot in their homes or their buildings.

And that is exactly what we did. We went to work.

The first episode of *This Hour Has 22 Minutes* was screened for the cast a few days before the premiere, in a boardroom at CBC TV. It was, in my opinion, and despite the freakishly strange opening credits, a masterpiece. Perfect from beginning to end. All these years later, even without the rose-coloured glasses, I have to admit it was pretty good.

It had a lot going for it. For starters, it didn't look like anything else on TV at the time. When the camera rolled up to the news desk, timpani drums signalled something very important was about to take place. For anyone just tuning in, we looked exactly like real news anchors at a real desk.

Immediately out of the gate the jokes from the anchors came fast and furious. And it was insanely topical. And there was real news footage! It was exactly as I had imagined.

And then we cut away to a commercial. Or rather a parody of a commercial. The NDP had released a campaign commercial just days before that featured supposedly regular Canadians angrily

demanding better of their politicians. I wrote the parody. Luckily for
us the NDP commercial looked intentionally low-rent. Low-rent we
could do. Our parody looked exactly like their commercial, and it
was devastating. Cathy, Greg and I were all in it, some of us playing
multiple characters, mine being decidedly head-injured. We ended
it by coming together and singing in unison "Free Nelson Mandela."
At that point Mandela had been out of prison for the better part of
half a decade. It was great satire, and it was short.

In fact everything was short. Gerald's greatest contribution to the
creation of 22 *Minutes* was what he called the ninety-second rule.
Nothing, no matter what, could be more than ninety seconds. And
sixty seconds was the sweet spot.

In those early years of 22 *Minutes* we followed that rule slavishly.
It meant that the show moved like a rocket. The viewer understood
that if they didn't fancy something, it would be over very quickly.

And as that first twenty-two-minute show progressed, four distinct voices were revealed.

Greg Thomey introduced Canadians to perennial politician Jerry
Boyle. Boyle threw his hat into the ring announcing that he would
be running in the upcoming federal election. He was broadcasting
from his campaign headquarters, which was also his brother's garden
shed. Boyle wrapped up his message by revealing his campaign
slogan: "If you can mark an X, you're my kind of people!" A star was
born. Everyone loved Jerry Boyle. He still is Bob Rae's all-time favourite comedic creation.

That show had my first rant. It was the only time anyone appeared
in the show not in character. Exactly what I wanted. It was also aired
in black-and-white, making it stand out even more. I was the angry
young man, the one who wanted Charles Lynch strung up, and now
I had a platform. Except instead of ninety minutes onstage I had
ninety seconds on-camera. I started to develop a habit where I would
write everything I wanted to say on a subject, filling pages and pages.
Then I would begin to edit and reduce, reduce and then reduce some
more. It was a long process, like reducing a full cow to a cup of hopefully palatable gravy.

Cathy Jones premiered her sassy '50s news reporter Babe Bennett. It was a tour de force of character work, funny and sexy. It was a character filled with joy and featured no malice. A sunny respite in a sea of anger. Cathy's characters were always happy. Every one of them also laughed. And it was always an infectious laugh. Laugh and the audience will laugh with you.

And then it was Mary's turn. It was Gerald who told Mary she would have to appear in the show and he would bring a camera to her bed. The show was, after all, being treated in the press as the new Mary Walsh vehicle. Nobody knew how that would work. It seemed like a tall order. Were we really going to cut away to a bedroom in the middle of a comedy show?

Yes, we were.

For the very first show Mary premiered Marg Delahunty, the saucy, opinionated woman who could and would say anything she wanted. Marg was so disgusted with the state of affairs in the country, she had taken to her bed and didn't have the will to get up. She did have the will to deliver a blistering commentary that went up one side and down the other of pretty much every major political figure in Canada. Marg, in her housecoat, and later in her Princess Warrior costume, would go on to become the most enduring character ever created on *This Hour Has 22 Minutes* and certainly one of the most famous Canadian comic creations of all time. And she did it while in Hell with a broken back.

All of this in one show was simply too much for me to handle. That day in the boardroom I can distinctly remember thinking, "This is the best show ever! I cannot believe I'm on this show! If this show happened and I wasn't part of it, I think I would jump off a bridge." I also remember thinking that if we played our cards right, this show could run forever.

Two days later the show premiered on CBC Television. Our time slot was a wasteland: Monday night at 10:30.

I watched the show the way a four-year-old watches Saturday morning cartoons. I stood in the middle of the room with my mouth open—in complete shock and awe. You only get one chance to launch a show. And this was it.

You have to be a die-hard student of television to make an appointment to watch a TV show's premiere. The entire world may have tuned in to catch the last episode of *M*A*S*H* and the end of *Seinfeld*, but precious few viewers made a point to watch episode one.

I have a distinct memory of exactly where I was when *CODCO* premiered on the network in 1988. I was nineteen. On that night, like this one, I was also off the island. I had arrived in Montreal a few hours before *CODCO* was set to air and immediately headed downtown to visit my great friend Dana Warren, who was in the city studying French.

It was my first time in Montreal, and I was intimidated as hell as I made my way alone on the shuttle bus from the airport to downtown. Finding my way from the bus station to Dana's apartment was an adventure.

I say I was intimidated not because I was afraid for my life or afraid of the big city, but because I have always had a terrible sense of direction. To this day, whenever I leave a hotel room, whatever direction my instinct tells me to turn to reach the elevator is more than half the time the wrong one. I have had to train myself to be counterintuitive and to go against my instincts when it comes to moving around in the world. I should have a guide dog.

Somehow, I managed to make my way from the bus station to Dana's place. Classic Rick, I made the twenty-minute walk in just under a slightly disorienting forty. I arrived less than an hour before *CODCO* was to air. Dana and her roommates had arrived just minutes before I did. I went through the open door to find an apartment that was surprisingly spacious and recently ransacked. They had been robbed. They were hysterical.

All of the women were in shock. Whoever broke in did a classic soul-crushing move of not only stealing anything worth a nickel but also dumping various intimate smalls on the floor. Big black muddy footprints were all over the living room. Anyone who has ever had their home broken into knows how deeply violating and traumatic it can be. There was disbelief and anger all around.

They hadn't even noticed my arrival when I glanced around the living room and I came to an unsettling realization. I am ashamed to say the first words I offered to my dear friends in distress were not words of comfort. Instead I said, "They stole your TV."

They looked at me like I was a mad person.

"We don't have a TV," Dana said.

There was an awkward silence, and then I said, "Oh, it's just that *CODCO* is on in less than an hour." And then, faced with blank stares, I began to explain to them the cultural significance and the importance of the evening.

Read the room, Rick. It's a wonder they didn't kill me right there on the spot.

Turns out that despite them all being somewhat aware that there was a CODCO TV project in the works, they had not cleared their schedules nor purchased a used TV in order to witness it.

I muttered that I was really sorry about the break-in and that I would be back. I left the house and wandered, where I had no idea, but I did see the lights of a busy commercial strip a few blocks away.

Once I hit the strip I immediately saw what I was looking for, a dive bar with TVs over the wood. Perfect. I walked into the bar with a simple plan.

I was not inside the door five seconds before I realized that my plan had a few flaws. The bar was surprisingly crowded. Everyone was over fifty, and to a person they were screaming in French.

Somehow, I knew in my heart of hearts that my requesting, *en anglais*, that everyone stop watching the game and instead switch over to the English-language CBC to watch a new show featuring cross-dressing Newfoundlanders insulting the one true church would not go over well.

I returned to the street, where I flashed back to an anomaly I had seen barely two hours earlier. In the bus station in downtown Montreal there had been a bank of small televisions in a row off to the side of the departures area. Each television was attached to a moulded chair that looked like a classic one-piece classroom desk-chair combo from the fifties. They were coin-operated televisions. It was the first time I had seen such a thing and I have not seen any since.

Who would be so desperate to watch TV at a bus station that they would pump quarters into one? I sprinted to the station.

Avoiding an elevated heart rate has always been a priority for me, so understandably I felt on the verge of cardiac arrest by the time I made it to the station. If I was going to go, it would be while watching *CODCO*.

The change machine next to the TVs miraculously worked. I settled in, and for thirty minutes pumped quarters into the slot and watched *CODCO*'s premiere on national TV. The luckiest Newfoundlanders on earth, as far as I was concerned.

And now, years later, I was about to watch another group of Newfoundlanders premiere a show on the same network. Except this time I was in it. I wondered if there were any young people in Newfoundland who were looking forward to this premiere as much as I had looked forward to *CODCO*'s; if there were any TV disciples out there who were aware of what we were up to.

Turns out there was one. Mark Critch tells me that just before *22 Minutes* premiered he stood on a table at the Ship Inn in downtown St. John's and yelled for everyone to be quiet, the show was about to start. There was a TV at the Ship, but it was almost never turned on. It was there for one reason only, so the owner could watch the World Cup. If it wasn't soccer, it wasn't watched. Knowing the Ship Inn of that era, I am impressed. Mark was taking his life in his hands.

I didn't know Mark well then. He was a young guy with a sketch troupe called Cat Fud. Clearly coming up with bad names for comedy troupes is a Newfoundland tradition. A few weeks before the *22 Minutes* premiere, he came through Halifax with his troupe to play the Fringe Festival. They sent out word through the usual pipelines that they were in town and penniless. I let him and his fellow comedians crash on the floor of my spare room.

I knew him only in passing. When he was in high school, he volunteered to work the door at the LSPU Hall for the run of the *Charles Lynch* show. He claims he stood at the back and watched every single night. I'm sure he is exaggerating.

He reports to me that, watching the *22 Minutes* premiere, he had the exact same reaction that so many actors have early in their careers. He thought, "That should be me up there." In his case it came true. Years later he would join the cast and become the new star, making it very much his show.

Mark wasn't the only one watching that night. Our premiere episode pulled in 468,000 viewers. Not too shabby for 10:30 on a school night. Our second episode, a week later, pulled in 535,000. Solid growth. Thanks in no small part to Canada's TV critics, who hailed our arrival as nothing short of revolutionary. I don't know if the Pfizer vaccine was given such good notices out of the gate.

In newsrooms across the country a debate was raging. In some quarters journalists were outraged that we were using CBC news footage and editing it for our own nefarious purposes. It simply had not been done before. Those people in particular focused their anger not at the comedians or even the network. They blamed the newsman on deck, Geoff D'Eon. He had been right. There would be no going back to the newsroom for Geoff if this didn't work out.

Luckily for Geoff, at least one of his old colleagues had no such problem. Geoff called up Arnold Amber, a man he describes as a "cranky old news guy and a really great programmer," to discuss the up-and-coming CBC election night special. Amber was executive producer. Geoff's pitch was simple—on election night, to lighten the density of back-to-back numbers and data crunching, they should on occasion cut to *This Hour Has 22 Minutes Live*. We would, he reported, do material pulled not from the day's headlines but that night's election. We would be as live as anything ever put on TV.

To Geoff's astonishment, Amber said yes. The decision had the backing of CBC anchor Peter Mansbridge and the head of English TV, Ivan Fecan. With just two episodes under our belt, the three most powerful people in TV had just given us the biggest vote of confidence possible.

Election night! We were going to the show! And nothing would be the same again.

———

I would say that a federal election is like the Super Bowl for political junkies, except more so, because they only happen every four or five years. The idea that we were going to be on the prime-time coverage of one was completely removed from what I thought was possible.

And it was a hell of an election. Kim Campbell started out with one of the highest approval ratings of any prime minister. And it all went down from there. Not her fault, really—she couldn't live up to the hype. Nor could she live up to her résumé, which was clearly padded. Note to any potential politicians who may be reading: do not claim to be fluent in Russian if you are not. Someone might ask you to say a few words in Russian someday. If that day comes and you simply mutter in English, "Hello, Mr. Yeltsin," things will go badly.

It's hard to pinpoint exactly what went wrong with Campbell's campaign because so many things went wrong. The death knell was when the Tories released an attack ad that seemed to be making fun of Jean Chrétien's looks, namely his partial facial paralysis. People were aghast, and when Chrétien spoke to reporters, he laid it on thick. He spoke of the deformity that God gave him, he talked of being teased on the schoolyard, he talked of overcoming adversity. He gave Meryl Streep a run for her money. *Sophie's Choice* was light entertainment in comparison to Chrétien's presser about his face.

But mostly people were bone-tired of the Conservatives. And on election night the voters, for all intents and purposes, wiped them off the face of the electoral map. The party won just two seats in the entire country. With a caucus of two they lost both official party status and any hopes for a *ménage à trois*. It was an unprecedented spanking for the Tories and a slam dunk for Chrétien's Liberals.

Throughout the night, as the results of the bloodbath flooded into election headquarters, Peter Mansbridge would say, "Let's see what the folks at *22 Minutes* are thinking." And then they would cut to our news desk. For most viewers it was the first time they had seen us or even heard of us. We delivered material from the desk, live to air, mining the night for laughs. Our adrenalin was on bust.

And when the final results were called and it became clear just how badly the night had gone for the Tories, Mansbridge went once again to Halifax for any final words from 22 *Minutes*. When the camera cut to us, Cathy, Greg and I were dancing a conga line around the news desk chanting, "Mulroney is no more, HA! Mulroney is no more, HA!" We were dancing on his grave. We were also doing what the entire country was doing, but out loud and on TV. Four million Canadians were watching.

The look on Mansbridge's face when the cameras cut back to him was hysterical. Later he would say that we summed up the mood of the nation perfectly, but in the moment, he was secretly wondering who at the CBC might lose their job.

It was a glorious way to be introduced to Canada's political junkies.

And then it was back to work. After all, we had a show to do that week, and the week after that.

In the early days of 22 *Minutes* we talked about politicians but never *to* politicians. It never crossed our minds. We were the jesters and they were the power. And never the twain shall meet.

The divide was generous both figuratively and literally. Politicians were the centre of an entirely different ecosystem. They strode around the hallowed halls of the Parliament Buildings. We were 1,400 kilometres away, jammed into a couple of old construction trailers in the CBC Halifax parking lot.

But for the most part we were kids in a candy store. From day one I was floating on air. I couldn't get to work fast enough. Every element of the show I loved. But one was causing mild consternation. Playing with real news footage and creating content from it was harder than I'd thought.

We had the best luck when we could access field tapes from a news story—the raw footage that was shot somewhere rather than the minute and a half of footage that might show up on the news.

This was not easy. Not every producer in the country was eager to part with the raw material and often such material had been erased before we came calling. Even when the footage existed, it was always (of course) shot by serious news camera operators, never by someone looking for the odd or misshapen moments at a news event. Why would they? As the show grew, Geoff would start getting calls from news producers around the country saying, "We have a piece of tape you might like"—but those days were a long way off.

So when we heard that Preston Manning was coming to Halifax soon after the election, Geoff and I decided to go and shoot our own footage. Instead of throwing to a story from the desk, I would be the fake reporter in the field. We had never done this before.

As news junkies we were eager to get a look at the guy in person. Manning was the western populist who'd founded the Reform Party. He was the man who'd dragged the Tories out behind the barn and put them out of their misery. Or at least he came very close to doing so. They were still alive, but only technically. The pulse on the Big Blue Machine was very low and they were breathing through a hose. Nobody was counting on much of a recovery. The right wing in Canada was represented by one man only—Preston Manning.

It was a spectacular turn of events. Before the previous election, the Reform Party was a fringe party with a single MP in the House of Commons. In one election they increased their seat count to fifty-two and became a major national force. The party was just three seats shy of forming the official Opposition.

Manning's problem was obvious. Fifty-one of his fifty-two seats were in the West. Easterners were very suspicious of a national leader whose message was "The West wants in." As a result, Manning was spending a lot of time post-election travelling through Ontario and eastern Canada, introducing himself to Canadians, trying to prove he was not the bogeyman.

And so it was that we found ourselves at a Reform Party of Canada meeting in Cole Harbour, Nova Scotia.

We were a three-piece fighting machine, a team who would spend a lot of time together over the next eight years. Geoff would become my road director, but that role had yet to be developed. Pete Sutherland, camera on shoulder, would be our director of photography. He remains one of the very best shooters in the country.

On that night, at the Reform event, the crowd was uniformly older. But it *was* a crowd, which was impressive. The first thing Preston did from the stage was to pass the hat to cover the room for the night "because Reformers believe in paying their own way." The crowd muttered in agreement and dug into their pockets.

It wasn't exactly a barnburner of a speech. In the early years of his career Manning was more of an anti-orator. He didn't preach the gospel of fiscal restraint so much as drone on about it in a nasal assault on the senses. Over the coming years he would morph into a much slicker politician, lowering his voice, getting contact lenses and experimenting with wearing clothes that fit. He would grow into a national figure who was confident and known to have a sense of humour. But in those early days the suspicion was that he was Attila the Hun with Coke-bottle glasses and mustard on his shirt.

After he spoke, Manning had quite a few people wanting to shake his hand. He was like a bird feeder for angry geriatrics. Geoff, Pete and I waited politely and then approached with a request. Manning agreed, and soon we were in the van heading home. We didn't know if the tape would fit into the piece, but Geoff was confident it would work.

On Friday night, when the segment played back, we could tell the live audience was into it. And not just because it was pandering to a hometown crowd; it was, after all, about Preston Manning trying to win over Nova Scotians. It was clear the audience was into the fact that I was playing a reporter in the field and was in such proximity to a national leader. It was not like I was in the frame with John F. Kennedy on his inauguration night, but I was there with that guy on the news from Alberta. The piece ended with me approaching Manning and saying, "Mr Manning, now that the election is over, will you finally appear on the show?"

Manning looked into the camera and said, "Under no circumstances will I *ever* appear on *This Hour Has 22 Minutes*."

Hard to believe, but just hearing him say the title of the show was enough to make the audience cheer. They loved that he was on the show and that he was in on the joke.

And a few nights later, when it played on national TV, a very small seismic shift occurred on Parliament Hill. We had a big audience there. The first people to find the show and watch the show were the people who worked on the Hill. The staffers, the press gallery and the MPs themselves were all watching.

And up until that moment Preston Manning had been accused of many things by many different people, but he was never, ever accused of looking cool. By appearing on 22 *Minutes*, he suddenly appeared exactly that. It must have been a strange feeling, not only for him but for everyone who knew him.

I won't say Preston Manning's appearance was the very moment that the relationship between 22 *Minutes* and politicians was consummated, but the heavy petting had clearly begun.

What evolved was what I can only describe as a mutually parasitic relationship. We wanted the politicians and they wanted us. Both parties benefited greatly when they appeared on the show. And if either party felt uncomfortable at any time, they closed their eyes and thought of the Queen. Or rather the eyeballs that were watching.

And so, any time a political figure came through Halifax, we were waiting for them.

I approached the Honourable Allan Rock, minister of justice, in the loading bay of the CBC. I declared myself a big fan and asked for an autograph. I had a book already open. He signed with a flourish. Once I closed the cover you could see the book's title: *Hashish—A Smuggler's Guide*. Good fun.

Mary went to a Conrad Black book signing. She fell to her knees and said, "Oh, Mr. Black, you have so much money, could I have some?"

Black reached into his pocket, pulled out a two-dollar bill and passed it to her.

Mary looked at it like it was soiled and said, "Just the two?"

During a royal visit Thomey did an investigative piece exploring whether or not the Duke of York had ten thousand men. He managed to get a question to Prince Andrew: "Your Highness, who do you like in the World Cup?" The prince looked confused and answered, "What an extraordinary question!" and then carried on his way.

These were all popular items, but they paled in comparison to what was about to happen. In season 3, Marg Delahunty went to Ottawa.

In the very early days of 22 *Minutes*, in fact before we had even gone to air, Geoff D'Eon had written to Prime Minister Kim Campbell, Jean Chrétien and Preston Manning and invited all of them to appear in some fashion on the show. None of them bothered to answer.

In fairness, that was before any of the people on those campaigns really knew who we were. And if they did, we were a show that was airing late at night and moving all over the schedule.

At the top of its fourth season, 22 *Minutes* was in prime time and killing it in the ratings. We opened that season with an audience of 1.4 million viewers.

This was the climate when Geoff wrote to Communications Director Peter Donolo in Prime Minister Chrétien's office and pitched an audacious idea. Marg Delahunty wanted to visit the prime minister in his office. The pitch said little else. Other than that Marg had advice for the PM and if he stood there and took it everyone would come out looking great. Donolo (after consulting, one assumes, the prime minister) said yes.

The result was nothing short of astounding.

The prime minister of Canada was seen working at his desk. There was a knock on the door and in marched, unannounced, the sauciest, most opinionated lady in television, Marg Delahunty. Marg, resplendent in golf attire, marched up to the PM, sat right on his desk, very close to him—*very* close to him—and gave him her two cents on how she thought he was doing as prime minister. The prime minister could not get a word in. And as fast as she had come in, she went.

It is safe to say that at this point we were way past heavy petting. We were in bed.

It was an incredible piece of television. No sitting prime minister had ever appeared on a comedy show before. Let alone while being lambasted by everyone's saucy aunt.

When it came to ambushing politicians, Mary set the bar impossibly high. The character of Marg was someone who could say anything and, more importantly, get away with it. And over the coming years nobody was safe. She said things to politicians that would make a longshoreman blush. And for the most part they stood there and took it. They had no choice. For them the silver lining was clear: being ambushed by Marg meant you were relevant.

Mary and I were nothing if not competitive. There was no way I could compete with her at the ambush game. So I began to cast my eyes elsewhere. Namely, south of the border.

Geoff claims—although I find this a little too clever—that the day after the piece with Mary and Chrétien aired, I went into his office and said, "Do you think you could get me in the White House? Do you think you could get me in the frame with the president?"

I wanted to go to America for a few reasons: to use Washington as a backdrop and to bring American politics into the show. I wanted to comment on American politics *in* America.

One thing I did not anticipate is that instead of all of those things, I would simply talk to the folks I encountered there.

But talk is exactly what I did. Did I ever.

17

Talking to Americans

Congratulations, Canada, on the adoption of the twenty-four-hour
    clock!
Congratulations, Canada, on getting eight hundred miles of paved
    road!

On April Fool's Day 2001, four and a half years after I'd walked
into Geoff's office and asked him if he could get me into the
White House, the CBC aired *Rick Mercer's Talking to Americans:
The Special.*

Neither Gerald nor I saw it go to air. This was unusual for us, as we
never felt any project was complete until we'd seen it on TV with
commercials.

But this time we were out of the country. We were in Jamaica, stay-
ing in a small collection of thatched-roof cottages on the cliffs of
Negril. Tensing Pen Resort was all about the view and the swimming.
Past that, the amenities were slim. There was no restaurant, just a
communal kitchen where you were expected to clean up after yourself.
There were no telephones, no televisions and no air conditioning.

Dave and Bernice, the Canadian couple who ran Tensing Pen, had become great friends over the years. Bernice was Acadian French from New Brunswick. One of the great saucy ladies I've known in my life, she had a laugh that sounded like a cement truck filled with gravel. Dave was a retired British and Canadian air force veteran. One year they had fled a Winnipeg winter for a few weeks in Jamaica, and they never left. They were wonderful hosts; their Canadian hospitality came naturally, and everyone was a repeat customer.

Because we were such great friends, I was granted an incredible favour that night. I was sitting in their little private house, at the little desk that doubled as head office. This was Bernice's sanctuary, off-limits to guests. This night she had made an exception. On the desk was the only telephone on the premises and one of the few in the area. I was expecting a call. It was to come in between six and seven. The lines were notoriously poor, and days could go by without a call coming in or going out.

Every minute past six was torturous. At 6:50 the phone rang. It was Slawko Klymkiw, the head of English-language programming at the CBC. There were no pleasantries, no greetings. As soon as he heard my voice he said, "Two point seven *million*."

This did not compute. I said, "What?"

"Two point seven million viewers."

I wrote the number 2.7 on a piece of paper, but it didn't look right. I didn't know numbers went that high. At least not when it came to ratings. I said, "What does that mean?"

He said, "It's the highest-rated comedy broadcast in the history of Canadian television."

And then the line went dead.

Later Slawko told me, "I thought you died."

I found Gerald waiting near the edge of the cliff. This was the place we watched the sun go down every evening. He was perched on a stone outcrop thirty feet above the Caribbean as if he was completely at peace with the world, one with nature.

I passed him the piece of paper with the 2.7 on it.

"Million?" he said.

"Million," I said.

He then, very calmly, said, "Those are Stanley Cup playoff numbers." He stood up and walked towards the edge. "Game five numbers." Then he leapt fully clothed off the cliff and into the ocean.

As always, I followed.

We laughed our asses off and whooped and hollered while the sun dipped below the horizon.

We were bigger than US Steel. It really didn't get much better than this. Two point seven million viewers! Not bad for a complete and total fluke.

Like Rice Krispies, *Talking to Americans* was an accident in the lab. I went to America hoping to do a lot of things for the show, but not this.

Before the camera rolled on the first segment, it had never been discussed, planned or even mused about. It happened in real time.

Everyone who works on the ground in the news business hates person-in-the-street interviews, otherwise known as streeters. They have been a staple of local news since the invention of the portable news camera. A junior reporter or an intern stands on a corner and begs civilians to comment on city hall's overnight parking ban or weigh in on the contentious issue of New Year's Eve resolutions. It's not journalism, it's filler.

In the early days of 22 *Minutes* I'd tried to find a way to turn the format into a segment. Early efforts were awful. No matter what we did, our product was no more interesting than any streeter you might see on any supper-hour news show. In fact ours were probably worse because, with the popularity of the show, people on the street knew we were a comedy show, so that made them hesitant to take part—or worse, eager to be funny.

I had no interest in the format.

On September 28, 1998, I found myself in Washington, DC, preparing to shoot the rant that would go in the premiere of season 6 of 22 *Minutes*. It was an easy day for us. We had rehearsed and blocked the rant. I had it memorized. All we had to do now was wait for the sun to start its descent and give us that beautiful magic-hour glow that the camera loves so much.

We were killing time on the East Plaza of the Capitol Building, sitting on a few benches and taking in everything that is Washington. At some point Geoff and Pete wandered away to read a plaque under a tree while I stayed back to keep an eye on the gear.

A few minutes later a well-dressed middle-aged white guy with a Capitol Hill security pass on his belt wandered up to me. He meandered to a stop next to the camera, feigning interest in the equipment. He looked down at one of the road cases. There was a faded sticker that featured the CBC logo, that respected symbol referred to by many inside the corporation as "the exploding butthole." Naturally, senior management frowns on this term, preferring instead "the multicultural pizza pie" or some such thing.

Anyway, the fellow looked at the sticker and underneath the logo were the words *Canadian Broadcasting Corporation*. He read the words out loud, rolling them over his tongue. He had a great accent. Broad and southern. He looked at me and said, "Canadian Broadcasting Corporation?"

"Yes," I answered. "The Canadian Broadcasting Corporation."

He pondered this information for a bit. Then his eyes lit up. He had an epiphany. He snapped his fingers, pointed at me with a big smile and said, "CANADA!"

This guy was no slouch when it came to connecting the dots.

I said, "Yup, we're from Canada."

"Wow," he said. "What are you doing way up here?"

Not really wanting to get into a long explanation about what it was that we did, I simply made up an answer on the spot. I said, "Oh, just doing a story about the presidential summit between Canada and the United States."

"Of course," he said. "Heard about that on the radio this morning. Great idea. I predict it will be a big success."

Now on the surface there was nothing wrong with this answer except for the fact that there was no summit. I had just made it up. I decided to push it a little and see where this would go.

"It's a big deal in Canada," I said, "But we can't figure out what to name the thing."

"Typical," he said. "That's politics for you."

I won't say that a light bulb went off in my head. I won't say that I heard a choir of angels. But it did dawn on me that this man, who might run the Pentagon for all I knew, was the kind of guy who would like nothing more than to talk at great length on subject matters he knew nothing about.

And so I uttered the words that would change my career forever. "Would you have a few minutes to answer some questions about the relationship between Canada and the US?"

"For Canadian TV?" he said. "I'd be happy to."

I hurried over to Pete and Geoff and said, "Let's do a quick interview with this guy."

They didn't know what was about to transpire but they went along with it. We were not in the business of interviewing people on the street. What could you possibly do with an interview with a random guy in Washington?

And then the Pentagon man and I were on-camera.

"The summit between the United States of America and Canada is about to begin," I pronounced. "President Bill Clinton is about to welcome President Ralph Benmergui of Canada to Washington."

Of course Ralph Benmergui was not the Canadian president at the time, he was a CBC TV and radio personality.

Behind the camera I saw Pete's eyebrow rise and a smile come to his lips. Geoff made eye contact but never broke. Every bit the professional newsman.

"The issue is," I continued, "neither country can agree on what this summit should be called. Should it be the Clinton–Benmergui Summit or the Benmergui–Clinton Summit?"

Our friend thought about it and took the diplomatic route. "I think it should be called the Benmergui Summit."

Well, he hadn't twigged to the fact that Canada doesn't have presidents so I hardly expected him to know that in the event of a summit it would be a Chrétien and not a Benmergui who would attend.

"Benmergui–Clinton?" I said "Why's that?"

"Well," he said, "it's alphabetical order."

I paused, and trying to look just a little bit confused said, "I'm sorry, it's what?"

He said, "Alphabetical order."

I began to sound out the word as if I had never heard it before. "Allpha . . . alpha . . . aphuoo? Alpha-bootya?"

He spoke very slowly. "Al-pha-be-ti-cal order."

I said, "Right. How's that work exactly?"

He began to explain it to me slowly and simply, as if talking to a child. "Well," he said, "*A* comes before *B*, *B* comes before *C*, and it goes on like that until you get to *Z*. So Benmergui begins with *B* and Clinton begins with *C*, so *B* comes before *C* so just call it the Benmergui–Clinton Summit. Alphabetical order."

"Ahhhh," I said, "alphabetical order! Cool. We don't have that in Canada."

"Well now you do!" he said. He looked into the camera and said, "Congratulations, Canada, on getting alphabetical order." He walked away pleased as punch that he was of such great assistance.

And he wasn't the only one. Over the next few hours, I interviewed many people about President Benmergui of Canada, and all of them were very pleased to hear that we had, with America's assistance, figured out how alphabetical order works.

"You won't regret it," one lady said. "It sure comes in handy."

We had perhaps a dozen of these interviews in the can when we realized we were losing the light. We switched gears and got busy with the task at hand: shooting the rant.

Geoff speculated that the interviews on the street could maybe make for a bonus piece that would run under the credits. I had my doubts. It was a season premiere, and competition for screen time would be feral. Everyone would be over-pitching, and I knew Geoff had been overshooting, not just with me but with Mary and Greg as well.

I put it out of my mind and turned to the rant. It went off without a hitch, the setting sun providing a golden glow to both myself and the statue of Ulysses S. Grant that stands guard over the famous Reflecting Pool. As a location Washington, DC never failed us.

That night we ate at one of our favourite restaurants in the capital, the Old Ebbitt Grill. Legendary newsman Henry Champ had introduced us to the place. I love this room. It is steeped in political history. It is the oldest restaurant in Washington and has been a watering hole for powerful figures since 1856. The crab cakes are delivered to your table by the ghost of Teddy Roosevelt. And when you go to the washroom, J. Edgar Hoover peeks at your bird when you pee.

It was a glorious night. Season 6 was about to begin. I was on the road with two of my favourite people. It was good to be back. We ate, we drank and we laughed, coming back time and again to that afternoon and how was it possible that so many people would accept that Canada did not have alphabetical order, or believed Canada had just finished the railroad we started building in 1805.

"What took so long?" one guy had asked.

"Well the truth is," I said, "most of the people we had working on it were Irish."

"Oh, yeah, that's a problem right there," he said.

Turns out my heretofore undiscovered superpower was the ability to look like a newsman and completely bullshit people.

The next morning we flew back to Halifax. Geoff went into the editing suite and I hit the writers' room. The next day was showtime. I still hadn't seen the bonus bit that Geoff cut together. He was in the suite with it until the last minute. He told me he'd named the segment "Talking to Americans." Sounded good to me. He created a simple graphic over an image of the Capitol and did the voice-over himself in the audio booth, trying to make his voice sound as big and bold and pretentious as possible. "TALKING TO AMERICANS."

When it was played back in the studio before our live audience, the reaction was like nothing I had ever seen. People lost their minds. Not only were the laughs fast and furious but the audience had a look of complete shock on their faces. They couldn't believe what they were seeing and hearing. Was this a trick? Was it real? These people clearly weren't actors. They were regular Americans who believed that in Canada people had no idea that *A* came before *B*. They ate it up.

When it was over there was huge applause. And as it died down someone yelled out, "Play it again!" The crowd began to clap in unison as if they were demanding an encore from a rock band. Gerald glanced at his watch and said, "Okay, let's play it again then," and it rolled again in the monitors. Second time around the reaction was the same if not bigger.

Sitting at the news desk, I caught Geoff's eyes in the wings. Simultaneously we mouthed the same thing: "HOLY FUCK!"

It was a busy week. The cast and producers departed Halifax for Toronto the next morning for the Gemini Awards. A great party of a weekend. At the Sunday night televised gala, 22 *Minutes* won the award for Best Comedy Series for the fifth year in a row. Unprecedented.

After the gala more than one CBC executive came up to me and mentioned "Talking to Americans." This was odd, I thought. The show was delivered that day to the CBC. It was hardly normal that so many so far up the food chain would have heard about the segment and sought it out.

Slawko Klymkiw came straight over to me. A giant of a man, he towered over me. "I saw the thing in America," he said. "I hope we will be seeing more of that."

Over the years I have been asked a million times about network interference. This was the only time I recall the network honchos saying anything about the show. And it's a bit of a stretch to call "I hope we will be seeing more of that" interference.

I didn't promise him anything, but privately I had my doubts that it would work a second time. There was no doubt it was funny, but I felt it was one joke and one joke only. It was just an updated version of the classic Canadian story about Americans showing up at the border with skis on the roof in August and asking directions to the closest ski hill.

Dissecting a joke is dangerous business. It's not that much different than figuring out how a frog jumps. Dissecting it might help you figure out how, but when the exercise is over there will be no more jumping because the frog is dead.

When I told Gerald that this might be a one-and-done, he was adamant.

"This is one of those moments," he said. "This doesn't happen in comedy very often. This is Bob and Doug McKenzie. If you don't do this, someone else will see it and they will start doing it. When something works this well you beat it like a rented mule."

I said, "Okay, we'll go back to Washington."

"The hell with Washington," he said. "It's 'Talking to *Americans*.' Go to the heartland—or go south."

With that I suddenly envisioned what my future might be like. Travelling on a regular basis to whatever city in America I would like to see. This was appealing.

The next night, "Talking to Americans" aired for the first time in the season opener. It had 1,319,000 viewers. An incredible number. There was much celebrating and there was a real buzz about the segment. I was getting requests from radio stations all over the country. They were playing the audio over and over again.

That night I was on the phone to my parents and my father brought up the segment. This was very strange for Dad. We spoke all the time but rarely about the show. Dad is the epitome of modesty and I have always felt he was uncomfortable with the notion of show business and certainly uncomfortable with anything coming close to fame.

"I watched the show this week," he said. "Saw that 'Talking to Americans.'"

I said, "What did you think?"

"Well," he said, "I can't believe how many people have brought it up to me. Jerry called to say it was the funniest thing he's ever seen. And the neighbours came over and asked me if you'd be doing more of them."

I said, "Dad, you have no idea. I've never had a reaction to a piece like this ever. People are mad for it."

Then Dad said, "Promise me you'll never do that again. It's in terrible taste."

So of course I spent the next few years doing just that.

As I have always maintained, my father is a saint and certainly a
better man than me.

Cameraman Pete Sutherland, road director Geoff D'Eon and me. I'm shaking hands with Governor Mike Huckabee, a man who will never be president of the United States in accordance with God's wishes.

Talking to Americans at Ivy League schools.

Myself and Prime Minister Jean Chrétien at our usual haunt, Harvey's.

Just a picture of legendary news anchor Knowlton Nash shotgunning a beer while surrounded by a galaxy of stars—and somehow me.

Sonja Smits tries her hardest not to stare at David Suzuki's bling. I can't get enough.

A name that stuck.

In Bosnia, hiding behind road director Geoff D'Eon and camera operator Patrick Doyle. When in a war zone I prefer to lead from the rear. It's safer there.

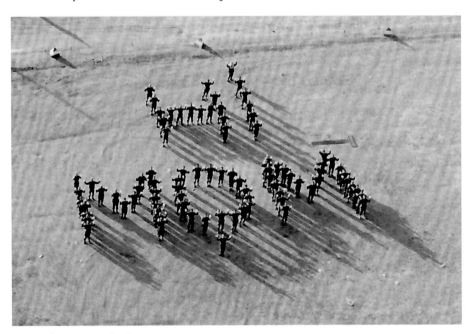

Not a dry eye in the house.

Ambition. Betrayal. Syndication. All in a day's work.

INDUSTRY

GEMINI AWARDS
Best Comedy Series
Best Ensemble Performance in a Comedy Series

Much to my chagrin, the sitcom *Made in Canada* was marketed as *The Industry* internationally (except in France, where it was known as *La Loi du Show-Biz*).

Surround yourself with the most talented, funniest actors you can find, they said. So Gerald cast Peter Keleghan, Leah Pinsent, Dan Lett (with bandaged ear) and Jackie Torrens (who's not in this picture, but seen in the poster).

Welcome to Kabul. That's a hell of a commute. When I called Tom Cochrane about taking part in *Christmas in Kabul*, he didn't ask about money or accommodations, he just said yes.

Rick Mercer charms the crowd with his Newfoundland charm during a Christmas night concert for Canadian troops at the Kandahar Airfield in the newly built Canadian gym. December 25, 2006.   *Photo by Corporal David McCord, Deployed Imagery Support Team, Kandahar Air Field*

Performing for Canadian troops in Afghanistan on Christmas Day 2006, three years after the CBC special. I love a captive audience—and there's no more captive an audience than the ones you find on a base in a war zone.

A new show and a new crew. With legendary camera operator Don Spence and *Mercer Report* road director John Marshall. We pledged to go everywhere and in all weather. And we did.

18

Prime Minister Poutine and the National Igloo

The next morning Geoff, Pete and I met at the airport bright and early. We were headed to Little Rock, Arkansas.

When we first travelled to the United States, we never considered for a second going anywhere other than Washington, DC. We were all about politics and so there was no better place to go in America. The realization that we could go anywhere in the country was a revelation. All we needed were Americans to talk to, and as luck would have it they were in ample supply in fifty states. The only question was where to start.

Geoff and I started throwing ideas around. Boston was close and convenient, as was New York. But there were so many iconic places we could visit. We both agreed that Mount Rushmore in South Dakota would make a killer location. I threw out the idea of Little Rock, Arkansas.

"Why Little Rock?" Geoff asked.

My thinking was that Bill Clinton was from there. I loved Clinton's accent and I could only imagine the folks on the street would have one far more pronounced than his. Also, I loved southern expressions. They were funny as hell and to the point. "That dog don't hunt,"

"Her wig is a little loose," "If you can't run with the big dogs, stay under the porch," "He came in here looking like ten miles of dirt road," "She's madder than a wet hen . . ." They reminded me of Newfoundlanders.

"What do they have in Little Rock?" I asked Geoff.

He said, "All I know is Bill Clinton and barbecue."

To be clear, Geoff, Pete and I were a great unit. We travelled well together, and we liked each other. We didn't mind putting in the hard work, and we were proud of that work.

But we were also connected on a deeper, more primal level. We were connected by the desire to have a great meal. We liked to eat, and we liked to eat well. That's not easy to do on the road. It takes commitment. The road is brutal food-wise. Far too many meals come from drive-through windows or gas station coolers. Food on the road is as glamorous as the early-onset diabetes it is responsible for.

Early on we decided among ourselves that if we were going to be on the road together, we would do whatever we could to avoid this classic pitfall. Breakfast could be skipped or eaten in the van. Lunch could be as fast and dirty as need be. But at the end of the day we would make every effort to avoid the tyranny of the room-service club sandwich. Room service or the restaurant in the lobby was nothing less than an admission of defeat. Life is too short.

So wherever we shot we always researched in advance where we could find that great culinary adventure. Something to look forward to at the end of the broadcast day. It didn't have to be the most expensive meal, just a great one. And there were many over the years. And when we talk about times we had together, we might talk about the shoots, we might talk about the laughs, but we always talk about the meals.

And so the truth is we settled on Little Rock, Arkansas, because that town has some of the best authentic southern barbecue in the entire USA. As Bill Clinton might say, "Ribs so good you'll wish you had two stomachs."

Now I know that Little Rock is actually a very groovy capital with a thriving cultural scene. There are two universities and funky neighbourhoods for days. The seat of government is the Capitol Building. If it looks familiar, that's because it is. It is a scaled-down replica of the Capitol in Washington. It's Washington shrunk by 30 percent.

We arrived on the last day of November. Coming from the Maritimes, the weather was a glorious nineteen degrees Celsius. The perfect day to stand around in a suit and tie and talk to strangers.

We made our way to the Capitol Building and, as advertised, it was beautiful and a perfect location for us to shoot. The place was humming with government employees and civilians.

I was eager to get going. I was worried the set-up script for my piece was a little convoluted and far-fetched. I couldn't help but think there wasn't a chance anyone would believe it. It's one thing to convince people the president of Canada is Ralph Benmergui or that drunken Irishmen took hundreds of years to build our railway, but what I had planned was a bit more of a push.

There was only one way to find out. Mic in hand, I approached a small group. "Excuse me, would you have a few minutes for Canadian television?"

They agreed. With Pete rolling, I put on a bold face and began my pitch.

"Well, thank you very much. We are here in Little Rock because—perhaps you're aware of this—your Capitol Building means so much to the people of Canada."

Turns out this was in fact something they were aware of, as there were nods all around.

"Your Capitol Building is a downscale replica of the Capitol Building in Washington, DC. And our Capitol Building in Ottawa, Canada, is a downscale replica of your Capitol Building here in Little Rock."

More nodding. I continued.

"But of course, *our* Capitol Building is made out of ice. It's an igloo. And we are very concerned about global warming and it's starting to melt, so we need to build a dome over it. Now to pay for it we're going to need to start a tourism industry. Would you ever consider visiting Canada to see our National Igloo?"

They were effusive in their endorsement of any building, made out of ice or not, that looked like theirs. They didn't commit, but they certainly said they would consider it as a vacation location.

We were off to the races.

After discussing the National Igloo with maybe a dozen folks, I became more animated. "We can't pass laws because the ice is melting and the water is dripping on the heads of the folks inside. All the paper is getting wet! We need a dome!"

Eventually I changed tack and told people I was doing a story on the fact that as of January 1, Canada was being made part of North America.

People were more than happy to welcome us to North America, although one lady wasn't convinced it was a good idea. She would have to look into it.

We were making great time and getting good content. A few more interviews and before we knew it we would be on the outskirts of town at a little hole in the wall Geoff had discovered during his research. Hard benches, sawdust floors, cold beer on tap and a brisket that was made in heaven. I couldn't wait.

Coming down the last stretch, I told a man outside the Capitol that Canada was getting a new currency, but that America didn't want us to use the word *dollar* because it was an American term, just like *pound* was a British one. I told him we'd decided that henceforth our dollar would be called a loonie. This was a bridge too far. He said loonie was a terrible name for a dollar and in fact refused to believe it was true. "Who would call any currency a loonie?"

The facts were harder to believe than the fiction.

People were thrilled to hear that I was doing advance coverage before the King of Canada made a historic tour of Arkansas on a fact-finding mission. They were more than happy to say "WELCOME TO ARKANSAS, KING LUCIEN BONHOMME OF CANADA." Silly stuff that made me laugh.

We had more than enough material and decided to head back to the front of the building to grab some more beauty shots. On our way we heard the sound that is the bane of any camera crew in the great urban outdoors: trucks backing up. The incessant beep was designed to ruin the audio during any take or conversation.

We rounded the corner and saw that in our absence a lot of activity had begun taking place. The Capitol Building was being decorated for Christmas. People were on ladders stringing lights. People were in electric lifts placing wreaths and others were busy putting what looked like the finishing touches on a nativity scene out front. By people I mean orange-jumpsuited males chained together at the ankles. Standing watch over them were a number of big-hatted dudes in mirror shades with shotguns.

I promise you will never forget the first time you clap eyes on a chain gang.

One fellow was watching the prisoners from the shade of a covered golf cart. I took it to mean that he was in charge. He motioned for us to approach. He wanted to know what we were doing and to tell us that in Arkansas the filming of prisoners chained together doing labour was prohibited due to privacy concerns.

I must admit this commitment to human rights and dignity for all was an inspiration.

That said, this man was amazing. This was central casting. This was the guy I had envisioned, the one who was going to give me the full southern special. Not for the last time in my life, I threw caution to the wind and asked the inappropriate or unlikely.

"Of course we would never show the prisoners, but perhaps you would like to answer a few questions?"

He looked at me and said, "You kin ask 'em. Doubt I'll answer 'em."

Camera rolling, we gave him the full spiel on the National Igloo. When asked if he would consider visiting, he said straight up, "Nope, I don't have any plans of ever going up that way." And then added, "And I never heard tell of no big old buildings made of ice."

I said, "Well, it's Canada!"

He snorted and said, "Yeah, that sounds about right." And then his eyes suddenly shifted right and he lifted his hand to block the lens, the international symbol for "this interview is over," and he shouted to one of his charges, "BE CAREFUL WITH THAT BABY JESUS, ROSCOE!"

Roscoe—well, I assume it was Roscoe as he was the only one with a baby in his arms—said, "Baby Jesus is safe with me" and laid the little guy in the manger as careful as, to use a metaphor, a prisoner laying baby Jesus in a manger while being watched over by a heavily armed, deeply devoted local sheriff.

Once we'd established that the Saviour was safe, and were preparing to head out, a motorcade showed up. Four Escalades and a police escort pulled up to the building. A gaggle of aides spilled from the vehicles, all deferring to and surrounding a portly man in a dark suit. At double speed they made their way indoors.

"Is that your governor?" I asked the man with the big hat.

"Yes sir," he drawled. "That's Governor Mike Huckabee."

I looked at Geoff and said, "Do you think we could put a governor in a 'Talking to Americans'?"

He said, "Do you really think you can convince a governor that our Parliament Buildings are made out of ice?"

To which I replied, "Those are fighting words." And then I raised my fist to the sky, summoning the gods of TV comedy, and said, "Bullshit powers on maximum!" Lightning flashed across the horizon. All eyes turned upwards to catch this seismic occurrence, but it was over as fast as it had begun. Dramatically I turned and walked up the limestone steps where just moments before the governor and his entourage had trod.

That may be an exaggeration. Actually, what I really said was, "Can't hurt to try," to which Geoff said, "We've got time," and the three of us, sans drama, meandered up the steps.

Those were the days. The days before 9/11 when a tourist or a camera crew could walk in the door of the frozen Parliament Buildings in Ottawa or through the doors of its larger stone lookalike in Little Rock, Arkansas.

Inside did not disappoint. A beautiful rotunda greeted us. Security guards stood by unconcerned. In the corner was an information table that was manned by a little old lady. I walked up to her and said, "We are a TV crew from Canada doing a story on our National Igloo, and we would like to see the governor."

She stared at me blankly for a solid minute as if she did not understand what it was I had said. And then right before I was about to start blathering, she said. "Of course, dear, stand over there," and pointed to an elevator bank.

The three of us headed to the bank and watched from a distance as she picked up a phone and dialed a number.

Five minutes later the elevator doors opened and out walked a young man in pointy shoes (they were everywhere). He said, "Canada, hey, welcome to Arkansas. What can I do for you?"

"Well," I said, "we would love a minute with the governor."

"Tell me about it on the way up," he said, opening the elevator and indicating we should pile inside.

On the ride up we made small talk. He asked and we explained the genesis of the show's name, that thirty minutes of television was twenty-two minutes of content. We avoided mentioning we were a comedy show. Like everyone else, he assumed we were news. We explained we were travelling the United States (true) visiting places of interest to Canada (true) and filing pieces that really spoke to the local colour one would find in the various locations (so true).

When we got out of the elevator he said, "So what would you like the governor for?"

"Oh just a quick minute. We would like him to congratulate Canada on preserving our National Igloo."

"You have a National Igloo?"

"Oh we sure do. We're very proud of it."

"Do you expect the governor to know anything about this igloo?"

"No, not necessary," I said. "It's a bit of a local story in Canada, not quite international news."

"Wait right here," he told us and went through a large swinging office door. As he walked through I glimpsed Huckabee sitting at an impressive desk. He had been talking to another young guy (red shirt) and now our guy (blue shirt) was addressing the both of them.

Blue shirt was, I assume, explaining that the camera crew outside had travelled twenty-one thousand kilometres to get his reaction to an igloo event.

This suddenly became nerve-racking. This wasn't a guy on the sidewalk who we would never see again. This was a state governor. We were easy to track down. We had a CBC logo on our equipment. The aide actually had my name, my real name, not J.B. Dickson. My thoughts drifted to the sheriffs that reported to him who were currently on the front lawn armed to the teeth.

All I could think was, "If they Google me I'm screwed." I looked at Pete and Geoff on either side of me, wondering if things went sideways would they let the three of us be chained together or would we be separated. Would I end up spending the rest of my days on a back road in Arkansas chained to Roscoe? Would I be his wife? Would we be happy? I was willing to do pretty much anything for a joke, but I didn't want to end up in a real-life version of *Cool Hand Luke* over a stupid igloo joke.

What was I talking about? It wasn't a stupid joke, it was a *good* joke. And the governor would make it better. God, I loved my job.

Minutes later the door swung open and our man was back. "He will be right out," he said. "He's just wrapping up." And he added, "He's in a good mood."

"Ah," I thought. "Perhaps he's closed some public housing."

Then the door opened and out walked the very tall (compared to me) governor of the great state of Arkansas. He sized us all up, said hello and then looked at me and said, "Tell me about your igloo."

I kept it simple. I talked about the vastness of the North and the national parks and the discovery of this igloo we believed was our earliest legislative building and how it looked just like Little Rock's building. I spoke of the pride it was bringing Canadians, and then he raised his hand to indicate he had heard enough.

I went silent. He looked at me. Or I should say he looked down at me and looked me straight in the eye and spoke. "Son," he said, "I am going to ask you one question and one question only, and I would appreciate a straight answer."

I said, "Of course."

He said, "This here igloo. This 'National' Igloo. This is not a controversial igloo, is it?"

I didn't bat an eye. "I promise you our National Igloo is far from controversial."

"Okay," he said. "Let's shoot this thing." And thirty seconds later he was saying, "Hi. I am Governor Mike Huckabee of Arkansas, wanting to say congratulations, Canada, on preserving your National Igloo." Then he gave me a smile and a handshake.

I answered, "Thank you, Governor, and thank you for appearing on *This Hour Has 22 Minutes*, Canada's most watched news program."

To which he responded, "Great!"

Soon we were walking down the front steps. None of us could believe what we had just done. In Newfoundland it's called "saucy," or in other words, "brazen."

Geoff and I looked at each other, we looked up at the rotunda, we looked at the convicts in chains and we looked at the sheriffs with guns.

I said, "What say we skip the barbecue—"

"And go straight to the airport," he said.

Pete added, "My thoughts exactly."

And that's what we did. We went straight to the airport and went up to the counter and said we needed a flight.

"Where are you flying?" the clerk said.

"Oh, anywhere," we said, "as long as it's out of the state. We'll work our way north from there."

A flight took off for Atlanta thirty minutes later. We were on it.

From the moment the first American described to me how the alphabet worked, I felt a little guilty about the entire thing. Odd, really, seeing as he was the one talking to me like I was head-injured.

For the record, the guilt had nothing to do with how easy it all was. I loved that part.

I'm a huge fan of anything easy. I will put in the hard work and the long hours necessary to get a job done, but if there is another way, if there is an easy way out, that is the option I will take time after time. When I come to a fork in the road, there is no dilly-dallying over whether or not to take the path less taken. I want a shortcut. I want a taxi.

I suppose I had a nagging feeling that "Talking to Americans" was a tad unsportsmanlike. They didn't stand a chance. It wasn't just shooting fish in a barrel; it was more throwing dynamite into a shallow pool. All I had to do was stand there with a net and scoop them up as they floated to the surface completely oblivious to what was happening to them.

And they just kept coming.

It really was a great gig. But we kept quiet about how easy it was. The fact that we could get a segment shot in half a day was the perfect crime. If the folks at head office thought it must take a full day and a half, no harm, no foul. We would get the segment and have an afternoon and evening to explore, eat, drink and be merry. Everyone was a winner.

Best. Job. Ever.

After the success we had in Little Rock we returned a few weeks later to Washington, DC. Old habits die hard. It was our favourite location. Nothing says America like Washington. Everywhere you look there's something iconic that screams "USA! USA!" The White House, the Capitol Buildings, the Lincoln Memorial and the Washington Mall. When the wind blows on a blustery day it's hard not to hear Jack Kennedy say, "Ask not what your country can do for you but what you can do for your country." And yes, look over there, it's Martin Luther King pronouncing, "I have a dream." Great big history is everywhere, from the March on Washington to the breathtaking spectacle of the AIDS Quilt.

But as wonderful as it was, we were beginning to exhaust the location. Our plan was to get two separate "Talking to Americans" segments on that trip, but after finishing one we started to rethink. There was no real way to make them look and feel different from one another. Also, if we ran two segments two weeks in a row and both were shot in Washington, the audience would figure out that we were shooting them two at a time. We wanted to create the illusion that we were shooting new material every week. It might have been easy to shoot, but we still wanted it to look hard.

So that night, while fortifying ourselves with Maryland crab cakes and American beer, we hatched a plan to fly out early the next morning to Boston and do the second segment there.

I didn't give much thought to the location other than "Boston." I figured we would just head to the historic downtown and stand on a busy corner. I imagined downtown Boston to basically be Halifax on steroids. Obviously my knowledge of Boston was limited. I knew the airport and I knew that Fenway Park was there, and that was about it.

We all wanted to see Fenway Park. As a location it was certainly iconic. And we knew that iconic architecture helped the pieces. But Fenway didn't seem right. The crowd there would be blue collar. I didn't like the idea of making fun of some regular Joes enjoying a ball game. That wouldn't be kicking up.

"What else is in Boston?" I asked Geoff.

"Harvard," he said.

Harvard was in Boston? This came as a surprise to me. I knew, by osmosis, that Harvard was in Cambridge, Massachusetts; I had always assumed Cambridge was some quaint New England college town. Turns out it's ten minutes from downtown.

Harvard would be perfect. Only the best and the brightest get to go to Harvard, and now that I knew where it was, I was going to go there too. The most prestigious Ivy League university in America. What could go wrong?

If you ever get the chance to go to Harvard, I highly recommend it. Either for a business degree or just to take in the sights. You will regret neither.

The campus appears like a walled city. And once inside its gates you feel like you have stepped through a portal into unimaginable privilege. It's stunningly manicured. Beautiful red-brick dormitories and restored heritage masterpieces are everywhere you look. Ancient ivy covers the stone walls and the lecture halls. This, I learned from reading a plaque, is where the term "Ivy League" comes from. I was barely there five minutes and already I was smarter.

It's an incredibly vibrant atmosphere. Beautiful young people with their lives ahead of them and with all the confidence in the world will do that to a place. Great optimism and privilege intersecting. America doesn't get much better than this.

We set up shop in front of one of the most famous buildings in American education: the Harvard University library. It is dead centre of the campus. And it was no doubt an incredible resource and inspiration to the eight American presidents and 161 Nobel laureates that studied there.

And on that hallowed ground we went to work, interviewing the next generation of great American business leaders, diplomats and academics.

I was very nervous.

This neck of the woods wasn't exactly far from Canada. And the likelihood of these kids having some knowledge of America's largest trading partner was high. They were, after all, at *Harvard*! One assumed they might read the occasional newspaper. We didn't know how we would proceed if suddenly we couldn't find anyone to take our bait.

If that happened, we would return with only one piece. That would be a failure. And we were allergic to that notion.

I sucked it back and approached a group of students and asked them if they had a few minutes for Canadian television.

We need not have worried.

When they heard that the Canadian government had reinstated the Saskatchewan seal hunt they were furious. Indignant! Outraged! And they had a message for the Saskatchewanians. STOP IT!

News that the crowd in Calgary (the Calgal-erin-ians) were also hunting seals didn't go over any better. "So, you're killing seals on both coasts now?" one guy said to me.

One university professor who looked freakishly similar to Wilford Brimley did suggest that tourism could save the fisherman. In fact he had long contemplated heading to the Saskatchewan ice floes to pet a baby seal. It was pending, he claimed, his wife's approval.

A professor! It had never even dawned on us that we would bag a professor. What a bonus.

Less controversial to the students was the news that Canada, Quebec in particular, had decided to allow the Irish to vote in an actual election. Most saw this as a positive move and were happy to find out that the Irish could be trusted in this way.

And numerous students appeared genuinely pleased to hear that Canada was finally opening its first university. This despite the fact that almost all of them claimed to have friends from Canada. They were very understanding that the Canadian school would for the time being only offer degrees in forestry-related subjects.

We were collecting congratulatory messages about St. Canuck University when campus security showed up and politely informed us that we needed a permit from the Harvard Film Office if we wanted to shoot on the property.

How famous is Harvard? They have a Film Office!

Thankfully we had just enough material, from thirty-plus students and three professors. We headed back to the van and skedaddled out of there.

We were pretty pumped. Nobody thought we would be able to top a US governor, myself included. And we had pivoted, and we came back with Harvard students. What a lucky accident.

Everyone on the planet wants to think that they are smarter than students at Harvard, and we let people believe it for three glorious minutes. The audience went mad.

Looking back, my only regret is that I didn't bump into Barack Obama, who must have been lurking somewhere, as he was president of the *Harvard Law Review* at that time.

Next up was South Dakota. Specifically Mount Rushmore.

Those heads could give any iconic structure a run for its money. And there is no doubt about it, it's a sight to behold.

Two million Americans make the pilgrimage to South Dakota every year. For many of them it has been a lifelong dream to stand on the observation deck, in front of the massive shrine to democracy, and say, "Wow, those are some really big heads." This is usually followed by praise for President Teddy Roosevelt's prodigious moustache and the observation that he looks like Cliff from *Cheers*.

I too was in awe of the sculpture. I too said, "Those are some big heads."

What I learned at Mount Rushmore is that Americans' love for their country is vast. The respect they hold for their national monuments runs deep. But nothing is more sacred than a buck.

Which is why the following exchanges occurred under the watchful eyes of four of America's greatest presidents.

ME: As you're probably aware, it's been widely reported that the mining rights to Mount Rushmore are actually held by a Canadian company. They say that they want to do preliminary explorations to see if there's any plutonium in the mountains. They want to do precision blasting in the off-season, but some people are saying that's not acceptable. They should be forced to drill into the heads from behind. What do you think?

WOMAN 1: I think probably from the back.

WOMAN 2: I think from the back of the mountain. Why mess up—you know, this is a national monument.

MAN 1: Choose the course which has the least impact on the environment, right? And if that involves precision blasting—which it should—I think that's probably okay.

ME: Do you think they should be forced, even though it's more expensive, to drill into the heads from behind?

WOMAN: How big would the scar be on their foreheads if they go through the front?

ME: Pretty small, I think. Well, relatively small. It would just look like they all got hit in the forehead with a rock.

What I found so surprising is not that people believed Canada had the right to mine for plutonium in the heads of the presidents, but that they were okay with that. Not a single person said, "Who sold the mining rights?" or "This is an outrage." They all agreed that if there was plutonium in there, it had to come out.

Their respect for private enterprise is so ingrained that they would allow a foreign entity to lobotomize their greatest presidents in the search for a radioactive chemical.

Drill, baby, drill! You can't stop progress.

And so we settled into a pretty set routine. When time allowed, we skedaddled south of the border and informed our good friends of more and more outrageous facts about Canada.

Every day would start the same way, with me thinking that this time I was going too far, that my premise was so out there, so outrageous, that I was going to get a punch in the head.

"They will never believe this," I would say to Geoff.

"Give it a try," he would say. And I would.

And no punch would come. The opposite, in fact. They oozed goodwill. Turns out that Americans' lack of knowledge about Canada was surpassed only by their desire to see us do well. Not only did they seem to think we were poor cousins but they were willing to believe we lacked everything that America took for granted.

And the congratulations kept coming.

Congratulations, Canada, on your first convenience store.

Congratulations, Canada, on allowing four-wheel drive.

Congratulations, Canada, on legalizing three-bedroom homes.

Congratulations, Canada, on completing the Chunnel to China.

Congratulations, Canada, on the completion of your fourteen-mile coast-to-coast trail.

And my personal favourite:

Congratulations, Canada, on legalizing insulin.

By the time we made it to our second Ivy League university, Princeton in New Jersey—then alma mater of forty Nobel laureates, two US presidents, twelve US Supreme Court justices and numerous living billionaires and foreign heads of state—petitions began to play a role in the segments.

I knew Americans were opinionated, but I wanted to know if they would put their name on a petition to back up their opinions.

Also, some critics of the show were beginning to suggest I was creating these segments entirely with the magic of editing (and, one supposes, hypnosis). It was further suggested that my unsuspecting victims had no idea what they were actually saying. I found this particularly insulting, not to me but to the people I interviewed. I mean, it was one thing to suggest they didn't know much about Canada, but to suggest they didn't actually know what the words *house, car* and *insulin* meant was a pretty tough way to defend them.

So we began to create petitions. This was a bit of a gamble. People don't just sign their names to petitions lightly, and one would think a critical mind might pause before signing a petition demanding an action be taken in a foreign country. I didn't stumble upon any critical minds at Princeton.

To illustrate that the folks knew exactly what they were signing, I would first have them read it out loud on-camera before signing with a theatrical flourish. One after another, students and faculty at Princeton looked into the camera and with great passion read: "To Mel Lastman, Mayor of Toronto, Canada, we the undersigned are strongly opposed to your plan to reinstate the Toronto polar bear slaughter."

I would then say, "Really enunciate the last part," which they did.

"We find this to be a naive and uneducated approach to what is clearly a serious environmental issue."

Pages and pages of signatures were collected.

But the most successful petition was one we pulled out at Columbia University. When the students at Columbia found out how we were treating our most vulnerable citizens, it really struck a nerve. Students lined up to appear on-camera and read out loud and sign on the bottom line. We didn't even have to move. All we had to do was say "Next!" and another person would step in front of the camera and say: "To the Right Honourable Paul Martin Jr., Prime Minister-in-waiting, Tête de Merde, Ottawa, Canada. Given that 2001 has been declared 'the year of the senior citizen' we demand that the Government of Canada discourage the Canadian tradition of placing senior citizens on northern ice floes and leaving them to perish."

Note that the demand was that the government "discourage" putting old folks on ice floes, not ban the practice outright.

And the reason I put "Tête de Merde" after Martin's name? I am at heart six years old. It probably was the only instance in "Talking to Americans" where people were in fact saying something they didn't understand. They thought it was his fancy French title. They had no idea they were saying "Paul Martin Jr., shithead, Ottawa, Canada."

Luckily we did not stumble on any French majors.

It was on our thirteenth foray into America, to Michigan, where we made our biggest splash. It was here we crossed paths with presidential candidate George W. Bush. Lucky 13!

In February 2000 it was not entirely accurate to say George W. Bush was the presidential candidate for the Republicans, but he certainly was the front-runner. Most Republicans had decided he was the best bet to take back the White House when Bill Clinton's presidency came to a close.

The only other candidate attracting attention was Arizona Senator John McCain. But McCain was polling nationally at 33 percent and Bush was at 57 percent. He was golden.

We felt a presidential primary would make an outstanding backdrop for a segment. So we headed to Michigan, to a place we had never heard of—Canton Township, just west of Detroit.

Our sources, or rather Geoff's sources in the Washington press gallery, told him that we were completely mad to entertain the notion that we would get close to a front-runner in a presidential primary. Bush was not taking questions, and there were reporters who had been travelling with him for months without having so much as exchanged pleasantries. And of course, as the front-runner he had a substantial Secret Service detail.

We took it to heart and made plans to talk only with delegates. At least we would get shots of Bush speaking at the rally.

We were on the plane to Detroit and I still hadn't decided what I would say on the off chance I got near him. If that happened, it would have to be a quick-and-dirty moment. This was more ambush than interview. I kept coming back to the fact that Bush had recently been called out for not being able to name the leaders of Chechnya, Taiwan, India or Pakistan. The notion that he was a bit dim was starting to stick.

I was trying to come up with a name for our prime minister that sounded French and sounded plausibly like "Chrétien." I was chipping a tooth. The closest I could come up with was "Jean Crouton," but I said to Geoff, "It won't work. The man was the governor of Texas. One assumes he's had a Caesar salad before, with croutons."

Geoff said, "What about Poutine?"

I thought, "That makes no sense—it sounds nothing like Chrétien. But then again, poutine is always funny." I made the call.

We landed in Detroit and drove an hour to an arena in Canton Township. The place was packed with Bush supporters. Michigan primaries are notoriously frenzied and this one didn't disappoint. I loved it. There were as many media crews as we have in all of Canada, including a huge CNN presence, CNN having just hit its stride as the leading cable news channel in the US.

We were allowed to stand on a camera platform, but it was absolutely no good to us. We spoke to some other crews and said we wanted to be in a position where we might get a question in. They looked at us like we were crazy. There would be no questions, they told us over and over again.

We did learn that Bush would enter and exit from a door behind the stage at the far right corner of the arena, and so we took up position. We were spotted by a campaign worker who checked our credentials and reminded us, "Absolutely no questions from here. Try that and you are off the tour." We assured him we understood. We didn't mention we weren't on the tour. We were in town for one night only—we had nothing to lose.

The rally began exactly on time. The Michigan governor warmed up the crowd and introduced the candidate. Bush appeared onstage to rapturous applause and made a stump speech promising tax cuts. This was the political big time. I was loving it.

No sooner had Bush wrapped up with "God Bless America" than our position got really busy with folks crowding around hoping to get a picture or a handshake from the candidate. We were suddenly the only media in a sea of hyper-Republican civilians. The same staffer pointed at us and repeatedly barked, "No questions! No questions!"

The first person to walk past, basking in the applause and whistles, was the governor of the great state of Michigan, John Engler. I waved my hands and yelled, "A question from Canada, sir!"

It was almost impossible to focus. We were being jostled and pushed.

And the Governor stopped, turned and gave me a great big smile. And why not? Michigan shares a border with Canada. We are neighbours.

I said, "Governor, Prime Minister Jean Poutine of Canada has repeatedly said that he would not endorse any candidate in the US election. But now he says George W. Bush is the man best suited to lead the free world into the twenty-first century! Is this an important endorsement?"

Engler looked pleased. So pleased it never dawned on him that a foreign leader would never insert themselves in an American election by endorsing a candidate in a primary. And I guess so pleased he temporarily forgot the name of the Canadian prime minister he had met with many times before and the fact that the prime minister was very much a Liberal.

Engler said, "I certainly think he's got *very* good judgment in making that statement about George W. Bush."

And that was it—we had our bit. Sort of. We had a governor and we had great interviews with some very excited political junkies. With the governor we had a solid double. They can't all be home runs.

The staffer was furious. He was waving to security and pointing at us. It was time for us to take our tape and get the hell out of there. And then suddenly there he was.

"Governor Bush!" I shouted "A question from Canada."

He turned, he looked bemused and drawled, "Yeah, what about it?"

I didn't miss a beat; there was no time. I expected to be grabbed by security any second. "Canadian Prime Minister Jean Poutine said that he would not endorse any candidate. But now he says that you look like the man who should lead the free world into the twenty-first century. So what do you think about that, sir? How's his endorsement?"

Bush squinted and went all statesman-like. "Well," he said, "I appreciate his strong statement. He understands I believe in free trade and he understands I want to make sure our relationship with our most important neighbour to the north of us—the Canadians— is strong and we'll work closely together."

And then he was gone. Geoff and I both said to Pete, "Did you get it?" No need to ask. Pete *always* got the shot.

And with security circling, it was time for us to go, too.

We spent the night in the hotel bar, which was filled with reporters from all over America and the world. The chatter was great. Some of them were quite taken to hear what it was we were up to. Some old correspondents told war stories from presidential campaigns past. A glorious night after a good day's work.

A few days later the Poutine item was played back to the Friday night live audience and got a delirious reaction. We seemed to have captured lightning in a bottle, and we were chuffed. That night the unit sent out a press release with a photo of Bush talking into the now famous 22 Minutes mic flag. And then it was the weekend.

On Sunday the *Toronto Star* picked up the screen grab and printed a short paragraph that George Bush would be appearing in the next "Talking to Americans."

Come Monday the phones started ringing. Interest was picking up based on the *Star* item, but as of yet no one had even seen the piece. That night the show aired, and a million people tuned in.

The following week there was no live show, so nobody was at work. Or at least that was the plan. Because on Tuesday morning the place went bananas.

Geoff called early that morning from the top of a ski hill with his kids. CBS Radio wanted me, the *Wall Street Journal* wanted me, CBS Television wanted the clip, as did CNN. Next I got a call from the newsroom in CBC Halifax to say I had fifty messages waiting for me—American news operations assumed we were with CBC News.

By Wednesday the shoot was front-page news in practically every newspaper in Canada. Front page not because of the audacity of the piece but because of the attention down south. The segment had become a legitimate US election story. Stop the presses! George Bush doesn't know who the prime minister of Canada is!

The *Washington Post*'s top columnist, Al Kamen, carried the story. We received reports that the segment had now aired on Fox News and Fox Extra—Ari Fleischer, Bush's press secretary at the time, was shown looking very stressed out, running a gauntlet of reporters and saying "No comment" to questions about the "Canada incident."

In Ottawa the Prime Minister's Office offered a short statement: "Clearly we are not in the Bush leagues."

That weekend Geoff received an email from a woman telling him that Brazil's biggest newspaper, *O Estado de São Paulo*, had carried the story on its front page, above the fold, under the headline "W. Bush Falls for Canadian Comedian's Prank."

I spent the entire week in my office doing radio interviews. There are thousands of radio stations in the USA and for a while they all wanted to talk to me. By the end of the week I barely had a voice. I looked at the pile of phone messages and thought, "That's enough."

There was no real reason to keep talking to the American press about a story that was already seventy-two hours old. It would be different if we had a show to promote in the US, but obviously we didn't. So I just stopped. I focused on the coming week and, as always, asked myself, "What's next?"

In the wake of the Bush score, what was Gerald's answer? Geoff's answer? George's answer? Michael's answer? The network's answer? Everyone agreed. *Talking to Americans: The Special.*

And then Gerald said to Michael, "Name above the title."

You would think this last request would be a no-brainer, but it was far from it. At this point it had been years since I'd uttered the name "J.B. Dickson" on the show. In fact I'd refused to say it. When "Talking to Americans" was taking off as a segment, when it was becoming the biggest thing on TV, I pushed my luck one day and introduced one of the segments by saying, "I'm Rick Mercer. This is 'Talking to Americans.'" Michael is a bit like me in that I don't get mad. He doesn't get mad. But this made him very mad. He had the piece recut and my name removed from the segment. He insisted I was J.B. Dickson.

After I saw the cut on TV, we had a heated exchange—really the only one in our years of working together. I said some things I regret and maybe he did too, I have no idea. But he won and I lost. It was his show, and as far as he was concerned, I would never appear as Rick Mercer. It was J.B. Dickson.

So when the notion of a special was floated with our company as co-producers, we had just two demands. I would be able to use my real name, and it would be above the title.

The rest is TV history.

Four years later, in 2004, President George W. Bush paid a visit to Halifax and gave a speech at Pier 21. It was very much a love letter to Canada and highlighted the historical relationship between the two countries and specifically Canada's help in the immediate aftermath of the attacks of 9/11.

He said, "I told Paul [Martin] that I really have only one regret about this visit to Canada. There's a prominent citizen who endorsed me in the 2000 election, and I wanted a chance to finally thank him for that—that endorsement. I was hoping to meet Jean Poutine."

The president got huge laughs. So in the end we both did.

19

Raising Hell on the Hill

Mary Walsh's success with the Chrétien ambush had inspired me to head south of the border. The US became a regular shooting location for me, but I did return to Parliament Hill, as did Greg Thomey.

Mary's ambushes and reign of terror continued. And thank god. Marg became a voice of reason in a sea of political bafflegab.

Initially I struggled with the question of how, in the face of her brilliant ambushes, I could carve out a niche on Parliament Hill. Again, Gerald had the obvious answer: "Just talk to them."

And it was true. While Mary was definitely making a dramatic impact on the body politic as Marg, you could not describe what she was doing as "talking to them." She was talking *at* them. She was delivering the tongue-lashing that the country wanted to give them. She was our surrogate. It was many things, all brilliant, but it was not a conversation. The politicians rarely, if ever, got a word in edgewise.

I would leave her to it. I would go another way. I would invite politicians to shoot with me and talk with me. And to a person, they agreed to appear.

I don't think it was my personality that drew them like moths to the flame. It was, if anything, our numbers. The numbers don't lie, and with our rerun we were pulling in just under two million viewers a week. Politicians leapt at the chance to appear on the show. It was a way to demonstrate to their constituents that they had a sense of humour. Also, there is nothing a politician loves more than to gaze into their own reflection in a TV camera lens.

I loved shooting in Ottawa. The shoots were beyond thrilling to me. Every minute I spent on the Hill was the real-life fulfillment of something I'd dreamed about doing for as long as I could remember.

Most men spend their entire lives never coming close to achieving their greatest secret desires. It's a fact of life. Many come to accept it. They have no choice. If a man's dream is to pitch a perfect game for the Toronto Blue Jays in the final game of the World Series or to marry Pamela Anderson circa 1991, he must, at some point, accept this will never happen. That is the cold, hard reality. Those who make peace with this may go on to lead a normal life. Others, the ones who keep waiting for the baseball club or Ms. Anderson to call, are doomed to a life unfulfilled. A life that is marked at the midway point with the purchase of ridiculously expensive sports cars and dubious hair plugs.

I dodged the bullet. I won the lottery. Walking around Parliament Hill with a cameraman and armed with a Parliamentary Press Gallery pass was everything I'd ever wanted. There was literally nothing else. I had made it to the top of the mountain.

When I was growing up, my father would always say, "Don't be in such a rush. You don't want to be like Alexander the Great. He sat down and wept when he realized that he had no more worlds to conquer."

I never understood why Dad would drop this nugget on me. I wasn't good at anything, let alone great, and world domination wasn't on my agenda. But on the rare occasion as a young man when I would zone out and daydream (which actually was a daily occurrence, often for hours at a time), I would fantasize about just this kind of thing.

It was a fantasy I learned to keep to myself. You only have to reveal that kind of thing to friends once before you realize it's something best not shared, something probably to be ashamed of.

When I was in junior high a rumour spread like wildfire that Heather Locklear, a star of the cop show *T.J. Hooker*, was going to appear in next month's *Playboy*. Upon hearing this, my good friend said, "I would give anything to look at that magazine. Seeing Heather Locklear naked would be the best thing ever."

I responded enthusiastically, "Yeah—and you know what else would be amazing? Working on Parliament Hill as a reporter or something."

The look on his face was that of a person re-evaluating a friendship.

I was never good at pulling off the small talk that adolescents have about seeing women naked. I did relate to my friend's desire to a certain extent. I too enjoyed watching *T.J. Hooker*, but it was the character of T.J. Hooker himself, as played by William Shatner in a girdle, that I found most appealing.

One of my favourite shoots on Parliament Hill was to be our last chance to play on the Hill before the 2000 federal election. Geoff cautioned me that, being so close to an election, the biggest fish might be somewhat reluctant to play. Any politician with a brain or a party whip looking over their shoulder knows that the period before a writ is dropped is the time to keep your head down and your mouth shut.

I told Geoff I wanted to go to the Hill anyway.

Who was the target, he wanted to know. At this point we had interacted with almost everyone on the Hill in one way or another. Who was left?

"Everyone," I said.

He wanted to know what I meant by "everyone."

"Everyone. All four caucuses in their entirety. All the leaders, the prime minster, cabinet members and anyone recognizable."

Geoff, bless him, simply said, "Explain." Nothing ever fazed him.

I replied with what I believed to be a brilliant idea and still do. It's one I would return to many times over the next twenty years.

But before you think I have gone completely mad with self-aggrandizement, let me be clear. The idea, while brilliant, was not remotely original.

My inspiration was *Solid Gold*, a show that's generally agreed to be a staple of empty eighties television. On it, disco artists performed live while backed up by the Solid Gold Dancers. The music was catchy, but the dancers were the stars. They played a big part in the show's success. Why? Well, it would be wrong to say they were fully clothed, but they were certainly fit and flexible. And the troupe was fully co-ed and diverse, so all the flavours were represented. There was someone for everyone.

The show was hosted by a coked-up and excitable Andy Gibb. He was famous for being the younger brother of the Bee Gees and for wearing the tightest jeans ever seen on American television. An hour before each broadcast, two members of the Teamsters stage union would put him in his pants and pull up his zipper with the aid of vise-grips.

At the end of the show, a segment often ran alongside the credits that featured civilians from all walks of life lip-synching to a number one hit. These segments tended to be fairly sloppy and appeared in many ways to be an afterthought. But I always thought the civilians lip-synching was fun, funny and, dare I say, joyful. It was my favourite part of the show. Even more than the dancers.

So, my idea was *Solid Gold* meets Parliament Hill. Members of Parliament would lip-synch—not to an American number one hit but to the Cancon rock classic, Trooper's "Raise a Little Hell." They would also, at various points, hold up signs that said "VOTE." And they would look into the camera and say "Vote!" I hoped I could persuade some of them to throw all caution to the wind and actually dance.

The pitch would be, "This is a non-partisan message from all members of Parliament to Canada." The message was simple. Vote. All members, regardless of party affiliation or ideology, would come together in a plea for all Canadians to exercise their democratic responsibility.

And the lyrics were perfect. I've always considered them the perfect rant set to music.

If you don't like
What you got
Why don't you change it
If your world is all screwed up
Rearrange it

Raise a little hell

If you don't like what you see
Why don't you fight it
If you know there's something wrong
Why don't you right it

Raise a little hell

In the end it comes down to your thinking
And there's really nobody to blame
When it feels like your ship is sinking
And you're too tired to play the game
Nobody's going to help you
You've just got to stand up alone
And dig in your heels
And see how it feels
To raise a little hell of your own

If you don't like
What you got
Why don't you change it
If your world is all screwed up
Rearrange it

Raise a little hell, raise a little hell, raise a little hell

We would have a "star" sing certain lines but get MPs, reporters, civilians and tourists to sing the chorus. We would bring cue cards and a portable stereo to the Hill and we would make a full-blown music video set to a classic Canadian song.

I was asking the impossible of Geoff, really. I wanted everyone. In fact, I needed everyone. If one leader was absent, the entire thing would not work. It had to be an all-for-one gesture. This meant we would be saying to all the caucuses, "Trust us."

The sad truth is, the various parties on Parliament Hill simply did not get along. They may have appeared amicable on occasion, but cross-party cooperation was rare. There was a nasty undertow, and we would be asking all parties to put that aside for the greater good and three minutes of network television time.

We managed to make it happen only because we didn't know how impossible a task it was likely to be.

So Geoff began to contact each caucus and the leaders' offices and outline our plan.

We were met with great suspicion. Yes, everyone liked the idea of encouraging young people to vote, but past that, they all had concerns. The Liberals thought the lyrics decidedly did not endorse the status quo—which, as the party in power, they represented.

Why would anyone think the lyric "If you don't like what you see / Why don't you fight it" was appropriate?

Why would anyone not like what they saw in the Liberal government? Why would they fight it? And suggesting that the people "right it"—was that not a tacit endorsement of the right-of-centre Alliance party?

Meanwhile, the Alliance's whip said that the party would do what they could to get their team involved but warned us that some caucus members would not say the word *hell* on TV as it was blasphemous.

I remember thinking, "If you people find Trooper blasphemous you will never form a government in this country." I assured the whip we would find an appropriate line that avoided any reference to that darkest of places where people like me go after death to receive our much-deserved eternal punishment. This was, after all, meant to

be a celebration of democracy featuring all parties. I would be nothing if not accommodating.

Geoff lined up a schedule that had us running around the Hill
non-stop from the moment we landed. For the most part people
were into it. It was as if they could see the finished product as it was
pitched to them. And as I suspected, the MPs, like the vast majority
of Canadians of a certain age, were familiar with the song and in fact
had learned the lyrics by osmosis.

But herding cabinet ministers, showing them dance steps and
arranging for the majority of a caucus to be in one room to sing
Trooper is not as easy as it sounds. We were run off our feet in so
many directions. And when we weren't having a star sing on-camera,
Pete was shooting B-reel to fill out the video.

The NDP came prepared and killed it with clever choreography.

Former prime minister Joe Clark, who was now leader of the once-
mighty PC caucus, appeared with his party of two pumping his fist
like a teenager at a heavy metal concert.

But the big three English leaders were all leaving it to the last
minute, each office wondering which other leader had already been
taped, and if they had been, what had they done? In the end we had
to gently threaten each of them. "What will it look like," we asked, "if
there is a video encouraging young people to vote and your leader
is the only one absent?"

It worked. Newly minted Alliance leader Stockwell Day appeared
and surprised us all by lip-synching like a theatre kid with a hair-
brush belting out Streisand tunes in his bedroom.

And Jean Chrétien, who sometimes has very weird instincts,
appeared coming from his office down the hall towards the camera,
holding a red file folder in front of his face. And then out he popped,
as if it were a game of peek-a-boo and said in neither official language, "*Vote!*" It was classic Chrétien. You never knew if he was
going to say hello, tell you to vote or punch you in the face.

And with that we had all our leaders.

The final product was every bit as joyful as the *Solid Gold* credit
sequences. Pete's shooting was impeccable. Al MacLean's editing was

masterful. Also Pete had somehow managed to get some incredible B-reel, including my favourite shot, a bunch of kids, Hasidic Jews, waving and clapping to the song in the Centre Block. What a country.

And it really was something to see all parties, all leaders, united. Unprecedented. Plus it was funny and had a great message.

And it went everywhere. MuchMusic, the country's premier music channel, at the time watched by millions of young people every day, put the video in heavy rotation. This was also unheard of. But hey, if all the leaders could appear in the same video, the CBC could let MuchMusic play their content on a rival network. The video also appeared on so many newscasts in Canada that we lost track.

It was one great big feel-good moment in a world where there is little co-operation or agreement. I liked it. I liked it a lot. I would have liked to see more of that on the show but I knew it was not in the cards.

We didn't design 22 *Minutes* to be an exercise in positivity, far from it, and the adage is, if it ain't broke don't fix it.

I decided to put the notion on the back burner for a future endeavour.

20

The Power Lunch

Everyone has different criteria for defining a "great Canadian," but I am certain I have met my fair share. I have pinched myself so many times I could be the cover boy for *Self-Harm Digest*.

"How did I get in this room?" has been a constant refrain for most of my life. I've met every member of Rush, every member of The Tragically Hip. I've met Martin Short, Dan Aykroyd, Eugene Levy and Buffy Sainte-Marie. That's royalty in my eyes. Great Canadians all.

And then there are the prime ministers.

I know that for many Canadians, chewing the fat with a sitting prime minister is not quite as exciting as spending time with a member of Rush, but for a political nerd like me it's pretty awesome.

I have never ambushed a prime minister, but I have spent time with, talked to, interviewed and gotten to know in my own little way every prime minister of modern times.

Jean Chrétien was my first. Go big or go home. I won't go so far as to say that Chrétien and I dated but we certainly did go on a date. At least by the Webster's definition of the word. And by that I mean I called him up and asked him to an intimate lunch at Harvey's and he accepted. Full disclosure: I picked up the tab, he drove me home.

I had known for a long time that Jean Chrétien's favourite fast-food joint was Harvey's. In fact, this ostensibly irrelevant fact had been whispered to me quite a few times over the years by Liberal staffers. They imparted this news with such a level of importance you would swear they were Deep Throat giving state secrets to Woodward and Bernstein.

One of the odd things about Parliament Hill and the idealistic young men and women who fill the roles of staff to prime ministers, ministers and members of Parliament is that those staffers collect and trade in mundane facts about MPs in much the same way adolescents memorize facts about boy or girl bands.

Over drinks at the Château Laurier a staffer will say to you, "I would never tell anyone I know this but between you and me the minister of natural resources will only drink water at room temperature, is sleeping with someone in the constituency office and is taking French lessons on the down-low."

And so this is how I came to hear that Chrétien likes Harvey's. It's also how I came to hear that his lovely wife, Aline, had found out he was hitting the Harvey's drive-through just a little too often after work and she'd put a stop to it because of his cholesterol.

Normally such arcane knowledge about a man's eating habits would be entirely useless. But before heading to Ottawa for one of our field shoots, this little nugget continued to resonate.

My idea was that Ottawa was the land of the power lunch. Who was seen eating with who was very important. And at the time, Ottawa was not so much obsessed with the current leadership as with who the next leader of the Liberal Party would be. The footsteps behind Chrétien put *Riverdance* to shame. The Paul Martin people (who were cultlike in their slavish devotion) wanted Chrétien gone. Yesterday.

My gag was, I would go to Ottawa for a power lunch, the pickings would be so slim that the only person available for a bite to eat would be Prime Minister Jean Chrétien. But would Chrétien want to be seen as a bad lunch date? For a prime minster, it's a bit of a stretch.

I asked Geoff to put in the request that Chrétien meet me for lunch at Harvey's.

Right out of the gate this proposal had some problems. First and foremost, the entire idea. It's one thing to request five or ten minutes of a prime minister's time in his office or in the hallway of the Centre Block. It's quite a different ask to request, at very short notice, a substantial sit-down chat. Also, prime ministers are used to people coming to them. Captains of industry, premiers, powerbrokers and journalists go out of their way to meet PMs on their terms, not the other way around. Ever.

I wanted him to meet me at Harvey's. Him come to me.

Also, the day we were scheduled to be in Ottawa happened to be budget day. One might assume that the prime minister is going to be busy on that day. It is the most important day in the parliamentary calendar. If the budget fails to pass, the government may well fall. It's a big deal.

I told Geoff I nevertheless had a good feeling about this. After all, I'd heard the man likes Harvey's.

Geoff pitched the PM's office. Initially they were incredulous. They seemed to think we had taken leave of our senses altogether. But Geoff just kept saying, "See what the big guy says."

Eventually it *was* pitched to the big guy and—surprise!—he said yes. He would power-lunch with me at Harvey's on budget day.

So we flew to Ottawa. It was all top secret and cloak-and-dagger. There was even a code word for the shoot. Wherever the PM goes must be cleared well in advance with security. Normally everyone who will be at a location the PM is going to spend time at would need security clearances. It's a giant pain.

But there is an exception. If it is a surprise, then there is actually very little need for layers of security. The idea is that if nobody knows the PM is coming, then it's inherently safe. So we were trusted to tell nobody. And we did not. Operation Cheeseburger was a go.

And that is how Geoff, Pete and I found ourselves standing on the side of the road on a nondescript industrial strip lined with car dealerships, fast-food joints and box stores waiting for the prime minister of Canada.

It was one of the more surreal moments of my career. So much so I was seriously entertaining the notion that the entire thing was a practical joke. I was giving it 50/50 that the PM would never actually appear.

And then we heard sirens. And out of nowhere there appeared a motorcade of black SUVs escorted by RCMP cruisers and motorcycles.

Pete reports that this moment blew his mind more than anything he'd witnessed in all his years on 22 *Minutes*. It was epic. Three schmucks on the side of the road with a little comedy show had summoned the most powerful man in Canada.

The motorcade blasted into the parking lot. The car was barely at a stop before the man himself popped out, shook hands with all three of us and said, "Let's eat." Before I could get a mic on the man, he was inside the Harvey's, shaking hands and flirting with the kitchen staff. To watch him work the room was astounding. He said hello to a gobsmacked family of four who couldn't believe what was happening. He shook all their hands too and then, without missing a beat, took an onion ring from the twelve-year old's plate and popped it in his mouth. The little guy from Shawinigan was on fire.

Eventually we managed to pry him away from potential voters and began to shoot our piece.

At the counter we ordered burgers, fries and onion rings. Chrétien, who had just overcome a scandal involving protesters in BC pepper-sprayed by police, said he wanted pepper on his fries.

I quipped to the server, "Do you have that in a spray?"

And then we moved to our table for the interview. But before we started, out of nowhere the prime minister's official photographer appeared and began to bang off shots at a million clicks a minute. "Eat the burger!" Chrétien snapped, and so I did, both of us taking big bites for the camera. And then the photographer said, "I got it," and he ran. I saw him jump in a Honda Civic in the parking lot and tear out of the place.

With that bit of unexpected business out of the way we settled down for a chat over burgers and fries. We talked about current events and, looking for any hints or insights, I teased him about the chances of his resigning. And then I asked a probing question about his life in politics. Chrétien had been minister of almost everything at some point in his career, and I knew he was proud of this. I also had a sneaking suspicion he could list his job titles in order. He could. And he did so in a hysterically monotonous way. It was a masterful monologue. And while he spoke, I finished a milkshake, making noises a nine-year-old would be shushed for. Noises a nine-year-old would find hysterical.

I won't lie, it was like doing a sketch with a master. It wasn't like shooting a segment with a prime minister at all. It was like shooting with Eugene Levy.

Jean Chrétien's timing is impeccable. And he understands what it means to be self-deprecating. Most politicians understand they *should* be self-deprecating, but very few have the confidence to pull it off.

At the end of the interview I thanked him and said I had been looking forward to this meeting ever since I'd read his memoir in junior high.

"You read it?" he asked.

"I did," I said.

"Did you like it?" he asked.

"I did," I said. "Good book . . . *Straight from the Heart.*"

"Next time," he said, poking me in the chest, "it will be straight *through* the heart." Zing.

It was comedy gold. Pure funny.

Outdoors we were saying goodbye when I decided to make a bold request. "Hey, these guys need to pack up. Do you mind giving me a run downtown? I can get out on Parliament Hill."

He paused for a second and then said, "Sure. I don't mind hitch-hikers."

I was bumming a ride with the PM. How cool is that.

He opened the door for me and I crawled inside. When we were in the back of the car together, I unplugged my microphone from the pack so he could see it was disabled. In fact it was clearly not even connected to a power source. I laid it on the armrest that separated us. Chrétien placed that small microphone, one that would normally be on my lapel, in the palm of his hand and closed it. It remained there the entire ride. No flies on that fella.

On the ride home he quizzed me about my upbringing. He wanted to know if my parents thought the Liberals were doing a good job. What, he wanted to know, did my parents think of Brian Tobin, Newfoundland's senior cabinet minister? He wanted to know a lot of things, actually.

There is an adage that sincerity is the most important attribute a politician can have and if you can fake that, you have it made. Chrétien, whether sincere or not, certainly appeared to be so. He had the ability to make anyone feel that their opinion counted and that he genuinely wanted to know what you thought.

He also had an incredible knack of coming across as one of the lads, the little guy from Shawinigan. He might have hobnobbed with the Queen, but the new Canadians behind the counter at Harvey's felt completely at home with him.

Later, when we were sitting around decompressing, Geoff asked me why I was so confident that Chrétien would go for this shoot in the first place.

I said I knew Chrétien liked Harvey's, but I also happened to know that his wife had told him to stop eating there. He was cut off. So my take was, he would jump at the chance to eat at Harvey's with us because when his wife found out he could say, "What choice did I have? It was work." He might be the prime minister but he was still a guy and that's the way guys think. They are all, to a certain extent, afraid of the wife.

I thought I was a genius.

Turns out, not so much.

It was, as I said, budget day. And not just any budget day but a very important budget day. Paul Martin's budget that year showed that the deficit had essentially been slain. Martin of course was the assumed heir to the Liberal Party and it was he who would get the credit for this very good news. Reports were that the relationship between these two political heavyweights was chilly.

The day after budget day in Canada you can be assured of one thing. No matter what the reaction to the budget, you can be certain that the front page of every newspaper in Canada will carry a picture of the finance minister standing in the House of Commons delivering the budget. It is his news day.

The next morning, we prepared to head back to Halifax. We soon found out that the pictures the prime minister's photographer had taken the previous afternoon had been sent out on the press wire at exactly the same time that Martin was making his budget speech.

As a result, the day after budget day? Yes, half the newspapers in Canada had a picture of Martin in the House of Commons, but the other half ran with a funny picture of me and Chrétien shoving burgers in our mouths at Harvey's.

That's how much they disliked each other.

So, despite my confidence in my own genius, lunch with Chrétien was nothing to do with me, the show or Aline or Harvey's. It was all about reminding Paul Martin who was boss. And who could get the headlines no matter when or where.

Nobody knew the dark arts of politics better than Chrétien.

And that kid whose onion ring he stole? Will no doubt vote Liberal for life.

21

Everyone Showed Up

This was such a busy time for me, and for everyone. Not only was I often flying to an American city every week and doing the full show in Halifax, but sketches had to be written and performed, as did rants. Week in and week out.

Everyone was on their A game. We were killing it in the ratings, and we were killing it every year come awards season.

Greg Thomey and I had a handful of duos that were popular with viewers. We played two pundits on a segment called "The Right Answer." I came up with increasingly outrageous right-wing comments on random subjects. I loved the segment. It allowed us to be wildly politically incorrect at a time when being so wasn't really an issue. If anything, I felt bad that we were presenting Conservatives as unbelievable caricatures with ridiculously intolerant views. (As it turned out, everything out of our mouths would seem mild in comparison to the Twitter feed of the man elected president of the United States in 2016.)

We loved playing hockey coaches in a segment called "Hockey Notebook," many of which were shot on frozen lakes that gave us the greatest, most Canadian-looking settings ever seen in Canadian sketch-comedy television.

I loved working with Greg. He was eccentric but he was pure. I've had the privilege of working with many different writers and performers in my life. Many of them, luckily for me, have been brilliant. But Greg is a genius. He is also a complicated, conflicted man. I love him dearly.

One night, in a hotel room, while making me and everyone around me laugh harder than we ever had before, Greg stopped, looked at me and said, "Heavy is the head that wears the lampshade."

I said, "Oh my god, Greg, that's the best title ever. That should be the name of your book or your one-man show."

He said, "You can use it."

I have been tempted over the years, believe me. But I await his memoir of that title.

In addition to a gruelling travel and shooting schedule, the cast of *22 Minutes* all began to freelance on the side. Together we hosted the 1995 Juno Awards in Hamilton, Ontario, the first time the music awards moved from a theatre to a stadium. When the cast of *22 Minutes* was announced, 8,500 people stood and screamed. You do not forget moments like that.

Likewise, *22 Minutes* hosted a gala at the Just For Laughs Festival in Montreal.

It was a great time.

But we were never a foursome per se, and we continued to work independently of one another. And for the next decade I busied myself with being the go-to show host in the entertainment world. I hosted the Juno Awards solo. I returned multiple times to host Just for Laughs Festival galas—on one occasion I was delivered to the stage of Montreal's St Denis theatre while riding on top of the Canadarm. The Gemini Awards, which celebrated excellence or at least competence in Canadian television, was a regular gig. And I went to Banff, Alberta to host the International Rocky Awards, my co-host being the beautiful but yet-to-be-Governor General Michaëlle Jean.

And what a thrill it was to walk out on stage on Parliament Hill, in the shadow of the Peace Tower, on July 1, 1996 and wish the 20,000

Canadians on the lawn and millions more watching from home, a happy birthday on Live TV.

I remember coming off the stage after the opening monologue completely exhilarated. Gerald was standing there with George Anthony, who was the CBC man in charge of the entire event. I went up to them and said, "Oh my god, there's some kids out there with a giant banner that says 'RICK FOR PM.' Can you believe it?"

Gerald and George said in unison, "We put that there."

Ah, show business. All smoke, all mirrors. I love it.

I really loved hosting shows. It was something I felt very comfortable doing. And it was always a pinch-me experience. It was also the only time any of us would come across other people in show business. On paper we were all colleagues, but I rarely crossed paths with other people working in the business, except at these events. For the Gemini Awards in 1999, I had an idea that we would create a cold opener featuring me walking through a "Gemini lounge," a private club where only previous winners could hang out.

Geoff and I invited as many people as we could think of. The pitch, basically, was "Come to this address early on Saturday morning to appear in a sketch with Rick for the opening of the awards show the next night." We really had no idea who would say yes. To do so meant putting on fancy clothes and travelling downtown. Who wants to do that on a Saturday morning? I felt like a grade six kid wondering if anyone would show up to my birthday party.

Who showed up? Every single one of them: Gordon Pinsent, Al Waxman, Sonja Smits, Maury Chaykin, David Suzuki, Mr. Dressup, Frank Shuster, Knowlton Nash, Wendy Mesley, the Royal Canadian Air Farce, Dini Petty, Evan Solomon, Peter Mansbridge, Lloyd Robertson, Pam Wallin, Steve Smith a.k.a. Red Green, Jonathan Torrens, Mike Bullard, Patrick McKenna and Dudley the Dragon. They just kept coming through the door.

And they began to hang out and enjoy the complimentary awful coffee we had arranged. If they were used to something fancier, not one of them let on. Collectively the egos in that room were no different than you might find on any given day at any Robin's Donuts in the Thunder Bay area.

Looking at the list now, I am in awe of the number of stars that showed up. To meet Frank Shuster, half of the legendary duo Wayne and Shuster, was a dream come true. To have him in a sketch I wrote? Mind-boggling.

And try to imagine how thrilled I was to meet Knowlton Nash. He was my news anchor growing up. He anchored every major event of my life, and every election too. I pretty much worshipped the man. Now I was not only meeting him, I was saying, "Hello, Mr. Nash. I would like you to sit in this chair and put this hose in your mouth, and Wendy Mesley is going to pour a beer into a funnel attached to the hose and everyone is going to shout 'CHUG CHUG CHUG!'"

He said in that oh-so-famous voice of his, "It's a bit early in the morning, but I guess I could chug one beer." He then took the hose and got in position. "Say 'Action,'" he said. Which I did.

And when I said to David Suzuki, "Dr. Suzuki, I want you to just be hanging out having drinks at the bar, but in your underwear. We will make it look like you're just hanging out naked," he nodded, took off his pants and said, "Where do I stand?"

To be fair, the motivation for this was a very well publicized fundraiser that both myself and Suzuki had taken part in that year. Allegedly famous people like myself and bona fide famous people like Suzuki posed tastefully nude for a good cause. Suzuki's picture caused a huge sensation because for a man in his sixties he was ripped. He was all abs and pecs. He posed naked holding a model of the earth over his head and a maple leaf over his no-no bits. I took *au naturel* to the next level and posed naked in a river holding a very large salmon over my parts.

Not that long after the photos were released I happened to bump into the good doctor and in a desperate attempt to make small talk I began to ramble. "I was a bit worried," I said. "I brought a salmon to the river for the picture, then afterwards I read you were very concerned with the notion of farmed salmon and the impact they may have on native salmon in rivers. Was I being reckless, bringing that salmon into the river? It was farmed."

Without missing a beat he replied, "Your salmon was dead, right?"

I said, "Oh yes. I bought it frozen."

He said, "I think you're okay, then." If it had been on tape, I'm sure that in slow motion you would detect the most subtle of eye rolls.

I said, "Is that the stupidest question you have ever gotten?"

He said, "No, but it's close."

How's that for bragging rights? I asked David Suzuki one of the stupidest questions he's ever received. And now he was here appearing in a sketch for the opening of the awards show I was hosting.

Everyone was on board, and more importantly, everyone seemed to trust me to make something funny that didn't make them look foolish.

Gordon Pinsent was smashing plates in a fireplace. Al Waxman was playing craps. Comic legend Jayne Eastwood was kissing his dice for luck.

The segment killed on awards night. Huge laughs.

Not bad for a side hustle.

22

Enter Doris

B ack at the mother ship we kept pumping out shows week after week. We always aimed high, and we all had a great batting average.

But occasionally, a segment would have ramifications far beyond a few laughs on show night. It happened to me on a few occasions, perhaps most memorably in relation to a politician you may remember called Stockwell Day.

Day had for decades been a leading Conservative voice in Alberta. When we started the show he was serving as minister of labour in the provincial government. Alberta's premier was the somewhat flawed but wildly popular Ralph Klein, whose hold on power was absolute. Being a Conservative MLA in Alberta under Klein gave Stockwell Day the job security of a hard-working postal worker whose uncle ran the union. It was a job for life.

But for a highly ambitious politician like Day there was a downside to the lock the Conservatives had on government. No matter how well known or allegedly competent one might be, there was zero opportunity to advance beyond the cabinet table. Barring a bolt of lightning directly from heaven, King Ralph was not going anywhere.

And so in the year 2000, Day, realizing that his prayers to the lightning gods were not being answered, cast his piercing blue eyes eastward, to federal politics.

It was an opportune moment in conservative politics. Big things were happening. It seemed like conservatives were finally uniting after a decade of infighting. In January of that year, the founding convention of what would eventually become the Canadian Alliance party was held in the nation's capital. It was there that Day made his national debut, as a featured guest speaker at the opening ceremonies. It was the first time most conservatives outside of Alberta would get a close look at him.

At the time, the federal conservative movement was looking for change. Many people felt this new party needed fresh new leadership. But who? The Reform Party leader, Preston Manning, made it clear he wanted to stay. But his was not a fresh face. No conversation about Manning's political acumen occurred without the words "awkward" and "stiff" being bandied about. According to Google, the word "nasally" has appeared in the same sentence as "Preston Manning" more than four thousand times. And that's just in the *Toronto Star*.

Conservatives were desperate for something, or someone, new.

So when Stockwell Day strode onto the stage at that convention it suddenly seemed like central casting had sent over a saviour. Day—a fashion-forward dresser and an avid runner with a lean build—was the antithesis of the awkward Manning and the slovenly Klein. At first blush the convention-goers liked what they saw. Then it got better.

Instead of going directly to the microphone and saying hello, Day moved around the stage like a conquering hero, bathing in applause like Cher on yet another goodbye tour. And then he did something no politician in Canada had done before. With dramatic flair he removed his tie. That alone was enough to raise some eyebrows. Then he tied it around his forehead so he looked like Christopher Walken in *The Deer Hunter* or a pale Ralph Macchio in *The Karate Kid*. Next, he ripped off his tailored dress shirt to reveal a too-tight T-shirt on his muscular body. He then launched into a demonstration of his karate skills, throwing kicks and punches with gay abandon.

Delegates from sea to sea to sea were wowed by his flair and his pectorals.

In Canadian history the only other political actor who pulled off that kind of stunt was Pierre Trudeau. He of the pirouette behind the Queen, the handstand and the bannister slide as he exited the Château Laurier. Everyone in that conference hall despised Trudeau. But to a person they would have sacrificed a digit to have a leader with just half of his appeal.

As the karate display continued, the women cheered and the men stared slack-jawed, like boys seeing breasts for the first time. They weren't sure what they were looking at or why they felt tingly; all they knew was that they wanted more.

Eventually Day stopped the punching and kicking and moved to the lectern where he spoke eloquently about the joys of fiscal conservatism. When he switched to French, the crowd reacted as if water had been turned into wine, or better yet, Crown Royal. At the back of the hall, ignored, upright and rigid, stood Preston Manning. A single tear rolled down his cheek and he emitted a tiny nasally sob. It was his party to lose, and that was exactly what was happening.

For the rest of the weekend Day was feted as a rock star wherever he went. Prominent Conservatives declared that they were "Stockaholics."

One purpose of the convention that weekend was to name the new party. After much debate, delegates settled on the Canadian Reform Alliance Party. When it was pointed out by someone with a passing familiarity with the alphabet what the new party's acronym would be, they went back to the drawing board. It was too soon to tell if the briefly adopted CRAP would turn out to be an omen for what was now the Canadian Alliance party.

Spoiler alert—it did.

But what followed immediately was a fairy-tale rise for Day. He threw his hat in the ring for the leadership and Preston Manning didn't have a chance. In September 2000, delegates of the Alliance gave him his victory on the first ballot. The man with the high kick was about to become the face of Canadian conservatism.

And while he was at this point a star in conservative circles, he was essentially unknown to the Canadian public. That was about to change in a dramatic way. With his election to the House of Commons he immediately became leader of the Opposition and one of the most powerful men in the country.

On the morning after winning his seat in BC, the nation's press was summoned to a beautiful lakeside resort in his new riding. It was time for the people to meet the next prime minister of Canada.

Buoyed by his success at making a great first impression at the convention months earlier, Day had something up his sleeve. The assembled press no doubt assumed the new Opposition leader would turn up in a town car or perhaps a minivan and emerge decked out in either a suit and tie or a casual polo shirt and khakis ensemble.

Then a child appeared out of nowhere, pointed towards a dot on the lake's distant horizon and shouted, as if he had spotted Superman, "There he is! It's him!" And sure enough, the dot grew bigger and bigger, and eventually a Jet Ski came into view. And the rider was not some laid-back West Coast dude burning fossil fuel for fun, but Stockwell Day himself. There was a new sheriff in town.

He pulled up to the dock, effortlessly hopped off his ride and strode up to the microphone, drenched in water and wearing a wetsuit that left little to the imagination. (He leans to the right but dresses to the left.)

Nothing very memorable was said at that press conference. It was mostly a chance for Day to introduce himself to Canadians and terrify Prime Minister Jean Chrétien.

Had Day left well enough alone and walked away to a waiting car or truck, it might have been a great PR coup. Instead, when the questions were over, Day returned to the dock, mounted his gasoline steed and headed back to wherever his secret lair was located.

An interesting decision, as this particular model of Jet Ski, when accelerating, throws a torrent of water into the air from the rear.

From the perspective of the news cameras it looked as if the giant plume was cascading from the newly minted leader's backside. It was as if he was expelling the world's largest barium enema on TV.

It was a sight that would have made ten-year-old me laugh uncontrollably for a week.

Turns out it wasn't just me. The entire country laughed, not with him, but at him. So much for first impressions.

But it wasn't all bad news. Stockwell Day inherited a party that was financially sound and perfectly poised to make a major breakthrough in vote-rich Ontario. That said, winning the leadership is just the beginning. Winning over your party faithful is one thing. After that you have to win over the country. The man had a lot of work to do if he wanted to become prime minister.

First and foremost, he had to take the time and travel the country. He had to introduce himself not only to his new caucus but the grass roots party supporters. Most importantly Day had to get out there and help average, everyday Canadians forget about his penchant for water sports.

But despite the daunting work ahead of him, the Alliance felt that they were well poised to give the Liberals a serious run for their money in the coming years.

Meanwhile, at 24 Sussex Drive, Chrétien was feeling the heat, not so much from Day as from his own minister of finance, Paul Martin. Many saw Martin as heir apparent of the party and were lately running out of patience. Team Martin were very hawkish, and there were rumours of a palace coup.

Chrétien, with two more years left in his mandate and excellent poll numbers, went to the Governor General and asked her to dissolve Parliament. He claimed he needed a new mandate. What for, nobody was really sure. He needed a mandate like he needed a place to sleep at night. That he called an election with a straight face was a lesson in moxie.

It was both a blow to the head of the Martin forces and a kick in the stones for Stockwell Day. In one fell swoop, Chrétien went ninja on his enemies. It caught them all off guard, but it shouldn't have. Jean Chrétien is nothing if not a scrapper.

When he was first getting his feet wet in Quebec politics, party insiders sat young Jean down for some unsolicited advice. They told him he could have a bright future in politics and in the Liberal Party, but he had to do one thing if he was serious: he had to stop punching people in the head when he was having an argument over politics in the bar—that kind of behaviour, they said, could only get him so far.

And so, while Chrétien might have heeded the advice and stopped the literal punching, the figurative punching continued. Forcing Stockwell Day to fight a general election before he could get his bearings was a punch that came from downtown Shawinigan.

Welcome to the big leagues, Stock.

I was thrilled, of course. Elections have always been my Super Bowl. This one was completely unexpected but, from a comedic point of view, most welcome. Politicians do absurd things during elections; they wear silly hats and they pretend they can operate farm equipment, with predictably hilarious results. They get caught flat-footed and off guard when obscure candidates say insane things or get caught on video urinating in someone's mug. It's a good time for both the press gallery and the court jesters.

And yet the issue that defined the 2000 election for me was one that I stumbled upon by accident, not by watching *The National* or reading the *Globe and Mail*.

Midway through the election I happened to read an article in a months-old issue of *Alberta Report* about the founding policy convention of the Canadian Alliance. There was a passing reference to a policy on citizen-initiated referendums, saying that a petition from any politician or civilian that was signed by 3 percent of the electorate from the previous election, would trigger a legally binding referendum. The article pointed out that the policy was endorsed by Alliance leader Stockwell Day. I had never heard of such a policy, and I paid pretty close attention to these things.

Why this wasn't being talked about—why it wasn't an election issue—I had no idea. Nobody was talking about referendums at all.

The notion of citizen-initiated referendums struck me right away as dodgy. It seemed like a clever way for the Alliance party, or any party, to advance hot-button policies and sweeping legislation without needing the guts to do so publicly. I saw it for what it was, a back-door method to clear the way for that triumvirate of socially conservative obsessions: introducing the death penalty, limiting access to abortions and, of course, banning gay marriage. This was a way to feed red meat to the base but in a manner that would not require anyone to lick their fingers clean.

Already groups were agitating and circulating petitions demanding legislation on these very issues. On the surface the petitions seemed like a waste of time, an exercise in tilting at windmills, but if the citizen-initiated referendum policy became law under an Alliance government, those petitions suddenly made a lot of sense.

I struggled for days with writing a rant about the policy. The subject was convoluted and not remotely funny. But it was driving me crazy that nobody was talking about it. As I saw it, the biggest problem with the policy was that under the right circumstances any idiot could get 350,000 signatures on a petition. I decided to be that idiot. Sometimes an idiot has to stand up for what he believes in.

In the writers' room I found myself asking, "What would stop me from getting 350,000 signatures demanding that Stockwell Day change his name to something stupid?"

A writer on the show, Luciano Casimiri, said, "Can it be Doris?"

And that is why Luciano Casimiri will always be, to me, worth his weight in gold. I may have kissed him on his forehead. Stockwell Day would hate that nickname so much.

But the truth was I had no idea how to go about doing it. Believe it or not, the internet was not the obvious answer. In the year 2000, barely half of Canadians had access, and those that did were using a slow dial-up service. Online commerce was theoretical, and news sites did not really exist. Watching a video online was impossible. Graphics were awful. The internet was not yet fun. It did not rule our world. Jeff Bezos was selling books online, but just barely and out of his garage.

Like everyone, I thought the internet was very cool and filled with promise, but I had yet to see how it could improve my life even one little bit. We could write emails to each other and that was about it.

But, I wondered, could this newfangled internet be used to collect signatures? If so, it would be a game changer. If you wanted to collect 350,000 signatures on a regular petition, you would need an army of volunteers nationwide. The pencil budget alone would be prohibitive. With the internet, in theory, it would be very simple.

I called Michael Donovan at Salter Street, our show's production company, and began to explain my idea. I knew that a division of his company was working on a website where investors could listen to the annual financial reports of publicly traded companies. To me that was about as appealing as shingles. I asked Donovan if this new department, Salter Digital, could help me with an elaborate piece of satire aimed at bringing down a political party in the middle of an election.

One thing about Michael is that he's always up for causing trouble. He connected me with Sudhir Morar, Salter Digital's programmer, to see whether it was technically possible. Sudhir was all in.

And then we went to work. If I was going to launch the petition during our next broadcast, the whole thing had to be live and ready in eight days.

But first things first. We quickly realized that despite having launched a digital division, Salter Street not only lacked a website for our show but had yet to secure the domain name 22Minutes.com.

The website we hastily created looked, by today's standards, like something a six-year-old would whip up on his iPad before breakfast. It was a single page with the text of my petition, which took up a single paragraph. You signed it electronically by entering your name and email address.

That Friday night before a studio audience I stood by a TV monitor and said:

"As we all know, Canada is a land of many different types of people. However, as Canadians, I think there's one thing we can all agree on and that's this, that Stockwell Day has lots of good ideas!

"I think his best idea is his proposed referendum legislation. Basically, if any group of Canadians presents a petition with 350,000 names on it, or 3 percent of the electorate, and the Alliance forms the government, they will hold a legally binding referendum.

"Now sure, critics point out that this type of legislation will tear the country apart, that it will drive the federal government into bankruptcy, as we face referendum after referendum. . . .

"So in preparation for an Alliance majority government, we're asking our viewers to take part in an exercise in democracy. We are asking you to sign a petition that you will find at 22Minutes.com. There are one million Canadians watching right now. All we need is 350,000 signatures. If we make it, the 22 Minutes referendum will become a reality. Now the petition simply states:

"'We demand that the government of Canada force Stockwell Day to change his first name to Doris.'

"And yes, any time there's a national referendum it costs about $150 million, but I think I speak for all taxpayers when I say it's worth every penny.

"So please log on now, or tomorrow at work, especially if you work for the government, and let's help force Stockwell Day to change his name to Doris Day. Why, you may ask? Because it'll be fun. And remember, this is not only an exercise in democracy, this is an exercise in national unity.

"Making Stockwell change his name to Doris Day is something we'd all enjoy, English, French, black, white, straight, gay. Especially gay!

"And in these bitter times of national unrest isn't it time that everyone in the country could enjoy a laugh at someone else's expense?"

My excitement about the piece was tempered by a somewhat lacklustre studio audience reaction. And to be fair, I understood. The problem with the piece was that because nobody in Canada was aware of the policy in the first place, I had to explain it before I could get to the joke. Other than calling him Doris, the only joke was the gay reference. It was a good one, though. Stockwell had been accused of many things but never of being a friend of gay people. The only discussion of gay rights he was interested in was how to limit them. Under oath I may have to admit this was part of my motivation.

That night after the show, the producers all put ten bucks in a hat along with a piece of paper with their guess at how many people would sign the petition before the next show aired.

The eventual winner, the producer who predicted a number closest to the final tally, was Michael Donovan. He predicted 30,000. He may have been the closest, but it wasn't that close.

The show aired on the evening of November 13, smack dab in the middle of the federal election. Within hours we were getting reports from India that the servers were lighting up like the night sky at a Punjabi wedding. Thirty-five people *a second* were reading the petition. It was an astounding uptake for a website that was created just days earlier.

The next morning everyone was calling Stockwell Doris and journalists were finally talking about the notion of citizen-initiated referendums. All the major leaders were scrummed on the idea and the notion of 350,000 signatures. Stockwell Day stuck to his guns. He claimed it would be a difficult threshold to reach.

Meanwhile, the number of people signing the petition kept rising. The entire country was keeping tabs on the site to see if I would hit the magic number. It was great fun. We were all the talk over watercoolers nationwide.

Within three days we hit the magic number, proving that the policy, or at least the number of required signatures, was ill conceived and maybe even reckless. Stockwell Day could have done karate moves on Bay Street from dawn to dusk and still he'd have had to answer questions about potential referendums on the death penalty and abortion, as well as questions about whether he'd changed his name yet.

We had become a bona fide campaign story.

The next week on the show I declared victory and pulled the plug at a staggering 1,043,925 signatures.

We were crowned the fastest-growing website in Canadian history.

In an effort to appear in on the joke, Stockwell dumped the policy and changed his campaign theme song to "Que Sera, Sera," Doris Day's biggest hit.

It didn't work.

A few months later on New Year's Eve, Gerald and I were at a friend's house in the Battery in St. John's enjoying the view. The harbour lights were gleaming and the fire was in the stove. We were listening to a "year in review" panel discussion on CBC Radio that featured a prominent Canadian pollster. He explained the Alliance's failure to break through by saying, "Blame Doris Day." He said that in seventy-two hours the petition had blown a hole in the soft support the Alliance had in Ontario. Support for the party had started growing from the moment the election was called, but stopped cold and began to dissipate within hours of the petition's launch. It may have cost them the election.

That, I decided, certainly called for some bubbles.

23

Bosnia

S how business is all about highs and lows. The hits are glorious and the misses are a punch to the gut. And there is no such thing as a failure in the privacy of your own home. By definition, there is always an audience.

And when something does hit, there is no time to savour it. Your immediate thought is, "How do we top this?" The dreaded "What's next?"

In business they say, "Success has many fathers, but failure is an orphan." In show business it's more a case of "Success has many fathers and failure is the sole responsibility of the nitwit in front of the camera." While I have always gotten credit for team efforts, I have always taken the blame for a collective swing and miss.

Whenever we knocked something out of the park, I had the nagging feeling that I had pulled a fast one, that I just got away with something. I never thought, "Damn, I'm good." I thought, "Damn, I'm lucky." Cameraman Pete was good. Producer Geoff was good. Me? I was lucky.

The amount of excitement generated by the Doris Day petition was unprecedented. Nobody saw it coming. And everyone, the network and Salter Street, wanted to know what I was going to do next. We had discovered the internet! Now what?

I had no idea. Another petition seemed bound to be a let down. What would I do? Ask people to change Joe Clark's first name to Petula?

I received a call from a company that wanted to use the momentum of the Doris Day petition to create a web platform devoted solely to petitions. People could post petitions on any subject they wanted. The Doris Day story would be the hook. They claimed deep pockets and partners in California.

I thought it was a terrible idea. Doris Day was a one-off, it captured the imagination of the country, but no way did that mean people would log on week after week to sign petitions. And even if they did, who would pay attention to them? Wasn't the biggest takeaway from the entire exercise that online petitions were absurd?

Eventually someone did follow through with that terrible idea. Change.org is now the go-to website for petitions from all over the world. You can sign a petition to free a political prisoner or to ban leaf blowers in your neighbourhood. If you think Boris Johnson should fornicate with a bike pump, Change.org will let you know how many people around the world agree with you. (Turns out it's in the tens of thousands.) They have 440 million users, and I dare say those users made a few people rich.

So here I was post-Doris. The last few weeks of the federal election were ahead of us but there was a problem. The next week's show was pre-empted, and the week after that we were to deliver a one-hour special. Unfortunately, that special would air a few days after the election. That meant it was pointless for us to cover any election events. Any material gathered on the campaign trail would be redundant.

Secretly I didn't mind. I was tired, and the last thing I wanted to do was get on a plane and go fishing for laughs at an NDP rally. Finding whimsy in a sea of sadness.

For the hour-long special Marg, Princess Warrior, had a great plan to go to Toronto and ambush Premier Mike Harris. He would be a big get. I knew Walsh would be successful. Closed doors and hostile staffers would not and could not stop the Princess Warrior from getting to the premier. Lately the Ontario Provincial Police, under the leadership of Julian Fantino, had started acting like a jackboot adjunct of Mike Harris's Common Sense Revolution, but I was pretty sure they were no match for Marg.

Greg Thomey was heading off to New York for the International Emmy Awards. That would be good fun, and more than likely he would have access to a host of movie and TV stars who would have no idea he wasn't an entertainment reporter. That sounded like a solid hit.

Me? I had nothing special up my sleeve and I didn't care. Let Geoff go to New York and Toronto. I would pull a Cathy and hang it down in Halifax.

But the website was still there, and the question was still there. What to do with it?

Salter Street was salivating over the fact that people were still visiting the site after the petition was gone. They wanted more "content."

I asked if we could post video there. The answer was yes but it would take the people at home a long time to download them, making moving pictures impractical. The entire country was on dial-up. Text and simple graphics were all that really worked. So far the only people who were actually making the internet hum were American evangelicals and Romanian pornographers. No doubt they had each other on speed dial.

I asked if we could have a caption contest. Yes, this was doable. I was told that people could post their answers on a "message board." I had never heard of a message board, but clearly it was a place to post messages.

I thought about who I would like to send a message to. Would it be the prime minister? Not particularly. Did I want to send a birthday message to someone? Nobody I could think of. And never mind me—was there anyone the entire country might want to send a message to? Who does everyone like? What could a plumber in Surrey, an engineer in Etobicoke and a lesbian in Lethbridge agree on? Not much.

It dawned on me that the technology was limited but certainly would have come in handy during the Second World War, when half the men in North America were overseas and simple correspondence with loved ones at home would take many months. But of course, we were not at war. That was a good thing. I wouldn't wish a bad government on Canada in order to get good material and I certainly wouldn't want us to go to war so I could nail a tidy three-minute segment.

But I kept coming back to the notion that folks in Canada could use the technology to send messages to troops overseas. And the one-hour special, airing December 5, was theoretically close enough to Christmas to expand on the holiday theme.

I wandered into Geoff's office. He was getting ready to fly to New York. "Do we have troops or peacekeepers overseas?" I asked him. Me, the Canadian news junkie, who allegedly had great insight into all things current in Canadian affairs, simply didn't know. I assumed there was a smattering of soldiers around the world and of course we had bases overseas, but I really wasn't sure if they were deployed in any great numbers.

"I think we always have peacekeepers somewhere," he said.

"Are there a lot of them?" I asked.

"I don't know," he said. "I should, though." And then, "Do you want me to find a guy?"

"Yes, please." Geoff could always find a guy.

In jig time Geoff called with the name of a lieutenant commander in the navy by the name of Jeff Agnew. Without hesitation I dialed the number. I say without hesitation because I know now one should hesitate in these situations. One should hesitate and say, "Why am I calling this guy? What am I going to ask him? Do I have even the remotest clue of what the hell I am talking about?" Also helpful is to ask oneself, "Am I going to sound like an idiot?" But unencumbered by facts or fear of humiliation, I placed a call to the navy.

Luckily Lieutenant Commander Agnew had the patience of Job. Either that or a lot of experience dealing with moronic civilians.

"Jeff," I said, "do we have peacekeepers overseas?"

I assume he took the pause to close his eyes and take a deep breath. "Yes, Rick," he said. "We have about 2,500 soldiers stationed in various theatres overseas."

"Good Lord," I said. "I had no idea."

"It's not exactly a secret," he said. Zing.

"Are any of them in harm's way?" I asked.

"Well, it depends," he said. "If you call being shot at or blown up 'in harm's way,' then I would say yes, affirmative, many of them are in harm's way."

"Where are they?" I asked.

"We have a sizable presence in Bosnia," he answered.

Of course. That made sense. I was certainly aware that a massive, ugly ethnically inspired civil war had gone on there a few years ago but I hadn't heard much about it lately.

It was about now that I realized I was sounding like an ill-prepared grade six student who hadn't done his homework. Something I had for the most part put behind me.

Not only was I asking stupid questions, but I was asking them to a man who wore the uniform of the Canadian Armed Forces. And not just any uniform but that of a lieutenant commander. I had no idea what the rank meant. I knew what a private was and I knew that a general was big, but everything in between was a mystery. I made a note to look that up.

I cringe thinking of that conversation now. There is no excuse for being unprepared.

I was deeply ashamed and suddenly inspired: 2,500 peacekeepers! I explained to Jeff that I was calling because I wanted to set up a portal on our webpage that would allow viewers to send Christmas messages to the soldiers.

Jeff loved the idea. In fact, he was surprised that I was suggesting it. He was the guy the media were supposed to call with questions about Bosnia and, he said, his phone rarely rang. He was sure the Forces would be grateful for the Christmas messages.

The word *grateful* struck me as wrong. When it came to civilians and soldiers, wasn't the gratitude supposed to go the other way around?

Out of curiosity I said, "How long does it take to get to Bosnia, anyway?"

I had already moved to a far wall on which hung a map of the world. My eyes were madly scanning the area on the globe that I suspected the former Yugoslavia to be.

Jeff said, "Wait—you want to *go* to Bosnia?"

Despite having not found the country on the map yet, I answered, "Absolutely." And I meant it. Suddenly I wasn't so bone-tired anymore. I found my second wind and located Sarajevo. "Wow," I thought. "That's far."

Five minutes later I was back in road director Geoff's office. "Do you want to go to Bosnia?"

He tells me my eyes were the size of dinner plates. I suggest that his were the same when he said, "Absolutely!"

And then he was gone. Off to the International Emmys with Greg. "I'm back tomorrow night," he said. "We'll figure it out then."

One of the great joys of 22 *Minutes* was the pace. With Geoff running the road team, we really did move like a news unit. We tried to plan as much as possible in advance, but more often than not there were sudden events to respond to and you could decide on a Monday morning you wanted to be shooting in Ottawa that night.

But Bosnia? This would be a little more complicated than packing a suit bag and hopping on a short-haul flight. Luckily, we suddenly had assistance in the form of seventy thousand soldiers, sailors and airmen and women in the Canadian Forces. The Canadian military is a big outfit, and of course being the military, the layers of the layers have layers. That said, when they decide to "deploy"—look out.

When our idea reached the top of the food chain and was given a green light, it took on a life of its own very quickly. Suddenly we had military logistics experts at our disposal, and they were amazing. And because we really didn't know what this piece was going to look like when it was finished, we didn't know exactly what to ask for. Despite our vagueness, though, the answer from the Forces was always yes.

Geoff liked the idea of finding some people with family members serving in Bosnia and offering them the chance to tape messages we could show to the soldiers on the ground.

I started thinking about hand-delivering either a Christmas present or a card to a soldier from their family. Then it dawned on me: "Should *we* bring something?" What does one get a soldier who is spending Christmas keeping two warring factions from killing each other? Chocolates? A nice tie or a sharp scarf?

I called the headquarters of Clearwater Seafoods in Nova Scotia and asked for John Risley's office. I had never met or spoken with the man before, but I knew that Risley was the founder of the company. I reached a gatekeeper, told him who I was and that I was calling from *This Hour Has 22 Minutes* and said I would be grateful for a minute of Mr. Risley's time. The guy put me on hold for a few minutes, came back and said he was putting me through.

Not for the last time was I taken aback and wowed at how quickly the name of the show opened doors. Access means everything in my racket, and with all our success, we had it.

It was a pretty short chat with John Risley. I told him we were headed to Bosnia to do a shoot with the Canadian soldiers stationed there. The theme was Christmas, I explained, and I would like to bring them a present from Canada. I thought it would be brilliant, I said, if I brought them some lobsters.

"That's not very much time," he said. "If this is for the week of the twenty-fifth, that's five weeks out."

I said, "Actually we're leaving Saturday. We're four days out."

"How many cases of lobsters do you want to take with you?"

I generally frown on answering questions with a question, but I responded with: "How many lobsters can nine hundred soldiers eat?"

He said, "That would be a lot."

I added, "Also, we don't know anything about getting lobsters to Bosnia."

He said, "I take it that's my job?"

I said, "It would mean a lot. There are a lot of Atlantic Canadians over there."

I heard him shout to someone about lobsters and Zagreb. Good sign.

I said, "I'll put you in touch with a logistics person in Ottawa. The Forces seem to be really good at this stuff."

"I should hope so," he deadpanned.

Before saying goodbye, I clarified what the ask was. "Oh, and John, we don't have any money. We can't actually buy any lobsters."

He answered, "I'll be in touch."

As soon as I hung up, Geoff called. "How many inches is the circumference of your head? It's for your helmet. And have you ever worn body armour?"

Not knowing the answer to the first question, I went to wardrobe in search of a measuring tape long enough for the job. Geoff called again. "I assume Gerald is your next of kin, right? And what's your blood type? And are you an organ donor? And if not, would you like to become one?"

This was really shaping up to be quite different from popping down to South Dakota to inform the locals that Canada had acquired the mining rights to Mount Rushmore and had plans to drill into the president's heads.

As for being an organ donor, I have been forever. When I bite it, they can have whatever bits and bobs they want. The rest of me can be shipped off to a med school. If my skeleton ends up at a house party in Wisconsin wearing Ray-Bans and smoking a wine-tipped cigarillo, I am okay with that.

"Yes," I told Geoff, "I am an organ donor."

"Okay," he said, "although they tell me it doesn't really matter because if you step on a land mine you become something they call 'pink mist.'"

I thought to myself, "This is going to be the most amazing badass shoot ever. Also, Pink Mist would be a great name for a band."

Not everyone was excited about the "amazing" shoot. Mary Walsh was preparing to go after Mike Harris and Geoff was supposed to go with her. To make matters worse, just days earlier I'd been the one who said he had no plans to go on the road. Walsh was not impressed that Geoff had chosen the Balkan Peninsula in southeastern Europe over Queen's Park in downtown Toronto. But even she could see that for Geoff it was no contest. He was at heart a newsman and he was on the phone informing the military that we would need a helicopter, and by the looks of it the conversation was going great.

The compromise was that Geoff would go to Bosnia with me and Mary would take Pete to Toronto. To replace Pete, we hired Patrick Doyle, a young cameraman from Cape Breton we had worked with in the past. He was a great shooter and a hard worker. And in those days he loved to party. First thing he said when he saw we had a stopover in Frankfurt was, "I hope they have a big duty-free area. I need to get some leather pants and some cologne." A slightly different vibe from Pete's.

On Saturday, November 25, Patrick, Geoff and I flew to Boston and then checked our luggage on a Lufthansa flight to Frankfurt. With time to kill, Geoff and I grabbed a cab and headed downtown to bask in local history, scout for a future "Talking to Americans" segment and, more importantly, find something good to eat.

We started at the Faneuil Hall market. It was here that Julius Caesar Chappelle, one of the first Black legislators in America, gave a famous speech in 1890. Because of this speech, by a former slave no less, the hall is referred to as "the Cradle of Liberty," a grand name that carries far less baggage than the actual name. Peter Faneuil, the man who built the thing, made his money in part as a slave trader. On the upside he died young of the hysterically named and terribly painful condition known as dropsy. At the time of writing, the market has yet to be rechristened Dropsy Hall.

After availing ourselves of some killer Boston chowder at Dropsy Hall we headed back to the airport for a night flight to Frankfurt. We landed in Germany at dawn. We checked our baggage onto the next flight and took the subway downtown. We wandered the quiet early-morning streets and listened to Geoff talk about how these were the people who bombed his grandparents' house during the war. Bit of a grudge there.

By noon we were back on a plane for the final leg of the journey to Zagreb, capital city of Croatia. In the arrivals hall we were met by Captain Bonnie Golbeck, our official media liaison for this whole shebang. She was accompanied by Master Corporal Kevin King, who was the official driver for the commanding officer of the Canadian Forces in Bosnia, Colonel Tim Grant. We got the big guy's driver! I was impressed. Along for the ride was a very serious, heavily armed young man named Jay.

The first thing we were told is that we must never step off the pavement. If for any reason our vehicle left the road, when it came to a stop, upside down or not, we were not to exit the vehicle—unless it was on fire. Exiting the vehicle would mean stepping off the pavement which, we were reminded, we must never do. It seemed to be the answer to any question. "How long have you been in Bosnia, Bonnie?" "Six months. Also, never step off the pavement."

I kept a diary on this trip, and will share some pages here. I hope they capture my amazement at being in such an extraordinary place, in such extraordinary circumstances.

It's a two-hour drive to Velika Kladusa in Bosnia and Herzegovina. It is from here that the Canadians keep the peace in northwest Bosnia. They are responsible for an area roughly the size of Prince Edward Island. The feeling is that the place could go up at a moment's notice.

The drive is spectacular. Our surroundings are dotted with villages and hamlets nestled along valleys and among steep forested hills. It is almost storybook. But on closer look one can't help but notice that many of the roofs of the cottages and farmhouses have been blown off and the properties are empty.

We arrive at Camp Black Bear in the late afternoon. It's not impressive. It's a ramshackle assortment of warehouses, ATCO trailers, shipping containers and outbuildings. It's one thing to produce a TV show out of old ATCO trailers, but surely our men and women in uniform deserve better.

We are told that before the war the camp was a poultry factory. It's been adapted by the military for its present use. Frankly I can't tell how it's been "adapted." The place is grim. I wouldn't wish this place on a doomed chicken, let alone Canadian soldiers.

My main concern, other than for the welfare of its inhabitants, is how this will look on TV. Slummy won't work.

In the warehouse where we first enter, the setting sun coming through the window highlights the flecks of fibre that seem to be floating down from the ceiling.

I say to a soldier, "Tell me that's not asbestos." He just shrugs and says, "Welcome to Bosnia."

People are really happy to see us. Everyone says the same thing: "Holy shit, I can't believe you actually came."

We are shown our sleeping quarters. It is evident that the three of us have been given the best available rooms. Somehow we qualified for an upgrade.

The rooms are cramped. The walls do not go all the way to the celling. There is a substantial gap between the top of the walls and the roof. Chain link fills the gap. (Security reasons?) I look forward to hearing what noises Geoff and Patrick make at night. My room reminds me of every kidnapping movie I have ever seen. I expect to see "John Paul Getty III was here" scratched in the floor.

I am so excited.

Immediately we are given a safety course. It includes a brief history of the war; a summary of the present situation and risks; and a LOT of emphasis on the danger posed by land mines, which litter the entire country. This is why we are told so often to never step off the pavement. Particularly evil are small, round mines known as "hockey pucks." People planted these mines under tufts of grass all over the country, and then winter high water from swollen rivers carried them downriver, where they were distributed on flood plains. Small, deadly and god knows where. The catchphrase we are asked to memorize is: "If you didn't drop it—don't pick it up." I am impressed by this advice. We are issued helmets and flak jackets, and told to use them, not lose them.

There is much amazement at the size of my head. I have the fattest head in the theatre.

At supper in the mess we have a decent meal of pork loin. It's amazing how happy the soldiers are to see us. As I expected, the place is crawling with Newfoundlanders.

We sit with Col. Tim Grant. This is his show. Dinner with the colonel, I assume, is like eating with the captain on a cruise ship. A big deal. We like Tim right away and are very grateful he is on board. This visit would not have happened without his say-so. He couldn't have been nicer or more co-operative. He tells us he was VERY curious as to what we had in mind. We apologize for any vagueness on our part, explaining that we really hadn't settled on a game plan until we were halfway across the Atlantic.

It was a great show of faith that they agreed to our coming with so little information, we say.

I explain my idea for shooting one of our rock videos, shades of the "Vote" one of a few weeks earlier. When something works . . .

This time *Solid Gold* meets the Canadian soldier. Maybe we would even get some of them to dance.

And then Geoff says, "One more thing."

Our idea was to get a group of soldiers standing in formation on the parade ground, and that on cue they would change formation to spell a word, and then another word. We would shoot all this from the sky, hopefully in the helicopter that Tim was going to find for us.

"What do you want them to spell?" he said.

"Hi Mom," we said. "First 'Hi' and then 'Mom.'"

Neither of us could tell what Tim was thinking. He would be good in an interrogation. He then spotted someone across the mess hall and yelled for him to come over. He gestured for the guy to have a seat. He was a warrant officer. Tim said to me, "Can you explain to this fellow what you need?"

We explained the bit to the warrant officer, adding, "We need as many soldiers as possible. Like a lot."

The warrant officer had an incredulous look on his face.

We added, "And it has to be fast. It's complicated but the whole thing has to happen in like ten seconds."

The warrant officer didn't look as convinced as we were. And quite frankly, what the hell did we know?

Fortunately, Colonel Grant answered on the poor man's behalf, saying, "I think we can do this." He then turned to the warrant officer and asked, "Can we?"

The warrant officer stood up, snapped to attention, saluted, said, "Sir, yes sir," then turned and ran. A man with a mission. And that was that.

At 2200 (10 p.m. for civilians) we went to bed. I lay awake in my bunk, not quite believing where we were.

Bright and early the next morning we start shooting B-reel footage of regular activity in the camp that hopefully we will set to music. Kevin, who has been assigned to us for the duration, drives us to a nearby firing range in Coralici, where a battle group is stationed.

Everyone seems surprised when I say, "Can I fire a machine gun?"

The guy in charge says "Sure" and starts to give me a quick lesson. I then spent 20 minutes blasting away hundreds of rounds on a C9 machine gun. Bonus.

Captain Golbeck is mildly scandalized and thinks we'll all get in trouble.

Geoff and I are thinking the same thing. Well, someone might get in trouble but it won't be us. We aren't in the army, we are in show business.

Patrick shot it all for use in the piece.

At noon our ride arrives, a Bell CH-146 Griffon helicopter, flown by the guys from 427 Squadron, based in Petawawa, ON. The Griffon is not exactly a fighting machine. It's a tactical transport chopper. Unarmed, to the best of my knowledge. But hell—it's a military helicopter and we're getting a free ride in it, so all aboard!

We fly south to Drvar. It's a spectacularly beautiful flight along the Una River Valley. Rolling lush green hills. It looks like every childhood fairy tale. But many of the small villages are abandoned. On closer inspection, it's clear that many of the villages have been destroyed. A sombre reminder that—notwithstanding the grand lark we TV boys are on—not long ago this was an active war zone. Two hundred and fifty thousand men, women and children were killed in this country from 1991 through 1995.

Everywhere we go we get footage of soldiers singing and carrying on in the small base at Drvar. It's a pretty spartan place, an old grain mill and storage facility. But the faces and the enthusiasm make up for it. Some of them even bust out a dance move or two. When we break out the boom box and play Trooper on bust, people's inhibitions go out the window. We work fast, not many second takes. We are slamming shots into the can. The soldiers step in front of the camera one by one and shout proudly the name of their hometown. Winnipeg, Regina, Moncton, Grande Prairie, Fogo Island, Iqaluit, the list is getting longer. Patrick is a machine. His days as a rugby player pay off in spades: he's draped in about 40 pounds of batteries and the 45-pound camera never leaves his shoulder. Any time Geoff or I suggest he take a break he says, "No way—this is the best day of my life!" That's enthusiasm.

We get to bed at 11, exhausted but totally pumped. We know at this point the video is going to work. We can all see it in our mind's eye. From now on everything else we get is gravy.

Back in Canada the polls in the federal election are starting to close. We wake up to find that Jean Chrétien has won a third consecutive majority for the Liberals, picking up seats in, of all places, Quebec. A blow to the sovereigntist movement.

First thing we do is go to the parade ground and sit on the roof of the cab of a military truck to watch the soldiers rehearse their moves for the aerial shot. They have been out there for hours. Despite this, the mood is festive. They are into it.

They have spelled the words out on the ground in something called parachute tape. This is brilliant. The tape is translucent, and while it can be seen if you're standing over it, it's invisible from a distance. It won't be seen from the helicopter.

Paul tells us that despite our asking for a full formation that turns into "HI" and then turns into "MOM," he's going to give us a third option where the formation spells both words together: "HI MOM." He adds, "Just in case."

Watching them from the roof of the cab it looks good but of course it's impossible to know what it's going to look like from the sky. I'm worried that the soldiers, when they get into place, are standing at attention. I think it might be more effective if they waved their hands in the air instead of standing still. Paul agrees. He tells me to address the troops. I explain to them what jazz hands are.

At some point I say, "I wish they could wave white handkerchiefs in the air. I bet that would look good."

This is the only point at which Paul pushes back. He says, "No, that would look like we were surrendering."

"Oh right," I say. "That's no good."

However, Paul has an idea. He sends a soldier running and he's back in minutes with a large box of white, I assume silk, gloves. Why the military has such a thing I have no idea but I am glad they do. I don't think many of these soldiers ever imagined when they signed up that serving their country would involve doing jazz hands in white gloves in prime time.

We leave Paul to rehearse some more and we leave to shoot more scenics. This time we have two Griffons flying side by side. Patrick is hanging out the side of our helicopter to get shots of the other. Geoff starts to make manoeuvre requests to the pilot over the headset. Geoff asks if they can fly side by side but closer, and then on his cue peel away in opposite directions.

"Say when," the pilot says. They are roaring along at full speed side by side with the mountains flying past us when Geoff yells, "NOW!" On cue both helicopters bank and separate at an incredible angle. This is a big shot. Patrick has on his face the biggest grin I've ever seen. Over the roar of the engine I yell to Geoff, "It's like we're in a Jerry Bruckheimer movie!"

From now on I want helicopters in all our shoots.

When the air manoeuvres are over we head back to the camp. As we approach we can see 100 soldiers in formation. We hover over them and when we have the shot lined up Geoff gives the go-ahead into the walkie-talkie. Suddenly the soldiers scramble like bees and come to a stop, forming the word "HI" perfectly. I can't believe how cool it looks. Three seconds later they scramble again and come to a stop spelling the word "MOM." They are in absolute perfect formation. Paul should be choreographing *Riverdance*. The term "military precision" comes to mind. White-gloved hands are waving madly in the air. And then in the third, "bonus" move, they scramble again and spell out the entire message. We land and jump from the helicopter and run towards them all screaming, "IT LOOKS AMAZING! HOLY SHIT! IT WAS PERFECT!"

They celebrated like they just won the Super Bowl. So many soldiers kept thanking me for doing this, thanking me for coming. Again, I can't believe it's they who are thanking me. They rehearsed this move all frigging day.

And then it's off to the mess hall where, glory be to God, there are Clearwater lobsters for all. We get great shots of soldiers REALLY enjoying lobsters.

I realize that at no point have Clearwater asked for a thank-you or even a credit in the show. I take a few crates from the kitchen and make sure they are in the shot, so they get a great commercial. I've never taken payment for product placement, but I don't mind giving credit where credit is due.

It is a really great touch. The lobsters, not the logo.

And then we were gone. That was the last shot. We hopped in a car and convoyed it back to Zagreb and the International Hotel. We were so tired we did something we never did. We ate at the place in the lobby.

The next morning, we flew Croatia Airlines to Frankfurt where we made a tight connection to Toronto. From there it was back to Halifax. We arrived totally bagged and not knowing the difference between up and down.

The next day was Thursday, and I had to shoot sketches in the studio and Geoff had to edit a rock video.

On Friday night in front of a studio audience, Gerald said to the crowd, "And Rick went on the road this past week too." The crowd cheered, because they thought he was setting up a "Talking to Americans" segment. The tape played. We'd shot the introduction to look like a rant, black-and-white in a nondescript industrial area with nothing to indicate where I was. I addressed the camera.

> Hello, and welcome to 22Minutes.com. As you know, in the past we have used the internet for evil. Well now that the holidays are approaching, we thought that the time had come to use the internet for good. Now don't worry, I promise we will use the internet for evil again in the near future. But now the holidays are approaching. Canadians are making plans to spend time with friends and loved ones. But for a lot of Canadian families a very important family member will be absent. I am talking about Canada's peacekeepers. If you go to our website, we can show you how you can send a holiday message to a peacekeeper this Christmas. And because they are so convinced that you are going to do this, they have already prepared a message for you. How do I know this? Well, I'm in Bosnia and [quoting the Trooper lyrics] "A very good friend of mine . . ."

At this moment the picture went from black-and-white to colour, the Trooper lyrics for "We're Here for a Good Time (Not a Long Time)" kicked in, we cut to the helicopter footage and the music video ramped up. The soldiers were singing, they were interacting with civilians, they were waving flags and most of all having a great time. We were pulling on *all* the heartstrings. It worked on so many levels. And it was clearly heartfelt. You could see that those soldiers, many of them kids, really did miss home. Some of them got great laughs for hamming it up. The studio audience cheered when the lobster came out. And when in the aerial shot they spelled "HI" and then "MOM," I could see literally half the audience spontaneously burst into tears. I had never seen that happen before. I didn't even think it was possible. There is no crying in comedy. It was wild.

To this day I believe our "HI MOM" is the greatest ten seconds in Canadian television history. Or at least, television that I have been involved with.

When it finished playing, the audience went nuts and the cameras cut to the news desk—it was time for Greg Thomey to do a story. He couldn't. He was crying. He has always been a softie, god bless him. He looked at me, tears in his eyes, and said, "You son of a bitch."

Two nights later 1,367,000 viewers tuned in for our one-hour special.

As predicted, Princess Warrior ambushing Mike Harris was a huge hit, and Marg also had a great bit with Dame Edna, and Greg at the International Emmys was a home run. But everyone was talking about the Bosnia piece. It was given multiple plays the next day on Newsworld. It played in its entirety on *The National*. The 22Minutes website racked up thousands of messages.

Along with messages for the troops, the site was inundated with messages from the troops and their families about the piece. Suddenly seventy thousand people wanted a copy on video. Canada's top soldier, the Chief of Defence Staff, wrote Geoff and me personal letters thanking us.

And the letter from Colonel Tim Grant describing watching the show in Bosnia brought me pure joy.

It was a great success. But for me it was so much more than just a good TV segment. I was proud of it in a way that I had never been before. It was the most personally satisfying thing I had done on television. I had felt that our soldiers were being ignored and I wanted to be part of changing that. I knew that somewhere, somehow, we would do it again.

24

Made in Canada

In the summer of 1998 Gerald and I were under the misguided assumption that we knew what we were doing when it came to making TV. Our confidence was on bust and we were eager to create something new. Because of this we embarked on a project that nearly killed us.

Originally it was supposed to be a summer job, something to do in the down months after 22 *Minutes* wrapped for the year. Where the energy came from, I have no idea.

It had to be something that could be done in the off-months because, while Gerald was ready to move on from 22 *Minutes*, I was content to stay there for the long haul. I was no different from someone who had landed a gig at the Department of Fisheries—I was in it for life.

The word was out that CBC was looking for limited six-episode projects. We wanted in.

The previous summer, Michael Donovan had hired me to write six scripts based on an idea of his. It was to be a sitcom set in a 1950s barbershop in Antigonish, Nova Scotia. Each script was supposed to be an allegory, a fiction set in the fifties that was in fact a comment on current events.

Creating thirty-minute scripts was a huge learning curve for me, but I loved the challenge. Everything on 22 *Minutes* was two minutes long or less. Writing episodic TV takes a completely different skill set. I felt it was very generous of Michael to tap me to write the project, since there was nothing to indicate that I was the guy for the job. Never mind the lack of experience—I knew more about quantum physics than I did about Antigonish in the 1950s. I researched until my eyes crossed. In the end I had scripts for a series I called "Haircut!" Yes, with an exclamation mark.

I was proud of the scripts, but I did have one nagging worry. It was not a show I would have watched. In the end the network decided it was a show that nobody would watch, and they took a pass. They claimed their main reason was that they were "not doing period." That might have been true at the time. TV is like that, slavishly adhering to trends. "We are not doing period pieces, until someone creates *Murdoch Mysteries* and it runs for the next two decades."

I decided to turn my attention to writing a project that interested me.

I liked the idea of a workplace satire. At first I worked on a proposal for a show set in the world of music video television. I thought the world of MuchMusic and MTV would make for a great TV series—something like a modern-day *WKRP*, a childhood favourite of mine that was set in a rock music station. But early on in the writing I came to the startling conclusion that I knew nothing about the music business. It is hard to satirize something you know nothing about.

Next up, I set out to write a show that would be set in the offices of a weekly entertainment newspaper, like *Now* magazine in Toronto or *The Coast* in Halifax. But the same problem surfaced. It sounded like a cool job, but I knew nothing about working on an entertainment newspaper.

If you want to satirize something you need to have a voice of authority. You need to know what you are talking about. All of my success on 22 *Minutes* stemmed from the fact that politics was my baseball. I followed it, I cared about it. Even when it angered me, it fascinated me. I knew what I was talking about.

So I decided to follow the maxim "Write what you know." I had only two interests in life, and they both bordered on obsessions: show business and politics.

I already covered politics on 22 *Minutes*, so I turned my eye to show business. I started to work on a TV show that would satirize people who make TV shows.

In hindsight, a tad self-indulgent—but I was young and fearless. Also, for some reason I was unfamiliar with the Broadway saying "Satire is what closes on a Saturday night." For those who are happily theatrically oblivious, Broadway shows traditionally open on a Wednesday, so to close on Saturday means to fail in a titanic fashion.

The TV business struck me as the perfect place to set a show. It is filled with oversized egos, backstabbing and intrigue. People are routinely rewarded for bad work and punished for quality. And popular entertainment is often a race to the bottom. There is a hierarchy that is both fascinating and nonsensical. And many TV people take themselves very seriously. Hysterically so.

Once at an awards show I found myself trying to calm down a TV director who was threatening to cross the room and punch a colleague because of a perceived snub of his work.

This indignation was coming from a man whose résumé showed that he directed three episodes of *Street Legal* and a pilot for a show that had something to do with a talking rabbit. TV is an industry of illusion, filled with delusion.

Around this time, while I was waiting for the muses to show up at my door and lend me a hand, something better arrived. A British miniseries entitled *House of Cards* showed up at my local video store. It was a political drama about the race to succeed Margaret Thatcher. It was revolutionary.

The lead character, Francis Urquhart—known affectionately as F.U.—was pure evil and relished being so. Of course, only the audience knew this. He would stop at nothing, including murder, to achieve his goals. The show was far ahead of its time. It would take decades for an American version to be produced.

What both Gerald and I loved about the show was that the lead character broke the fourth wall, by which I mean in the middle of a dramatic scene he would gaze directly into the camera and speak to the audience. This was simply not done in television. Ever. It had only really ever been done in the theatre—and *House of Cards* clearly wanted F.U. to remind viewers of Shakespeare's Richard III.

We had never seen anyone break the fourth wall in Canadian or American television, and we immediately became obsessed with the idea. We would create a show where my character would speak directly to the camera. In a nod to Mr. Shakespeare, I would name him Richard.

Neither of us knew if I would be able to hold my own in a sitcom, but Gerald had faith that I could look into a camera and talk. After all, that's exactly what I did every week in my rants.

Michael Donovan loved the idea. He had lots of ideas for a show about show business. Michael had an incredible amount of clout at the network. With him on board we could get the thing made.

Gerald and I had great admiration for Michael. What he created with Salter Street Films was truly astounding. He started out as a movie producer in Halifax when there was literally no film industry. He just declared he was producing a movie and somehow persuaded the business community there to finance his project, a post-apocalyptic thriller written and directed by his brother called *Def-Con 4*. Even more astounding, that film became a drive-in-movie hit in America and the investors got their money back. Later, with *CODCO*, he single-handedly turned CBC Halifax into a production hub for the national network.

What Michael had accomplished at that point in his career was astonishing. What he would go on to achieve would be even more so. He would eventually win an Academy Award as the producer for *Bowling for Columbine*. He would then go on to chair one of the world's largest international creators of children's content and animation. At one point he owned *Teletubbies*, *Inspector Gadget* and the entire Charlie Brown/*Peanuts* franchise.

Our yet-to-be-written TV show would be a co-production between Salter Street and Gerald's and my own company, Island Edge. Gerald would be the showrunner, and I would be the lead.

We got to work. The first thing we did was approach Mark Farrell and ask him if he wanted to come on board and write the show with me. Mark was a relatively new hire at *22 Minutes*. He was a successful stand-up comedian and an actor, and funny as hell.

And when it came to the CBC we had one very important ask. We wanted to do the show with George Anthony. George was the CBC creative contact for many shows at CBC but not for scripted half-hours. We didn't care. To paraphrase Brian Mulroney, "You dance with the one that brung you." If we were going to do a new show with the CBC, it would be with George or nobody. Besides, nobody knew more about the industry we were going to satirize than George.

Michael pitched the idea to the CBC, and pretty soon got back to us to say they were on board. There was much celebration all around—until the other shoe dropped. The amount of money available to do the six shows was astoundingly low. I thought, "Here we go again."

And so we got to work on the series that would be known as *Made in Canada*.

It was not an easy birth.

To be fair nobody, to a person, knew what they were doing because nobody, to a person, had ever done anything like this before. The writers, Mark and I, were first-timers. Gerald had never produced a half-hour episodic. Henry Sarwer-Foner had directed *22 Minutes* brilliantly, but he'd never directed a half-hour before. The CBC crew that made *22 Minutes* could shoot sketches better than anyone, but they had never come close to making something like this. Alan MacLean, the editor of *22 Minutes* and a great friend who had thus far edited everything of mine of any consequence, was brand new as well.

And of course, I was the lead actor. Something I had not even come close to doing before.

What a wonderful exciting long shot we were.

———

The scripts came fairly easy to Mark and me. We were very happy with them. We knew they were tight and we knew they were funny. And when they were read by casting agents in Toronto, they caused a huge buzz. Every actor in the country wanted to be a part of the production.

It may seem like a no-brainer, but when creating a show around someone who has little or no experience as an actor, the best plan of attack is to surround the guy with the funniest people you can find.

The most obvious example of this is *Seinfeld*. Jerry Seinfeld was a stand-up who had never appeared in a sitcom. In the early days of his show this was evident. He was a really funny guy who initially couldn't walk and talk at the same time. By surrounding him with brilliant comic performers, the show survived while Jerry grew into the job as a sitcom actor. We followed his lead.

Gerald sat in on hundreds of auditions. The cast he assembled was stellar.

Peter Keleghan was cast as Alan Roy, the handsome, dim owner of a production company that prided itself on being number one in the country when it came to producing second-rate TV. Alan made his money and built his reputation as a filmmaker early in his career by producing a series of successful teen comedies, each one of them having a plot that involved a bet and a box of condoms. Leah Pinsent was the office manager and the real brains of the operation. Dan Lett was Victor, the hapless head of the film division. Ron James, who I consider one of the funniest men in Canada, played the head of the TV division. Janet Kidder, every bit the spitting image of her aunt Margot, played a young film producer. Emily Hampshire, who would later star in *Schitt's Creek*, played Alan's daughter. Jackie Torrens was Alan's long-suffering secretary.

Because we had no money for a set, the decision was made to shoot the show entirely on location in Salter Street's actual offices. They would double as the offices of the show's Pyramid Productions. One person at Salter's office liked this idea—Michael. Many staff revolted at it. How could they carry on being a TV production company if a TV show was being shot in the office? It was decided that the only way to make it work was to shoot each episode Friday through Sunday, at night.

It was a completely deranged idea that saved us not one cent. Shooting every weekend meant loading all the equipment and crew in and out every single week. Time-consuming and hard work. The offices were on the fourth and fifth floors, with one very small elevator. We needed an army of sherpas just to go to work each weekend.

Conditions were the most difficult I have ever encountered. The massive amount of lighting needed to light the large space caused the rooms to heat up to an unbearable temperature. Picture all the actors in business attire attempting to appear cool and collected while surrounded by crew members in T-shirts and shorts dripping in sweat. The air conditioner, as small and as ineffective as it was, could not be turned on, as it was noisy as hell.

The sound department was also severely challenged by a venting system attached to the pizza restaurant in the basement. The building, a gentrified old brick factory, creaked, belched and farted like an octogenarian.

And the CBC crew, while excellent when working in the CBC studio during business hours, had little appetite for being on the job at four in the morning on a weekend in July because I wanted a vanity project. How could you blame them? We were expecting a mutiny at any moment. The entire vibe was that of a slow boil.

The actors were the only ones who knew what they were doing, but the tendency to get punch-drunk from sleep deprivation made for very long hours.

Everyone had so much at stake, and the stress was unbearable. Henry, a perfectionist director at the best of times, seemed unwilling to compromise at all when trying to get the shots he envisioned. He was constantly at high risk of getting punched in the head by any number of crew members.

But somehow, we got it done.

Nobody may have known what they were doing at the beginning, but their talent and instincts were for the most part formidable.

And Michael Donovan did the show the greatest service any executive producer could deliver. He watched while we created a show that was somewhere in the neighbourhood of $1 million over budget. His money, not ours.

He supported the show and he put his money where his mouth was. Any other executive producer would have pulled the plug or forced us to deliver something cheap and shoddy. Michael's gamble was that if we delivered a show that was a hit, the $1 million in red ink could be retrieved, or at least amortized over future episodes.

I believe that's what is called a long shot.

The only thing we did know for certain was that if there were to be any more episodes of *Made in Canada*, they would not be shot at night, in that building, in a steam bath.

Post-production is the process that occurs once all the actors and the crew go home. This is when the show is edited, the opening created, the sound added and mixed. This is when you work with what you have. There is no opportunity to go back and make changes. There are also no magic buttons you can push to make everything better. If the sound is bad, the sound is bad. If the lighting is bad, there is no way to fix that. The expression is "Garbage in, garbage out."

Henry delivered a good-looking show. All the money, real and imagined, was on the screen. The cast was brilliant.

The opener was slick, and its theme song was the Tragically Hip's "Blow at High Dough": "They shot a movie once, in my hometown. Everybody was in it, for miles around . . ." I have fifteen Hip songs on my top-ten favourites list, but this one has always been number one. This was a gigantic coup for a little show with no money, and one I will always be grateful to the Hip for.

My relationship with the Hip was minimal at the time. We were at best passing acquaintances. They had come through Halifax a few times on tour and were kind enough to send some tickets our way at *22 Minutes*.

I had called the Hip's manager, Jake Gold, a few months previous to enquire about licensing the song for the opening of the show. I told him straight up that I had very little money to work with. I will not divulge the amount, but it's safe to say that it wasn't so much an offer as an honorarium.

Jake has been in the music business for a long time, and he is not in the business of making small, insignificant amounts of money for his clients. His job is to make them as much money as possible. And one of those ways is by licensing music to film and television. And the Hip was probably the biggest band in Canada at the time.

I could tell Jake was entirely unenthusiastic about the money that I was offering, but he said the licensing decision would ultimately rest with the band. And these decisions, he said, had to be unanimous. As luck would have it, the band was meeting the next day for the first time in quite a while. He said he would see if he could get it on the agenda.

Late the next afternoon, Jake called me and said the decision was unanimous and it was a yes. What an incredible vote of confidence by five artists at the top of their game.

It was in post-production, though, that we encountered some mistakes that were potentially fatal. The scripts were all a few minutes heavy, and they were dense. Shaving the few minutes needed to bring the show down to time was very difficult. There was no fat to trim, just muscle and bone.

But the show looked great. And it moved like a rocket. We had very high hopes.

So did the network. They scheduled the show to premiere that fall immediately after *This Hour Has 22 Minutes*. It was the best time slot we could have hoped for.

Watching the premiere at home, Gerald and I were so giddy it was ridiculous. It really did look good. And despite my reluctance to watch myself on TV, I had a feeling not unlike the one I had when I watched the first episode of *22 Minutes*. This is a show I would watch. This is a show I love.

And then the phone rang.

It was an old friend of ours, Justin Hall, calling from St. John's. He said, "Guys, I just wanted to call and tell you I love the show, it's amazing. And I hate everything on television."

Afterwards I said to Gerald, "That was nice of Justin."

Gerald said, "I'll tell you one thing about Justin. He's not lying. He does hate everything on TV. If he's our audience, that could be a bad sign."

If Justin's endorsement was open to interpretation, there was no denying the message we received first thing the next morning. As always, we walked to the office and as always, we stopped in to the local magazine shop to pick up the day's newspapers. When the kid behind the counter saw me, his eyes lit up like saucers. "Hey, guys! I saw your new show last night . . . IT'S AWFUL!"

After we left the store we began to laugh. One of those laughing jags that once started cannot be stopped. In fact, I don't know if we had ever laughed so hard. And when it threatened to stop, one of us would say, "IT'S AWFUL!" and we would start again. We were steeling ourselves for what was to come.

The time slot was a godsend. We opened with 1.2 million viewers. And by and large the critics loved us. As did, it seemed, most people who worked in the industry.

The people at home? Not so much. Over the next six weeks *Made in Canada*'s ratings began to hemorrhage. Every week another hundred-thousand-plus people made the decision to change the channel the second the opening bars of "Blow at High Dough" came out of their TV sets.

The biggest complaint about the show was that my character was so bloody mean. And he was. There was no denying it. Each week he became progressively more so. By the final episode he was hiring thugs to kneecap actors and was guilty of insider trading. Where do you go with a character like that? Other than municipal politics, I mean.

Don't get me wrong. The show was funny, but it was very dark. And it was dense. And there was a lot of inside baseball. Funny is always good. Dense and dark is, to paraphrase the Broadway expression, what gets you cancelled after six episodes. Each episode was also in effect "to be continued"—if you missed one episode you would have no idea what was happening the next time you tuned in.

Mark and I had essentially written a movie, split it into six parts and called it a TV series.

When the final credits rolled on the last episode, 50 percent of our initial audience was gone. Justin Hall liked it, but a lot of folks didn't. To this day, whenever we have done something that fails to resonate with the crowd, Gerald will say, "Justin Hall on line two."

Gerald and I were very proud of *Made in Canada*. But it was evident, looking at the first season, that the show was decidedly not mainstream. Which was odd for us. We like mainstream.

The critics loved us. To them we had all the makings of a cult hit— which is show-business talk for not very accessible with low ratings. And the entertainment industry at large, for the most part, really liked the show. It was, after all, about them, or rather us. Many people in show business are convinced their industry is endlessly fascinating. We fell into that trap.

Slawko Klymkiw and George Anthony at the CBC were big supporters of the show, but this is a cutthroat business. Eventually the time would come for Slawko to look over his TV schedule and decide who would live and who would die.

And then the Academy of Canadian Cinema and Television weighed in.

The "Academy" is the non-profit professional organization that represents film and TV professionals in Canada. Membership hovers around four thousand people. Three thousand of them barely have enough to eat on any given day.

Like any professional organization, say the teachers' union or the farm equipment sales association of Canada, the academy raises money from membership dues. Also, like the farm equipment people, they hold an annual awards show, a chance for everyone to get together in one room, slap each other on the back and celebrate themselves. In the academy's case it's televised.

The academy looked very kindly on the first six episodes of *Made in Canada*. And come the 1999 awards season the entire cast was nominated for Best Performance in a Comedy Program. But more importantly we landed a nomination for Best Comedy Program. This put us head-to-head against a serious heavyweight, namely *This Hour Has 22 Minutes*, which had won the award the previous five years in a row. It was a chilly day at *22 Minutes* when those nominations were announced.

What they say about show business awards is true: it's an honour just to be nominated. But it's still better to win. And more than a few jaws dropped on the broadcast night when *Made in Canada* won Best Comedy, beating perennial winner *22 Minutes*. I had beat myself. Michael and Gerald accepted the award.

The CBC ordered thirteen shows to be made the next summer. I would like to thank the Academy . . .

And so began the evolution of *Made in Canada*—from a six-part dark satire of the TV business to a somewhat lighter episodic comedy about office politics.

Everything changed, starting with the crew. Thirteen episodes was more than the CBC crew could logistically handle. They had their hands full with *22 Minutes* and a host of other programs. Also, they were still suffering from post-traumatic stress after the torturous nighttime schedule we'd subjected them to the previous summer.

A full independent film crew was hired. Halifax was in the middle of a film boom. American productions were regularly being shot there, and we had the pick of phenomenal professionals. They were a machine.

Pete Sutherland, my cameraman for every *22 Minutes* rant and every "Talking to Americans," was the only CBC crew member who was there for season 2. He was joined by cameraman Don Spence. The only debate about these two cinematographers is which one is better. It's a tough call.

A permanent set, designed by Stephen Osler, was built in the new sound stage that Salter Street had opened in an old power plant on the Halifax harbourfront.

Creatively, we decided the show would no longer be serialized. Each episode would stand alone. No longer would it be a show that you had to watch every week if you wanted to understand what was going on. And my character was changed. He was still conniving but he was no longer on his way to becoming a serial killer.

And while we'd had great fun poking fun at this wonderfully ridiculous business I've spent my life in, we accepted that not everyone is obsessed with the TV business. In fact the vast majority of people don't care about it at all. So we shifted the focus to office politics. People mightn't have first-hand experience with TV actors and producers, but almost everyone has experienced a dim boss, a conniving co-worker and a cutthroat work environment.

It was the best summer job a man could have. Mark Farrell and I ran the story department, and together we worked with the best comedy writers in the country. The writing and the rewriting never stopped. Mark deserves so much credit. The man never stopped working, never stopped improving the scripts. It was our college; it was here we learned how TV actually works.

Gerald brought in a guest star for each episode. His casting was brilliant. What a dream. Everyone wanted on the show. We had a reputation for running a sane, tight ship. And it didn't hurt that our studio was in downtown Halifax right next to the water. For most actors based in Toronto, the appeal of fleeing their city in the blistering heat of August for a few days' work in beautiful Nova Scotia was overwhelming.

Not only did I get to work with the permanent cast, who I loved, I got to work with actors I really had no business on a stage with. Gordon Pinsent, Kiefer Sutherland, Shirley Douglas, Margot Kidder, Sarah Polley, Colin Mochrie, Don McKellar, Maury Chaykin, Cynthia Dale, C. David Johnson—the list went on and on. And how surreal it was to do scene work with public figures who played themselves, such as Peter Gzowski and Moses Znaimer.

It was the hardest work I have ever done. 22 Minutes was a Swedish neck massage compared with Made in Canada. And I loved it. It took over my life for five seasons. We shot sixty-five episodes and held our own in the ratings for the entire run. The critics stayed in our corner, and so did the academy. The show won twenty-three national awards during its five-season run, including multiple Geminis, Writers Guild of Canada Screenwriting Awards and Canadian Comedy Awards. In the United States, Australia and Latin America, the show was syndicated as *The Industry*. In France, it was syndicated as *La Loi du Show-Biz*.

And we were given the greatest gift in show business. We were afforded the luxury of wrapping up the series when we felt it was time.

I wrote and directed the final episode. It was a hell of a run.

25

Untitled Rick Mercer Project

Made in Canada had spoiled us. Gerald and I had complete creative control over it. That's a rare thing in the TV business. And we both knew that if there were going to be any more projects, that was the bar we had set for ourselves.

Easier said than done. The TV business is not that much different from the restaurant business. You could be a successful chef in a popular restaurant, but at the end of the day you are a cook. You are an employee. There's nothing wrong with that, of course. Most of us work for someone else. But whoever owns the restaurant is ultimately in charge. They can arbitrarily do whatever the hell they want. If they decide it's liver and onions every day, that's their prerogative. If they want to come in the kitchen and start waving the salt shaker around, they can do it. If they want to sneak in late at night and put gas-soaked rags in the ceiling tiles and then burn the place to the ground for the insurance money, they are free to do so. In fact, it's encouraged.

And at any restaurant, if a cook protests too much, the owner can always find another cook. That is the free market. And that was *22 Minutes*.

I knew I would never be a producer of the show and certainly not an owner. And nor should I. It wasn't built that way. And if it ain't broke, don't fix it. I was one cook out of four. The restaurant was owned entirely by Salter Street Films. Mary, Greg, Cathy and I were the face of the show. We created the bloody thing, but we did not own it. We were employees. Our contracts were renewed annually and entirely on Michael's whim. That show was the best thing that ever happened to me, but it was time to move on. At the risk of beating the previous metaphor with a shovel until it is dead, Gerald and I wanted to own the restaurant.

We called a family meeting and we decided that the time had come to do what we had talked of doing from the very earliest days of the one-man shows. We would create the Rick Mercer show. It would mean leaving *This Hour Has 22 Minutes* and Halifax, the city we had lived in for almost a decade. There was no other choice. If we were going to do the show we had in mind, we needed a studio. The studios were in Toronto. It was time to make a move.

A simple press release went out in which I was quoted as saying that I was leaving the show to pursue other opportunities and Salter Street Films was quoted as wishing me well on my future endeavours. Short, terse and to the point.

I agreed there would be no exit interviews. It would be a low-profile exit designed to protect the mother ship. Regardless, the press had a field day. It must have been a slow news week in the world of entertainment.

On the phone my father said, "That was a pretty funny article about you leaving the show, I thought."

I asked him what was so funny. He said, "The headline says, 'Mercer Departing 22 Minutes, Can He Be Replaced?'" My father followed this up with his own take on the situation: "Winston Churchill was replaceable. I'm sure as hell you are."

There is no getting a fat head with my parents.

I never thought for a single minute that my leaving *22 Minutes* would damage the show in any real way or for any amount of time. They would be fine. If they kept the cast at three, that was three of the funniest people I knew. And if they decided to replace me? Well, it's a big country with lots of funny people in it. If they wanted to stick with the Newfoundland palette, there were also many options. Including Mark Critch.

Mark Farrell was now in charge of 22 *Minutes* and he quickly put an end to any speculation about how hard I would be to replace. He hired Colin Mochrie to fill my chair. Colin was a huge star both in Canada and the USA for his work on *Whose Line Is It Anyway?* Canadians love Colin. If anything, adding him to the cast made the story go from "Can he be replaced?" to "Rick who?"

Gerald and I left town. When 22 *Minutes* premiered with Colin in the chair, we were out of the country. I wished them well, but I wanted to be as far away as possible. Eventually we sold our house in Halifax and made the move to Toronto.

We didn't rush into launching a new show right away. We didn't want to appear like we were leaving one show for the other. But Slawko was clear: when we were ready, he was ready. There was still a home for me at the CBC.

So we took some time. We travelled, and I began to perform live around the country.

There is a circuit in Canada that keeps the heads of many people in show business above water. It is for the most part a secret, because these gigs are not ticketed events and they are not advertised. It is the corporate event circuit.

For years I'd been offered work there but I was always busy. Suddenly free of any TV production, I could accept them. And accept them I did. I took all of them. It allowed me to hone my chops and practise my live presentation. For almost two years, if more than five hundred professionals assembled in a hotel ballroom for a convention, I was on the bill, doing stand-up, talking current events and regaling delegates with behind-the-scenes tales from "Talking to Americans." I talked to nurses and teachers, mayors and plumbers, oil and gas folks and farmers. I spoke, it seems like, to everyone in every nook and cranny of the country.

I loved it. Still do. There's nothing quite like performing live, even if sometimes it has to be at seven a.m. in front of a hungover room inhaling coffee and eggs.

But eventually Gerald and I sat down and went to work creating a new show.

First person we called was George, and then Slawko. We were given an order for seven shows starting in January 2004. It was called "Untitled Rick Mercer Project." Gerald and I were the executive producers: it was to be owned 100 percent by our own company—there were no partners.

It was our restaurant. And only ours. Whatever happened, there would be nobody to blame but ourselves.

The first thing we had to do was put up our house to guarantee interim financing from the bank. If things went sideways, we would be very much in the hole. Sometimes owning the restaurant is not all it's cracked up to be.

I would be lying if I said my departure from *22 Minutes* did not create any bad blood. But the truth is, there was very little. It was a flesh wound at worst. Any fear that my departure would be damaging was negated quickly by my replacement. And for the most part we all got along—although conveniently, now that I was in another city, we never saw each other that much either.

Things did get a little dicey when *22 Minutes* director Henry Sarwer-Foner asked us if he could direct the new show. This was awkward, because when we departed we had said we would not approach or poach anyone from *22 Minutes*. But the truth is, Henry came to us.

Some people saw Henry's departure as disloyal or a vote of non-confidence in *22 Minutes*, but the real reason was far less dastardly. Henry lived in Toronto, had a house in Toronto and had small children in Toronto. Toronto was where he needed to be just at the time we were moving there.

Also, Henry had created the opener and the director's template for *Made in Canada*. That's his high suit. The chance to birth another show on the network was greatly appealing to him. At *22 Minutes*

Henry felt he was in a velvet rut. He certainly wasn't being challenged. The bugs had been worked out long ago.

Creatively I was nervous. I knew I would have a news desk, but that would be a very small part of the show. The main element of the show, we concluded, would be me in the field. But try as I might, I couldn't see exactly what the show was going to look like.

Gerald was infuriating. All he kept saying was, "That's the least of our worries. You're going to talk to people. You're good at that."

And when I said, "That makes no sense. It's not going to be a talk show, we know that. Who the hell am I supposed to talk to, lobster fishermen?"

He said, "Exactly, and farmers, and teachers, and plumbers and people at county fairs." It was unnerving, the faith he seemed to have in me. "We'll send you out on the road and you'll do what you do best. I'm not worried about that part."

Fine for him. I was worried enough for five actors.

To accompany me on these road trips, Gerald hired his old friend John Marshall. They went way back. When Gerald was a bartender in Ottawa, John was the busboy. Based in Toronto now, John was a long-time producer and road director with *The New Music*, a long-running show on Citytv in Toronto and on MuchMusic. Don Spence agreed to be the principal cameraman but warned us that he never did a job for much longer than a year or two. "After that," he said, "I get bored and move on." Gerald said, "Well if you're lucky, we'll be cancelled after six episodes and you won't have to worry about it."

But privately Gerald's theory was that unless I completely tanked, we would get a second season.

Again he assured me, "You can talk to people. It will be good."

In the meantime we had a show to design, an opener to create, a template to figure out, music to get scored. We had a team to assemble—writers, researchers, makeup and wardrobe. We needed an audience co-ordinator. We learned that we were going to have to buy chairs for our studio audience and build bleachers to place them on. We had to come up with a bloody title.

We were getting very close to this really happening. And then Geoff D'Eon sent me an email.

26

Christmas in Kabul

Travel advisory. October 23, 2003: "Canadians should not travel to Afghanistan. There is little law and order. The security situation remains extremely volatile and unpredictable. The potential for violence and unrest remains high. Bombings have occurred in Kabul. No area can be considered safe. Warlords control many areas. Banditry by armed groups is common. Journalists are particularly vulnerable when accompanying military units."

The advisory was in a brief email from Geoff D'Eon that included the question: "Want to go?"

A few minutes later I responded, "With reviews like that, how can I say no."

Geoff and I had been through a lot together. Every "Talking to Americans" shoot and every road trip to Ottawa. We had banked thousands of hours on the road. But the shoot in Bosnia had been the most personally satisfying for both of us. We had talked of doing something overseas with troops ever since, but it had never panned out.

And of course, in the three years since we had gone to Bosnia, the world had changed dramatically. The role of the Canadian military had changed dramatically as well. In 2001 Canadian troops were in Bosnia as peacekeepers. In 2003 Canadian troops were in Afghanistan. They were not keeping the peace; we were at war with the Taliban.

The majority of Canadian soldiers there were stationed at the main base for the Canadian contingent in Kabul, Camp Julien. It was in the news a fair amount as the frequent target of mortar rounds fired by Taliban sympathizers.

We had long bandied about the idea for a proper Christmas special overseas. Maybe now was the time. And let's face it, we had a pretty good track record when it came to one-hour specials.

And so, *Christmas in Kabul* was hatched. A one-hour comedy and music special shot entirely on location in a war zone.

Geoff flew to Ottawa to pitch the idea in person.

Canada's Department of National Defence was very receptive. Or at least receptive enough that they agreed to take the meeting. But the idea of shooting a variety show for the soldiers raised some serious logistical concerns. One through five being that Camp Julien was in a war zone.

Turns out they took this war business very seriously. They were particularly concerned with any civilians that were allowed "in theatre."

I told Geoff to assure them that if asked, the theatre is where I got my start.

But it was clear that because of our Bosnia visit, the Department of Defence trusted us and took us seriously. That made all the difference. They assured us they would carefully consider the proposal.

George Anthony, our man at the CBC, loved the idea. It was pure show business. But there was some hand-wringing at some levels of the CBC. And understandably so.

The CBC is in the business of sending employees into dangerous circumstances—they know all about that. But usually, when it comes to a conflict zone, they send in a seasoned, battle-tested war correspondent who's used to being shot at. Someone like Adrienne Arsenault, who came out of the womb wearing body armour.

That was not us. We were show people. We were circus. I could teach a course on wigs and makeup, but helmets and flak jackets were still a relative mystery to me.

And although our crew was a CBC crew, they were essentially a studio crew based in Halifax. They were used to shooting *22 Minutes* and the East Coast Music Awards. The closest they had ever been to a war zone was the annual broadcast of the Maritime Fiddling Championship.

But the TV special angels shone on us. In mid-October both the CBC and the Department of Defence approved the show.

We were headed to Kabul.

There were a thousand questions that needed answering and a thousand needles that needed needling. In short order I received mandatory shots for tetanus, diphtheria, polio, measles, hepatitis A and typhoid fever. Malaria drugs were prescribed, but because of their possible severe side effects, they were not compulsory.

My arm felt like it was used for dart practice.

The crew fared a bit better. As veterans of the aforementioned fiddling championships they had already been inoculated against diphtheria, hepatitis A and dengue fever.

Geoff and I disagree on whose idea it was to approach Tom Cochrane for the show's band. Success has many fathers. We both wanted someone who had radio hits. Tom certainly fit the bill. He'd had a whack of hits in his career. According to the society of Canadian recording artists, "Life Is a Highway" has been played a gabillion times on North American radio. When it is broadcast, the number of speeding tickets issued increases 200 percent.

A quick aside: my first concert as a teenager, at Memorial Stadium in St. John's, was Tom Cochrane and Red Rider.

Now I was calling Tom.

RICK: Tom, Rick Mercer here. We haven't met.

TOM: Hello, Rick. What's up?

RICK: I'm doing a Christmas show called *Christmas in Kabul* on the CBC. It's an old-fashioned variety show for the troops, shot in Afghanistan, just before Christmas. We were thinking—

TOM: I'm in.

A short conversation. It was like I was asking him to move his car. He didn't ask about money or accommodations, he just said yes. A very big fish had been landed in very short order.

Next, Geoff approached Damhnait Doyle, she with the beautiful voice and stunning looks. From my home province. Damhnait is so talented it hurts. She, too, took seconds to answer in the affirmative.

Rounding out the band was Kevin Fox, a master of the cello, the guitar and everything else with strings. He was to be the musical director.

Geoff was on the hunt for some Afghan musicians to be in the show. Also, we were musing about a choir of soldiers.

The number of details Geoff worked out prior to our leaving is mind-numbing. In total, fourteen of us were to make the trip. A lean, mean TV-making machine. Every piece of equipment required a redundancy. If anything failed, there would be no running back to the studio for a replacement.

We were, in a record amount of time, going to create a one-hour TV show.

And on top of that I was just weeks away from opening our new series. Gerald was swamped with the start-up details—putting an office together, hiring writers, negotiating studio access in the CBC's Toronto Broadcast Centre. It was a herculean task, during which I was somewhat distracted by the Kabul project. Probably not the wisest thing to take on just before launching the most important show of my life, but Gerald and I were committed to the special.

Because we were so close to the launch of the new show, John Marshall came along for the ride with the idea that we might get some content for the now-named *Rick Mercer's Monday Report*.

When we hired John, we told him he would report to work in the first week of January, but in early December Gerald asked if he could start early and shoot a road piece for the new show. John, knowing by now exactly what our vision for the new show was, figured this meant he would be headed to the Cape Breton Highlands or the foothills of Alberta. He was pretty surprised when Gerald said the Hindu Kush mountains. But he was in, big time.

It would be our first road trip together, something we would do roughly 175 more times over the next fifteen years.

It was the beginning of the second week in December when John and I met up with Tom, Damhnait and Kevin at Toronto Pearson Airport. Turns out Tom Cochrane is not only a gifted singer-songwriter but also a great raconteur. Tom talks as much as I do. We blithered and blathered all the way across the North Atlantic to London Heathrow.

Later that night in the bar of an airport hotel we met up with Geoff and the entire Halifax crew. The excitement was on bust and the nerves were too. We stayed up a little too late for a group of people who had to be at the airport by six to fly to Frankfurt and then Dubai, where we'd spend the night.

The next morning everyone was early for the lobby call. A very good sign.

In the Dubai hotel I bumped into a group of Canadians, among them a doctor who had just come from Camp Julien. The doctor gave me some sound intelligence, the upshot being that Kabul was a massive dry and dusty city that, thanks to neglect and war, has experienced a catastrophic failure of its sanitation and sewage systems. His advice: constantly wash your hands and never put your hands in or near your mouth or eyes. And when possible, especially in dusty areas, which is just about everywhere, wear a face mask. He said the mask was very important, as some estimates put the fecal count in the dust at 40 percent.

Naturally I told the doctor that I believed in freedom and it would take more than a high fecal count to make me cover my nose and mouth. I contemplated leaping on a chair to implore everyone not to buy into dubious conspiracies from medical professionals who were hell-bent on us not licking our fingers and rubbing our eyes. "Ignore the science," I would cry. "That's not poo dust you're inhaling, that's the sweet taste of freedom."

But instead I double-checked with Geoff to see how many masks we were travelling with and was relieved to hear that we were packing enough for a crew twice our size. I then vowed that while in Afghanistan I would keep my mouth covered and my hands sanitized whenever possible.

Thank god, I thought, that I live in a country where medical officials would never have to implore citizens to wear a mask at all times in public. The notion was too horrific to contemplate.

The good doctor's only other advice was, if so inclined, to feel free to take a sedative before the next day's flight over the mountains into Kabul. That piece of advice I actually did ignore. I have never taken sedatives before and I certainly wasn't going to start simply because we were flying over mountains.

Twelve hours later, standing on the tarmac looking at the plane I was about to board, the suggestion that I take a happy pill prior to takeoff began to make sense.

The fight-or-flight response is a physiological reaction that occurs in response to a perceived harmful event, attack or threat to survival. Such events include being held up at gunpoint or gazing for the first time at a battered blue-and-white Airbus A300 proudly labelled Ariana, Afghanistan's official airline.

Ariana had been the national airline of Afghanistan for a very long time. But under the Taliban regime it became the personal plaything for Osama bin Laden. Apparently he liked the legroom, and he found the airline a convenient way to ferry drugs, guns, money and like-minded ding-dongs around the Middle East with impunity. But with the advent of sanctions against the Taliban the airline became a pariah in the world of aviation and collapsed.

The Taliban reacted to this the way they always did. They blew up the planes and used them for target practice. When one is convinced that the zipper is a symbol of evil, it's not that great a leap to think that multi-million-dollar aircraft are best used for target practice.

When the Taliban fell, and the NATO-led mission of international countries attempted to stabilize the country, the Indian government donated three Airbus A300B4s to Afghanistan so it could once again be a country that had a commercial airline. One country's ancient, decrepit airplanes are another country's triumph in aviation.

This was our ride.

It was perhaps the greatest "We're not in Kansas anymore" moment in my life.

Standing at the bottom of the staircase, I could see the exterior was dented, scratched and patched. It reminded me of the old Datsun B-210 that my brother drove into the ground. Some windows had been replaced with what looked like metal patches. I now understood the genesis of the airline's nickname: Scary Anna.

I contemplated heading back to the hotel where I could hang out in the swim-up bar for the next few days while the crew shot the special without me.

That would never fly, so I took a breath and walked up the stairs with the rest of our brave and now suddenly very quiet TV crew.

Inside the plane all the instructions and signs in Hindi had been covered up with black spray paint. New instructions in Pashto or Dari, Afghanistan's official languages, were written on the walls in marker. Numerous overhead compartments were missing their doors. If contents were going to shift, they would be shifting onto heads. The carpet was badly frayed and completely torn up in areas. The walls were battered beyond belief. This was clearly a plane that had for a very long time been used for cargo, not passengers.

I took my seat. A member of the crew next to me was alarmed when he realized his seat belt had been cut off. The cigarette butt in the ashtray of my seat did not evoke nostalgia for travel in a bygone era.

Airplane jokes have been a staple of stand-up comedy since Alcock and Brown made the first transatlantic flight from Newfoundland to Ireland in 1919. And so during takeoff and the early minutes of the flight I distracted myself by jotting down first impressions of the flight—maybe to be included in my monologue at the base.

"So we flew in on Scariana. Everything I ever said about Air Canada I take back."

"You know it's a bad sign when the flight attendant pushes his cart down the aisle and he's asking the passengers for food."

"Now I know why we needed tetanus shots to come here. I stepped on a rusty nail while walking through business class."

"It's a little unnerving when the laminated safety instructions in the seat pocket are just instructions on how to surrender."

To be clear, none of these "jokes" were ever used. In a fit of clarity, it dawned on me that the people of Afghanistan were rightly proud that they had planes, any planes, in the sky again. And the last thing they needed was some spoiled Westerner making fun of them because the service wasn't up to scratch. I poked them away in the event that twenty years later I would write a book.

And then the mountains came into sight. Majestic and stunning. Although less so when the plane suddenly began to plunge towards them. I didn't know commercial aircraft could plummet like that. We were suddenly literally skimming the mountaintops.

A man across from me, who turned out to be an airplane mechanic, told me in broken English that this was an evasive manoeuvre, and we were flying low to avoid radar, a tactic he said that is common but also dangerous, as low-flying planes can be targets for hand-held surface-to-air rocket launchers. "But," he said, "rare in the mountains."

No sooner had he said that than we all heard the unmistakable sound of the landing gear being deployed. A voice came over the speaker and said in English, "EVERYTHING IS NORMAL! EVERYTHING IS NORMAL!"

Tom Cochrane, despite the insane turbulence, stood up and walked calmly down the aisle towards me. He was like a Zen master or John Wayne. Tom, himself a pilot, drawled, "Just to be clear, dropping the landing gear fifteen hundred feet above mountains is not normal—this is some crazy shit." Then he returned to his seat.

Dare to dream to be as calm as Tom Cochrane in a crisis.

Thirty minutes later we landed at Kabul International Airport. The end of the runway was littered with the wreckage of planes, burnt-out fuselages painted in colours identical to the plane we were in. As we deplaned, I couldn't help thinking that once we were clear, the plane would just taxi over to the pile, collapse in a heap and fit right in.

For the first time I related to the Pope, with his penchant for kissing the ground he lands on.

The airport was pretty much as I expected. There was one small luggage carousel and hundreds of people pushing and shoving. It was kind of like the arrivals section in St. John's airport before they renovated. The only real difference was the bullet holes in the walls. Mixed in with the crowd were Canadian soldiers who were part of the International Security Assistance Force. They were happy to see us, and we them.

All fourteen of us, stunned, shocked and awed, stepped out of the airport flanked on both sides by Canadian soldiers carrying automatic weapons. Parked directly outside the doors were two large Bisons, a couple of SUVs and a flatbed for our equipment. The Bison is Canada's armoured personnel carrier. It looks like a tank, but if you call it a tank they look at you like you're an idiot.

Each of us was given a helmet and two layers of clothing lined with metal plates. None of us really knew what went where. We needed assistance from the soldiers, particularly in adjusting our helmet straps; we looked like kids getting help with our hockey gear.

The soldiers were super-efficient, polite and very serious. We were told that we would be travelling through downtown Kabul. We were warned that if anyone shot at us, we would be shooting back.

Speaking casually, the top soldier stated that if we encountered any roadblocks or interference or if for any reason a car or truck stopped and blocked our way, we would not stop or attempt to go around, we would "bust through." It was also mentioned that actors and musicians were forbidden from touching the guns in the Bison under any circumstances. Also, do what we were told.

During the drive I took a turn standing in the back of the Bison. This allowed me to see Kabul close up. The streets were complete chaos. Functioning buildings were side by side with buildings that had been gutted and destroyed. The tail gunner standing next to me scanning the streets and the rooftops may have tweaked to my alarm. Over the roar of the engine he said, "Don't worry—I've got my eye on you." I shouted, "Thank you!" He said, "I'm from Plate Cove."

"A Newfoundlander is guarding me," I thought. "This is a good omen."

Camp Julien was impressive. Home to two thousand Canadians, it was a combination of permanent buildings and tents. Completely self-sufficient, it came with its own power generator and its own sewage and water filtration systems. The accommodations were tents but very secure and neat, with their own cooling and heating units. The camp was designed and built by SNC-Lavalin. Say what you will about that scandal-ridden outfit, I know for a fact that given an unlimited budget they can build a fortified small town in very difficult circumstances.

At a briefing we were told over and over again what not to do—and of course, told what to do, which is to always do as you're told. We were warned of the dangers of land mines, which were lying in wait everywhere. We were told that there were more guns in the country per capita than any other place on earth. And of course, there was a very active Taliban and Taliban-sympathizing community very close by whose entire raison d'être was to cause us serious bodily harm. Also, they do in fact target VIPs.

My thought was, "Well, thank god we aren't travelling with any VIPs."

Then we were informed that all fourteen of us fit the bill.

CBC technicians and people in show business have been called a lot of things in Canada but never VIPS. A great place to start.

But for all the talk of warlords and land mines, the most startling part of the briefing was being told to check our boots in the morning and our sleeping bags at night for scorpions. Oddly enough, that was the only time there was an audible gasp from the crew. If there was a clear and present danger that concerned us the most, that was it.

Despite the late hour we headed to the junior officers' mess where the rank and file hang out. The reaction there was insane. A giant cheer greeted us all when we entered the room. This may have had something to do with Tom Cochrane or it may have had something to do with the fact that there was a very strict maximum of two beers per day per man in effect and on that evening they were waiting for us to arrive before the bar opened. Hip hip hooray!

It was a great night. People were generally stoked for the show. It was a surreal experience to be constantly thanked for doing something we felt honoured to do. Also, very strange to hear people excited about a show when none of us yet knew what it would look like.

I hadn't met so many Newfoundlanders outside of Newfoundland in my life. Instead of calling it Camp Julien, they should have called it Julien's Cove. There were close to four hundred on the base. They were all totally pumped because they had just held a Newfoundland Night that raised $12,000 for the Newfoundland and Labrador Children's Wish Foundation.

Everyone there had a story. One soldier showed me pictures of young girls walking to school near the base. He said he sees more and more women and girls in public every day. He showed me a picture of his own little girl, who he told me is very smart and very good at school. School was her favourite thing in the world. Of course, he hadn't seen her in many months.

Another soldier, a young guy, told me this would be his first Christmas away from home. He said he was not looking forward to his Christmas Day phone call because he was afraid he would get emotional, which would upset his mother, which in turn would upset his brothers and sisters and ruin everybody's Christmas. He'd agreed to spend the holidays on base so another guy with kids could spend two weeks at home.

Despite the congenial nature of the evening, you could see the stress of this posting on the soldiers' faces and in their eyes. There had been numerous attempts to attack the camp, and two of their colleagues had recently been killed less than two kilometres from the camp gate.

After we said our good nights, we headed back to our tents, although not to sleep but to work. Or at least some folks went to work. Geoff and me? We were treated to a magical night of sipping completely illegal, smuggled-in Bushmills whiskey and listening to Tom and Damhnait rehearse along with Kevin on cello. It was a thorough rehearsal. Tom and Damhnait would be singing solo but also backing each other.

The music went forever. And that night I slept soundly.

And why wouldn't I? I was being protected by two thousand Canadian soldiers and Kevin Fox on cello.

Morning came far too early. I was awake at five and wandering the camp, jet-lagged. It was three in the afternoon in my head.

While wandering I came across a monument to Sergeant Robert Short and Corporal Robbie Beerenfenger, the two Canadians who had lost their lives on this mission. I noticed that whenever a soldier passed the monument they saluted, even in the pitch-black. I saw a Dutch soldier running across the square. When he reached the monument, he stopped dead in his tracks, stood at full attention, and saluted before continuing on to work. He had no idea anyone was watching him.

I wandered by a huge tent and heard a Donna Summer song. I pulled back a flap and there was a guy in short shorts leading a group of about thirty soldiers, half male and half female, in a step class. "Three more, two more, one more, change." A sign on the door indicated that the yoga class had been moved to another location. This was a modern armed force.

And then sunup and the day began.

As in Bosnia, I was taking notes . . .

Our request to take aerial shots of the base had been approved. This was an international mission, and the Germans were lending us a helicopter. We were going up with the Luftwaffe!

And we didn't have one helicopter, we had two. And not just any helicopters, but the meanest, coolest helicopters you can imagine. These were serious heavy-lift choppers, made by Sikorsky. They are referred to as Super Stallions. They are beasts, with a range of 1,800 kilometres while carrying thirty-six armed soldiers. They are known for their superior low-level flying capabilities.

I was so excited I could have peed.

The helicopters typically fly in pairs for security reasons. Which is why, bright and early on day one, two of these monsters landed in Camp Julien so we could get our cute aerial shots for our little TV show. One thing you can say about the military: they have good toys.

There was lots of room in these birds, but the only person dubious about going up in the helicopter was Damhnait. I didn't know if she wanted to rest, relax, rehearse or simply retreat. But I went to her tent and gave her my spiel. I said straight up that this would be an experience she would never forget. Also, that this kind of opportunity only comes along once in a lifetime. She grabbed her makeup bag, put on some lipstick and said, "I'm in."

And so the entire band went airborne with the Luftwaffe. Tom, Damhnait, Kevin, Geoff and me—along with Pete Sutherland, who was tied on and dangling out the back to get the visuals.

Once our shots were complete, things got real. The Germans on board stood up on each side of the helicopter and took their positions at these big-assed machine guns. We were going on some sort of patrol. The female soldier manning the gun nearest to me was built like an Amazon warrior.

And suddenly we were flying over mountains, down canyons and following riverbeds. These suckers have a top speed of 480 kilometres an hour. And the pilots, bless them, showed us exactly what that felt like. We were so low, and we were going so fast, if there was any error in judgment, we all would have been gone in a nanosecond. But yet my confidence in them was absolute. I'm a sucker for a man or woman in uniform. It was at once exhilarating and terrifying.

I have no idea if Damhnait is grateful that I persuaded her to come along or resentful, but I do know she remembers the ride very well. Perhaps more than any of us. As we were coming down to land, we did one more sweep over the camp. We came in low over the tents we were residing in. Each tent in a row, ten feet apart from one another like a miniature suburb. We could see the undertow created by the rotors making the tents shimmer and shake.

And then suddenly one tent, one random tent in the middle of a row, simply rose up about twenty feet in the air and then dropped in the middle of the road. It was as if the hand of God had reached down and given it a flick. And once the tent was gone the personal belongings inside were scattered in the wind like dry leaves in a hurricane.

Damhnait looked at me and screamed, "THAT'S MY TENT!" Followed by: "$&%#$@!!!"

"Good thing you didn't stay behind. That would have been a hell of a wakeup call."

For the rest of our time at Camp Julien, Damhnait was approached on a fairly regular basis by men and women in uniform who would sheepishly pass her random items—a T-shirt, some socks, a makeup kit, a bra or some underwear, while saying, "I believe this might be yours."

Memories.

The rest of that day was spent shooting one of our music videos for Tom's song "Life Is a Highway." My happy place, it turns out, is encouraging soldiers to dance, sing and do jazz hands.

Meanwhile, Tom and Damhnait did a series of small impromptu concerts around the base.

I had fourteen interviews with soldiers scheduled. They knew I wanted to talk to them but didn't know why. With cameras rolling, we showed them videos of their families, wives, husbands, children and parents wishing them a merry Christmas and telling them they missed them.

This might have made any reality TV producer blush, but it was honest and raw. There was not a dry eye in the tent.

That night we did our first of three shows. I opened it with a twenty-minute monologue specifically about Afghanistan and the mission. Normally in television the "studio audience" is secondary and the "TV audience" is all-important. Everyone involved in this show believed the opposite was true. Which was why we were doing three shows. It was the only way we could ensure that everyone who wanted to see the show live could do so.

Tom killed it. He left nothing on the court. It was spectacular. And the reaction to Damhnait's singing was spectacular, and the reaction in certain quarters to her simple black cocktail dress was near hysteria. They loved her.

The next night we would do the same show again, but twice. But in the meantime, we had a few holes to plug.

First off, we heard that Dr. Abdullah Abdullah, the Afghan foreign minister, had accepted our invitation to be interviewed by me for the special. Nobody at the Canadian embassy had thought this would happen. Suddenly I was not a goof doing a comedy show, I was Mike Wallace with *60 Minutes*. Dr. Abdullah's imminent arrival created a whole new level of security and protocol issues for the camp. This man was the face of Afghanistan in the world's media. Getting him to appear in this Christmas show was a huge coup. Clearly, he didn't have Google.

The Afghan musicians showed up. Nobody spoke English, of course, and Kevin didn't recognize the instruments they were carrying, but that night they would be performing on said instruments with Tom, Damhnait and a choir of soldiers.

With just an afternoon of rehearsals, we pulled off the final two shows that evening. The highlight was the local musicians, who brought a whole other level to the show. It turned out they were like the Paul McCartney and John Lennon of Afghanistan.

We learned that the leader of this group of three had been jailed and tortured by the Taliban for the crime of owning and playing a musical instrument. He told us that he never believed he would be able to play in public ever again.

Later that night a cultural impasse occurred. The musicians refused payment for the show because their tradition prohibited them from charging friends to play music for them. They were steadfast in their refusal.

Geoff explained through a translator that it was a CBC tradition to pay great musicians when they performed on a TV show. "It's out of our hands," he said. "Blame the union." By Western standards, they were just getting paid for a few hours' work, but by Afghan standards, they had just won the lotto.

And then all there was left to do was to fly back to Canada and turn forty hours of footage into a tight fifty-minute TV special.

And John Marshall and I had our own footage as well. The very first rant for the first episode of *Monday Report* was in John's briefcase, along with a sketch I wrote that starred about two dozen of our country's finest.

It was a hell of a week.

27

To Be Continued

Christmas in Kabul aired on CBC Television on December 23 in prime time. The reaction was extraordinary. In show-biz parlance, "The switchboard lit up." Which was odd because in 2003 people normally didn't call the CBC on the phone, they sent an email.

But call they did. They called newsrooms and radio stations and tip lines. They left messages for the folks at *As It Happens, The Nature of Things* and *The National*. They called the bloody sales department. All positive.

It was like nothing I had seen before.

And to be clear, the insanely positive response had little to do with me or the music. Those things are relative and subject to an individual's taste.

No—Canadians responded as they did because of the soldiers and their stories. In these men and women they saw themselves and their neighbours, their sons and their daughters. It was a celebration of regular Canadians who, regardless of one's feelings about the mission, were tasked with a very difficult and very dangerous job—a job they were doing on our behalf.

In the grand scheme of things, it was a small show, but it had a huge heart. TV that wore its heart on its sleeve. I never saw that coming.

Perhaps it was a consequence of getting older, perhaps I was getting tired of being an "angry young man," but my act was changing. And I liked it. I realized I was actually becoming less cynical, which was shocking to me because historically I'd spent so much time being cynical the state of mind qualified as my second residence.

But if there was ever a time to figure out what this meant it was now.

Because while I was gallivanting around the Middle East making TV with Tom Cochrane, Gerald was in Toronto dotting the i's and crossing the t's on the biggest gamble of our life: the new TV show that was all ours.

We had huge champions at the CBC in Slawko and George. But so far the only thing Gerald had set in stone with the network was the title. It was to be *Rick Mercer's Monday Report*.

What was it going to look like? What was it going to feel like? What in God's name was I supposed to do all alone for 30 minutes each and every week? There were many questions and fewer answers. But all roads led to this place. Everything we had done together for the last 15 years led here.

It was terrifying but it was well-trodden territory.

How many times had Gerald sold the powers-that-be on a project or a vision, only for the both of us to find ourselves staring at a blank page, a blank stage or a blank screen asking one other, "Now what?"

It's an incredible privilege to walk into an empty TV studio and know it's your job to create the show that is going to fill it.

That will never get tired. But it's scary as hell.

And the studio for this particular show was in the Broadcasting Centre in Toronto. It was bigger and slicker than any studio I had been in before.

It felt exactly like walking out onto the stage of the National Arts Centre opera house in Ottawa long ago—except this time no stagehand chased us out the door.

Yet again I found I was asking myself: "How did I get here?"

It felt like only a few years had passed since I was in a high school library surrounded by misfits creating a play that would feature a punk band.

And it seemed like yesterday Gerald and I had left St. John's and flown to Ottawa to mount a one-man show that wasn't written yet.

But it all prepared us for the task at hand. The creative conflict that birthed *This Hour Has 22 Minutes*? The experience of creating a scripted sitcom when neither of us had done it before? That was our PhD program.

We picked up a few things along the way and we certainly learned from our mistakes. I always had a knack for learning from my mistakes. Even as a child I didn't need to smash my hand with a hammer or touch a red-hot element more than three times, that's for sure.

When you create a show, you can't help but dwell on the shows that inspired you to get into the racket to begin with. That's the magic you want to capture. And for me nothing had ever come close to *The Wonderful Grand Band*. I was too young to realize at the time but in hindsight I could see that what made the *Grand Band* so special was the audience's investment in the show. The people of Newfoundland and Labrador knew it was for them and only them. They felt a pride of ownership.

How, we wondered, could we do that nationally?

Well for starters we would create the most unapologetically Canadian show we could imagine. A show that could be embraced from sea to sea to sea but would make no sense five feet past the 49th parallel.

And it was Gerald who nailed the substance and the theme of this as-yet-unseen show in one word: *celebrate*.

He said I was very good at pinpointing what was wrong with the country, that the rants that had made me famous proved this. "But," he said, "what the country needs now is someone to point out what's right about the place. That's what you should do."

And he was right. Since we'd created *Show Me the Button*, Canada had been through a lot. Never mind a few constitutional crises, there was also a referendum that nearly tore the entire country apart.

The Canadian psyche was taking a beating.

And the very people whose job it was to fix these problems, our politicians, seemed hell-bent on doing the opposite.

Rural Canadians were being pitted against urban Canadians and vice versa. The West and the East were forever at odds and there were more than a few political voices on all sides willing to exploit this. French and English Canada were still in constant need of marriage counselling, the wounds of the near breakup had yet to heal. People were starting to throw the word "elites" around, creating an entirely new group of people to dislike. There was anger. Everywhere.

And in the face of all of this Gerald kept repeating: *celebrate*. It may be hard to believe, but what he was talking about was actually revolutionary.

It is every comedian's instinct to tear down or to criticize. It's what comedians do best. And there is a reason for that. You don't get laughs in grade five by celebrating the teacher. You get laughs by taking them down a few pegs. This is a primary survival rule in the comedy jungle. You ignore it at your peril.

But the more we talked about it, the more sense it made. And the show began to take form. Yes, I would keep ranting. It's what I did. But tearing down or being critical would have its place. And for the most part that place would be Parliament Hill. We hadn't taken complete leave of our senses.

But when we left the Hill, the tearing down would stop. And wherever we went (and our plan was to go literally everywhere), we would celebrate the people and celebrate the place.

We developed a philosophy heading into those first days and stuck with it for the next fifteen years. It was very simple: "At this show, we don't shit on Thunder Bay."

And we never did. Wherever we went, whether it was Thunder Bay, Fort McMurray or Ball's Falls, Ontario, we had one agenda: to show the country why this place and these people were the absolute best.

It was to be a show for and about people who know what it's like to wear out a pair of steel-toe boots. Fishers, farmers, nurses and autoworkers. Sure we might cross paths with some rock stars and politicians but for the most part I would talk to people who never in a million years thought they might end up on television. We would treat them like gold and make them look like stars.

And we had a few aces in the hole. Don Spence would be holding the camera, because a country so beautiful it's like a smack in the face deserves the very best in scenics. And I already knew from our brief sojourn to Kabul that Gerald had made the absolute right call with his choice of road director, John Marshall. It was a fantastic team.

If Gerald ever had any doubts about my ability to do my job, he certainly did a masterful job of keeping them from me. When I felt my performer's insecurity rising, when I was feeling overwhelmed at the notion of carrying a show on my own, he would say the same thing: "Stop thinking that this is a one-man show. There's one name in the title, but if this works, you'll have a cast of thousands."

If I wasn't so excited, I might have fallen over from the stress.

Excited to get on the road. Excited to develop a new kind of relationship with the viewers. The Doris Day campaign involved the audience to the point where they actually signed a petition. The trip to Bosnia convinced folks in the thousands to send Christmas messages overseas. Our vote video had engaged people at home in untold ways. I wanted more of that. I wanted a show that was funny but also an advocate. God forgive me, I was contemplating audience participation.

All of the pieces were slowly falling into place as we approached our initial air date.

The pressure on both of us was immense.

This would be the highest-profile launch of my entire career. I knew the network was going to haul out all the bells and whistles. Cripes, they were going to put billboards in Vancouver, Toronto and Ottawa. Not since the launch of New Coke was a company so committed to selling its latest offering.

As we got closer to opening night there was much talk of what it was that we could do on the premiere episode. CBC in particular wanted us to grab the attention of the millions of potential viewers who lived in the Greater Toronto Area.

Great ideas were floated. We could have The Tragically Hip perform live in the studio. We could get the prime minister to appear in
the studio as a guest. A friend had a personal relationship with Mike
Myers—could we get Hollywood's biggest comedy star, and a proud
Canadian, in the very first episode?

All great suggestions, and if one or two of those ideas came to
fruition, it would make for a hell of a launch. But it didn't seem right.

You only get one chance to make a first impression and we didn't
want to leave anything to chance. So we went with our gut.

We realized when it came to this whole "celebration of place"
thing, we could talk a good game or we could put our money where
our mouth was.

We went with the latter.

John, Don and I went to the airport and headed out to shoot the
first road piece for the first show.

We didn't know what would be in it, or what it would look like.
You can't write or prepare for the unknown. All we knew was that we
were going to the greatest place on earth via Bearskin Airlines out of
Ottawa. We were headed to Iqaluit, Nunavut. They had an election
coming up and I had just found out they didn't have political parties
but believed in something called "government by consensus." Clearly
that was worth looking into. Also, apparently, there was a guy there
with a funny story about a road. Also, he wanted to feed me some
raw caribou and take me out on his dogsled in search of a polar bear.

In other words, it sounded exactly like the kind of show Gerald
and I would watch. Would anyone else? We had no idea but it was a
hill we were ready to die on, or at least bet the house on. Literally.

Before I left for the airport, Gerald had one piece of advice: "Just
do what you're good at, just talk to people. If you do that, the show
will take care of itself." And then he added, "In fact, we probably
should just call the bloody thing 'Talking to Canadians.'"

I said, "Good title. Let's save that one for another series."

"Sure," Gerald said. "Or the memoir."

It was the beginning of a great adventure.

Acknowledgements

While I enjoyed writing this book very much, the subject matter tested my patience.

On more than one occasion I wished that I was writing not a memoir but perhaps a biography about someone else or even anything else. Didn't have to be a person, really. The story of an inanimate object would have sufficed.

So, I am indebted to the few bodies who were kind enough to read pages in advance. It was these people who said, "No, stick with your story, it's funny. You can write about a rock or a tree next time."

Asking someone to read a rough draft of a book is a huge imposition. It's like asking to be picked up at the airport multiplied by ten. For agreeing to read advance drafts I wish to thank Geoff D'Eon, Greg Eckler, Alison Gzowski, George Anthony and Tom Stanley. Wise, funny people. Your words of encouragement and honest criticism meant the world to me.

And also, of course, thanks to my partner in both show business and in life Gerald Lunz, whose notes, as always, made everything better. I owe an additional debt of gratitude to Geoff D'Eon for providing me with incredible access to his personal 22 *Minutes* archives. It made telling this story so much easier.

The Centre for Newfoundland Studies at the Memorial University of Newfoundland Libraries was a fantastic, vitally important resource for my research. Colleen Quigley, Joanne Cole and Linda White went above and beyond, during a Covid lockdown, to allow me access.

Many thanks to my literary agent Suzanne DePoe at Creative Technique.

I am so grateful to the good folks at Penguin Random House Canada, especially Kristin Cochrane, CEO; Terri Nimmo, Creative Design Director; and Scott Sellers, Associate Publisher, and at Doubleday Canada: Amy Black, Publisher, Emma Ingram, Marketing Lead, and Assistant Editor Ward Hawkes. Thanks also to freelance copy editor Shaun Oakey and freelance proofreader and fact-checker Lloyd Davis.

This book has been edited by Tim Rostron. A finer fellow or a better editor I have not met. He has great skills and a wicked sense of humour.

And finally I would be remiss to not thank all of the brilliant creative individuals I have had the great pleasure of working with in my career—it takes a village.

Thank you, Lois Brown, for being where you were, when you were. I can't imagine how things would have turned out if you had not been there.

And to my mother and father, Pat and Ken Mercer, for never once saying "What the hell are you doing with your life?" Thank you for everything. Literally.

Picture credits

Drama club (page viii): photo by Tina Riche.

Rick and Donna Pinhorn in *The Twenty Minute Psychiatric Workout*: photo by Tina Riche.

Corey and Wade's Playhouse: photo by Jamie Lewis.

Rick and Andrew Younghusband shooting a commercial: photo by Jamie Lewis.

Rick in *The Vacant Lot*: photo by Dan Callis, courtesy of Picture Plant.

Show Me the Button poster: original photo by Justin Hall; silkscreen by Derick Caines.

I've Killed Before poster: photo by Sheilagh O'Leary.

This Hour cast: ©Salter Street Films.